Cernitha St. Jean Presents...   In This Lifetime **Vol1**

"In This LifeTime"

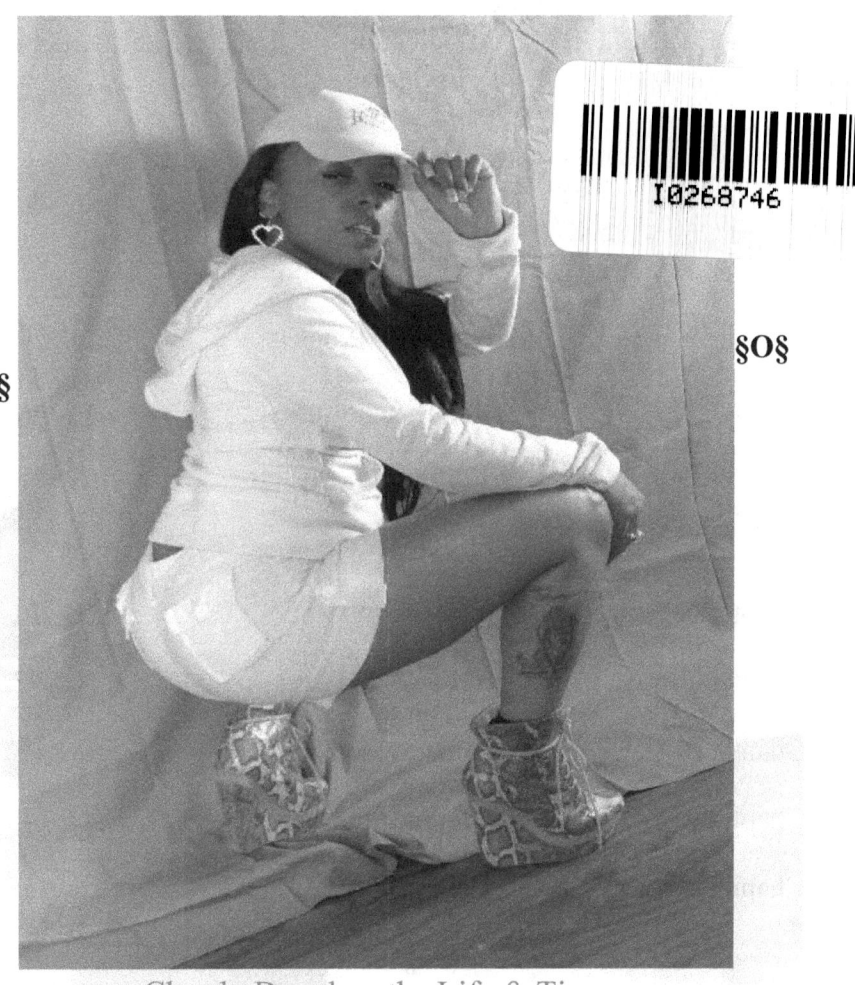

Closely Based on the Life & Times

Of

CerSire   By: Cernitha St.Jean

§~Index ~§

Page II............................ Index ....pg 2
Page III............Legalities, Copyrights, ISBN ....pg 3
Page IV-V..................... Dedication ....pg 4-5
Page VI..................... Epilogue ....pg 6

§O§

§~Chapter 1~§......... Too Young For Sex pg.8

§~Chapter 2~§......... Too Much too Soon pg.22

§~Chapter 3~§......... Lincoln Park Projects pg.29

§~Chapter 4~§......... Always Goodbye pg.49

§~Chapter 5~§......... I Will Fight for Myself pg.55

§O§

§~Chapter 6~§......... Heavy & the Vydoc pg.70

§~Chapter 7~§......... No Fucks to Give pg.97

§~Chapter 8~§......... Welcome to the Fast Lane pg.137

§~Chapter 9~§......... Time to Face the Music pg.145

§~Chapter 10~§........ The Fire Inside pg.157

§O§

§~Chapter 11~§......... Cinnamon pg.178

§~Chapter 12~§......... The Mirage pg.195

§~Chapter 13~§........ Dan /Dumb Ass Nigga pg.214

Cernitha St. Jean Presents... In This Lifetime **Vol1**

THIS NOVEL is closely based on real & fictional characters and the life events that unfold around them. This book has been comprised in this manner to protect the innocent as well as the guilty characters perpetuated in this novel. The Author has received permission to use the likeness of the individuals named under real name and or alias. Clearance, Non-Compete & Use of Name Likeness are available on-file with Dynasty~1Enterprises, LLC.

If you have purchased this book with a dull or missing cover, you have possibly purchased an unauthorized or stolen book. Please immediately contact the publisher advising where, when and how you purchased this book.

Compilation and Introduction copyright
©2016CerSireProductionsInc
P.O. Box 11166 W. McKinley St.
Phoenix, AZ 85323
www.cersire.com

LOCC: 1-3125391506
ISBN-10#:0-692-64359-1
ISBN 13# 978-0-692-64359-4
Author: Cernitha St. Jean'
Editor: Dynasty~1Enterprises, LLC
Consulting: Dynasty~1Enterprises, LLC

Copyright © 2016 by Cernitha St. Jean'
Dynasty~1Enterprises, LLC. All Rights reserved. No Part of this book may be reproduced in any form without permission from the publisher, except by reviewer who may quote brief passages to be printed in a newspaper or magazine. Trade Paperback Edition Printing December 2016

DYNASTY~1ENTERPRISES PUBLISHERS

§~Dedication ~§

To My Life: Baby CJ. aka Cernitha Jean I wish I could go back to the day when our heart was taken, our soul left shaking, and our innocence broken. If we still suffer from that body of pain, I'm telling you today, to let it go and be free. I want you to know that you are not alone, nor the only one who has and will experience such pain and violence. In Your Life Time, You will go through many trials and tribulations but the Joy and Blessings you have and will continue to receive In This Life Time is worth you choosing life, choosing right and always choosing you. You're a blessed woman; your children and peers have and do rise and call you blessed. You have been and will be called and titled many things, but enjoy and relish in your favorite title: Loved.

To My Children, my 3rd Worlds, The Universes God, and I Co-Create: Arailya-Mona "My Queen, Over/Underboss! DonPierre "My Prince Don the Prophet" & Aubriya-Sanaa "My Princess Model Diva".

On the day of each conception, my life changed. You must have power, a sense of humor and a strong core to have decided to travel this life with me. On the day of each delivery So much Joy and so much Pain, yet the temporal pain cannot be compared to the joy that has and will continue to be revealed. Throughout this journey as your mother; I've grown, I've gained, I've lost & I've found: Wisdom, Knowledge, Power, Substance & Truth. I've made plenty mistakes and I'm sure there is more to come, but your lives are the very reason I strive to do better, be better, show better. I love you more than this life itself. Each heartbeat is my every reason; wrong or right. You have no Idea what your lives mean to me.

I met each of you at a very young age (16,19,22), and for you choosing me in the Heavens to be your mother, the guiding light beside God; I humbly thank you. I also ask your forgiveness for the wrongs I failed to make right. I pray I shape you, direct you, and raise you into your God-ship correctly. My peace, my deepest love and blessings I pray forever for you's.

Remember this if nothing else: God is With You, You are powerful, words shape your world, you're at minimal a magician. You can have and make, speak and say the life of your dreams.

Dream-Visualize, Believe-Execute in Faith, Achieve that in which you create and desire. (My Salaams)

Abracadabra: Means I create what I speak. Thank you my angels for allowing yourselves to be a vessel that God shows himself to me through you! & PS stay off my last nerve thou ☺ #THEISLAND

Mom, I love you. I'm thankful for this life; I would never attempt to disgrace you. You are my friend when there are none. The hardest teacher I've ever had. Dad, My Introduction to man: thank you for the Dictionary and all my words, thanks for pushing me and being the voice of wrong reality. You & mom are still my first love, & I love you. You know my struggle better than anyone and I thank you for your real word, real approach in this life. Through your wisdom and ignorance you've shaped me greatly I thank God for you both.

Leila Sophia (RIPIH) I love you for teaching me right; to go hard with no apologies. The Just man falls 77x+ and I'm Just Cernitha.

My Family: I was forced to be & find the example because I was first. I love you all!

To Momma Rita, my lady friends and the women that have impacted my life #Love #Wisdom #Blessings Thank you…
To My Folks 7-4 Til the World blow #Growth & #Development #GrowOnGodBaby

Lord I'm Alive, forgive me, as I've asked you a million times. And for your continued blessings, wisdom's, graces and mercies I am Alive Today. All Praise Due to The MOST HIGH GOD!

-In This Life Time, your beginnings do not determine your ending; your daily choices do! MakeLife. ~CerSire

§~Epilogue ~§

"You better bust Star! That's all the fuck I know!"

I pleaded nervous with the pistol sitting on my lap; trying not to grip it so he couldn't see how bad my hands were shaking.

"Scared my mother fucking ass, on BOS, you bust, on BOS you bust! ON BOS!!"

My body and soul shook! The hell in his voice was the trigger in my ear. The fear as the bullet left the chamber the first time was all the power of hell I could stand to gain.

"BOS!!"

I pulled the trigger again. This time trying to aim through the blur of the tears that filled my squinting, blood shot red, traumatized eyes. I didn't know who I was shooting at. I didn't know why. I just knew I loved him; I had to prove to him I loved him. Brownstones "If you Love Me" played on repeat for the hundredth time.

The fear, anxiety and sorrow that engulfed my body was now hate, a beast's snarl of protection: As I imagined my targets harming Looney. Life without Looney was the catalyst behind my trigger finger. If you love me the song questioned and I was letting off the 6th bullet. The engine revving stopped. The jerk from us skirting off was worse than the kickback in my wrist from the Nine. The same Black Nine that would later change my life forever.

"Babe I love you! You hear me? You hear me Star? I love you! Wipe your face." He said hitting the corner damn near on two wheels, then taking his rugged right hand in a quick effort to rub my tears away. We played the "Prove You Love Me" Game all the time; this time was the worst of all. If mom found out about this, it would be more than her extension cord on my soaking wet body. An ass whipping for this stunt would be far worse than her throwing the lit packet of firecrackers on me while I was damn near naked.

You think you popping? Oh I got some pop for that ass; she said as she took the firecrackers and the lighter out of her pocket. I guess her splicing my skin 35 times with her switch wasn't enough.

"Baby ain't shit ever gone come between us." Looney said snapping me back into reality.

"You down to ride out ride for me on life. Fuck the tears Star you're that bitch, your that Boss Bitch! I'll bust for you. You bust for me, We Bonded for Life Star. Wipe your tears, I got you Ma. You gone be my wife…"

I tried not to think about just ruining my entire life on our high-speed drive back to the hood. I can't wrap my mind around what just happened. But this on BOS would be much worse than prison. Lord I love him, Let him protect me and love me forever and ever and eva.

§O§ ~ §O§ ~ §O§

§~Chapter 1~§
TOO YOUNG FOR SEX

    The knock on my closet door let me know that my next door neighbor wanted some company. Shawn was 16 and I thought she was the best thing since recess. It was 1986 and I was six years old. My family shared a duplex or a half a double that was owned by my estranged grandfather; with another black family who was trying to buy the property from him. Shawn had a brother named Bradley who I thought was super fine. They were all adopted so they all looked different.

Bradley was light skinned with hazel green eyes, he kept his hair in a wavy fade and all my cousins and neighbor friends thought he was the bomb! At-least he was considered the bomb back then. Shawn on the other hand was dark-skinned regular brown eyes and her perm stayed dry and fried looking. I didn't care she was still the closest thing I had to a big sister, when Michelle wasn't around.

 I ran down the dark oak hard wood stairs praying mom was in a good mood. It was around the first of the month so I figured she was happy as she normally was; when she got her check and food stamps. The scent of marijuana was a constant in my house; my father smoked like a freight train. I believe my mother smoked on occasion to entertain him. Running barefoot through the cloud of smoke I interrupt my slow dancing parents slow grinding in the living-room while Freddy Jackson's: You Are My Lady played in the background. I watched my father blow my mother a shot gun from his joint. Her coughing seemed to excite him as he grasped her butt tighter with his right hand pulling, the joint with his left.

"Yea you know I like blowing your head back. Momma get's a little freaky once the Cess get in you." He said dry humping my still chocking mother.

"Chucky you crazy." she replied fanning the cloud of smoke lingering in her face.

"Stuff, I'm crazy about you, you freckled faced red-bone." He said now leaning in to kiss her.

"Yea nigga that's why we got three kids now." She sassed in her I got yo ass tone.

"Come here." He motioned trying to blow her another shotgun.

"Mom!" I yelled startling the two love birds. "Can I go next door and spend the night with Shawn? She's going to braid my hair." I lied, adding more reason for my mother to let me go.

"Did you ask her mom?" Stuff questioned still dancing with Chucky now pulling the joint into her own mouth.

"No Ma'am Shawn came through the attic and said it's ok for me to stay."

"Go ahead!" She blew. "Be back before noon we're going to see Grandma tomorrow."

"Oh hell no, Stuff! You know your old mean ass Geechie grand-momma don't like me, I ain't going to sit over that woman's house!"

"Chucky; she's over that little showdown, bullshit between yawl. You didn't think she was going to pull her pistol on you when you had her daughter at gun point?"

"That's cause your old crazy ass momma pulled the gun on me first, what was I supposed to do Stuff? Then your grandma pulled up in the cab pulling her pistol & shit. All yawl motha-fucking Miller women are crazy!" He yelled grabbing at his beer chugging like he was in a race.

"Yep and your ass still here with my crazy ass, Geechie got you stuck Chucky?" She laughed sipping on her Pepsi "Come here baby" she teased rubbing her 40DD on the side of his angry face."

"Nah go on with that Stuff you just pissed me off with that bullshit." He said nudging at her breast.

I wanted to turn and run but seeing them together always captivated me. When I grow up I'm going to be cool with my husband like that. We're going to put the kids to bed then stay up and eat the good food, have drinks, smoke and slow dance under the red light. Hell my momma knew about the Red Light Special before TLC was ever invented.

"Come on Chucky baby, I got some kisses that are going to make you forget everything." She grabbed his free hand while he scurried to grab his sack and the remains of his Colt 45. Sashaying past me she looked down at me.

"Lock the bottom lock whenever you unfreeze yourself.
Oh baby grab my cigarettes." She motioned her left hand towards the Cherry Oak Coffee table that matched her curio that matched her furniture. My dad was now badly singing Lionel Richie's Three Times a Lady.

"Ughhh…" I interrupted.

"Hurry Up babe!" She whimpered to my father one hand balancing herself on the dining room table while the other hand she made swirls in the air with the Dobie of the joint. I rushed out locking the bottom lock, struggling with my belongings.

Shawn opened the door in her normal bossy attitude. "It took you long enough little midget." She smiled. "Hurry up and close the door why you standing there looking stupid. My mom and Step dad left and I found something I wanted to show you."

"OK!" I said like any other time my Big-Sister told me anything. She pressed her finger to her mouth as to indicate silence as she grabbed my sleeping bag and hand simultaneously and rushed me through the living and dining room to the upstairs. Her bedroom smelled just like my living-room.

"You been smoking that weed Shawn?" I asked with a shocked curious smile.

Startled she looked back at me while sitting my things on her guest twin bed.

"Can you smell that shit, how'd you know?" She rushed passed me slamming the door and I couldn't stop laughing at her fear. Shawn was fearless her and my Aunty Lisa stayed in some trouble and like them I'm going to be a bad girl when I get older. She pulled a can of air freshener from under her bed and began to spray.

"Open that window." She said to me while turning on her lamp with the black florescent light, turning off the bright overhead.

"I figured we'd have ourselves a-little party tonight since my parents are gone and I couldn't get anybody else over here." I didn't know at that time she was dissing me as the last resort but I was glad the big homie asked me to hang out.

"Here try this." She smiled, handing me a blue cup that had that transformer: Optimus Prime scrolled across it.

"Drink it down real fast and don't stop!" She bossed me. The taste was something I never experienced before; my first reaction was to throw up. Well it was more like dry heaving because nothing was coming up; my mouth was watering and my stomach was becoming hot.

"You are so young; you should probably go home since you can't hang with the big dogs." She laughed in mockery pulling a joint out of her brush box. My mouth dropped to the floor.

"You actually about to hit that?" My six year old mind questioned.
"And so are you!"

"No I'm not! I don't want that stinking stuff." I said rolling my neck in the traditional matter of fact.

"Oh yea little Diva, well don't more for me!" She blew the smoke in my face and pushed the cup back up to my lips.

"I thought you wanted to be like me?" She questioned, flipping her ponytail inhaling another cloud of smoke. I instantly started feeling light headed. My mouth was still watering from:

"What is this stuff?" I screamed, her laughter was making me mad.
"Aw babe its E&J erk and jerk; I got it out of mommy's wine cabinet. She got a gallon of that shit so I figured she wouldn't miss a glass or two."

"Ok watering from the Erk and Jerk." I wined.

Again she blew the thick cloud of smoke in my face. Her smoking stuff didn't smell like my dad's.

"You know what Shawn, I think you smoking on some homegrown shit, that doesn't smell like my dad's shit." She busted out laughing hard, as if I was Eddie Murphy and just told her one of the funniest goonie goo goo jokes she's ever heard.

"Oh shit you must be feeling yourself, cussing and calling my shit home grown, what the fuck you know about some home grown shit?"

Her enjoyment made me feel cool. I was the shit hanging out with the big homie. Shrugging my shoulders weaving my head sided to side.

"Shit you know you got that good Cess and you got that home grown shit. That's what my dad says and at home my dad was smoking that good Cess and your shit must be the home grown."

I took another swig of her erk and jerk and that was it. "I got to pee my stomach hurt, I want to lay down." She continued laughing at me.

"CJ you got me fucked up. You're funny as shit. Go fucking pee, you need an invitation?" She carried on in her laughter, "I'm-a tell ya Aunt about you cussing."

"And I'm-a tell her about your erk and jerk." I quickly replied making my way to the door.

"No you're not either!" She shouted throwing her pillow hitting me in the back of my head as I opened the door."

"Yes I am, and that's why you're a black bitch!" I laughed hurrying to slam the door. I laughed down the hall-way, pleased with my big girl talk, covering my mouth as if my laughter was going to wake up her brother. He always said I was cute whenever my mom freshly pressed or braided my hair. I remember crying for two days when I saw him kiss his girlfriend on the porch. Approaching the bathroom door before I could grab the knob the door swung open and Bradley stood there in just his boxers. I never thought I'd see him without his shirt on; let alone in his boxers.

"Uh…" I caught my breath realizing I was about to pee on myself.

"Hey little C.J.!" He smiled rubbing the top of my head like a little dog. "You might want to plug your nose. I set off a bomb in that bad boy." He bent laughing rubbing his stomach in relief, taking a deep breath.

"I know Shawn ain't smoking no weed up in here. Is she in there smoking?"

"What?" I ignored his question brushing past him intentionally touching his bare stomach, doing my best pee-pee dance. Slamming the door, I could barely get my pants down before the stream of piss came rushing. I tried to rush the piss out so I could hurry up to see him in his room before he closed his door. The piss must have lasted every bit of 15 seconds but it felt like 15 minutes. As soon as I felt the end of the stream I grabbed a wad of toilet paper and dabbed the front and folded then the back and she was off. Racing down the hall, still pulling up my pants, I had to see him one more time.

I stopped in my tracks right at the crack of his door. His light was on and my future husband lie there on the bed while some white girl I never seen was pulling his penis in and out of her mouth. My own mouth hung open wide. I never seen nothing like that before and his mouth was wide open, while his hands were both wrapped around her red hair seeming to pull her head up and down. I wanted to open his door all the way to see everything. I couldn't wait to tell my cousin Tasha everything that was happening. She made this humming sound as I walked closer to the door my gaze was now fixed on his stomach muscles rising up and down. The more she made the crying sound on his penis the more he pushed her head, the more his mouth stretched open the more his stomach pumped up and down.

Shawn's voice scared the shit out of me; I thought I was in trouble for damn sure.

"What are you doing?" She asked sticking her head out the door into the corridor.

"Oh!" I jumped back realizing that Brad and his white girl heard me at the door. I looked at Shawn then back into the room, then at Shawn again. Apparently Brad was still in Hornville with his mouth wide open as I turned to look back in the room the girls eyes starred directly at me. She pulled her long reddish brown hair back with her left hand while she stroked his long brown penis with her right hand. She pulled it all the way out and pointed it towards me. She stroked and spit on it then smiled at me as she dropped her gaze to focus back on his penis. I couldn't move as she looked at me again; this time smiling; asking him if it felt good.

"Get your nosy lil ass in here," Shawn whispered in a low firm voice pulling his door shut with one hand snatching me by the collar with the other.

"You a nasty little girl." She said closing her door flopping down directly across from me on the other twin bed.

"No I'm not Shawn, don't say that." I didn't know what else to say, was I a nasty girl? I couldn't stop looking at that nasty girl sucking Brad's Penis. I couldn't believe I seen a penis; Brad's Penis!!!! I couldn't believe that girl was sticking his penis in her mouth!!!

"What you thinking about nasty girl?" Shawn snapped her fingers in front of my face.

"And you better tell the truth, matter of fact here." Motioning the transformer cup back in my face. I snatched the cup dreadfully hoping my stomach wouldn't burn and my mouth wouldn't water this time.

"Here drink some of this, after-wards." She smiled pulling the can of Pepsi from underneath her bed post. I took another big gulp then quickly chased it with the Pepsi. She laughed genuinely amused as I drank the entire can.

"So back to you nasty girl, why were you standing there looking in my brothers room Hun? Did you see what you were looking for?" She rolled her eyes and her neck at me as if she caught me sucking the Penis myself. Shook I didn't know what to say in response.

"You ignoring me?" She leaned forward into the walk space that separated us.

"No!"

"No; what?" She asked pushing my shoulder.

"No; I'm not a nasty girl, no I didn't see nothing".

"Shut your o'l lying ass up. I know you was standing there watching her suck his dick, she been sucking his dick off and on all night. So I know that's what you were looking at." She said matter of fact; pushing my other shoulder.

"Did you like watching Terra-Lynn suck on his Dick? Did it make your little pussy throb?"

"What are you talking about?" Leaning over placing the empty can under my bed post.

"Have you ever played house?"

"No what is a house."

"Not a house, just house." Shawn corrected me.

"No! What is that game like?"

"Well it's when two kids act like grownups. You make each other feel good like the grown-ups do, accept you can't tell no body because kids aren't supposed to play house." She leaned back on the bed turning up her radio that was playing 'Before You Turn Off The Lights' by the: World Class Wrecking Crew.

"No I've never played that, how do you play house?" I questioned wondering if I even wanted to play house and If I had to go play house with Bradley who I kind of didn't like anymore.

"First we're going to open the vent, I'm about to light this joint back up and were going to watch Bradley and Terra-Lynn play house." She demanded.

I was excited about that. I still liked Brad a little bit, enough to keep watching this real live nasty movie. I was fascinated with Terra-Lynn looking at me and making his body move like that. Shawn opened the vent slowly looking back shushing me to a quieter silence. She waved her hand for me to scoot closer to the vent. In our duplex the two smaller rooms shared the same heating cooling vent. The old style vents that gapping's were big enough to stick two fingers into each section. I was surprised that she was still sucking on his Penis or Dick as Shawn called it.

Vigorous is what I would now call Terra-Lynn's efforts, she was going up and down on his penis so hard her face was turning red. This time he wasn't holding her head palms open but his fist gripped her hair pulling harder up and down; his stomach still pushing in and out. She wasn't using her hands now and I was trying to figure out if he was pushing his thang down her throat since her head was all the way down.

"Yea Baby; Come on Baby." She moaned taking a deep breath before plunging his thang back into her face.

"Come on T, don't stop, don't stop its building baby don't stop!" He whined to her.

I couldn't see his face because his position on the bed but I could see his chest and stomach and her face. Her red face whose cheeks were caving in, as she made this gurgling sound her eyes bulged open and closed. I felt like she was looking at me again through the vent. Did she like me looking at her? Was I a nasty girl?

"Ooh, huh, huh, ahh! His stomach hardens and he let go of her hair. His hands were open in a grasp and she kept going up and down, this time I could see more penis from her mouth.

Ahh... And it happened!
"Look!" I pointed: Shawn jumped on top of my back putting her hand firmly around my mouth. I didn't move her I stayed fixed on the white pee shooting into Terra's face from his penis. I thought I was tripping when I realized Shawn was still on top of me now moving her vagina back and forth on my butt. I didn't know what to do. I wanted to close my eyes but I was glued to the white pee that she kept sucking and the more she sucked the white pee the more Bradley's body shook like he was getting electrocuted.

She reached in-front of me and closed the vent still grinding back and forth.

"I told you, you were a nasty girl. Only nasty girls like to watch live porno."

I didn't know what a live porno was like many things she use to say to me, but I guess I was a nasty girl because I couldn't stop watching.
"See that's how we play house" And at the end you feel very good she whispered in my ear.

"You're gonna play house with me, and I'm going to play house with you."- "No I don't want to play house with you."

"Shhh yes you do. Turn over." She whispered while forcing me over; pulling down my panties and pajama pants. "I'm-a show you how girls play house together, and if you don't like it then we won't play anymore but first you got to try it." I held on to my pants from the front as she tugged from the side. She tugged again getting my undies a-little further down.

"I don't feel good Shawn; I want to go to sleep." I pleaded.

"Exactly; that's why I'm going to make you feel good, then you're going to make me feel good then we can both go to sleep and go to buy lots of penny candy from Talley's in the morning."

She took one hand and began to rub on my vagina through my pants. With the other hand she pulled up my shirt, baring my flat chest. I wanted her to turn off the Blue light; instead she began to suck on my nipple. The firming of my nipple scared me and I closed my eyes wondering if I had to suck on her nipples. The many thoughts began to dance across my mind as she slid her hand into the side of my pants and down onto my private part.

"That's a good little nasty girl… Look at your bald little pussy. This is what girls do!" She exclaimed now pulling my bottoms all the way down to my knees then off my ankles.

"Don't move." She whispered spreading my legs apart climbing back over me on the bed.

"Your aloud to moan but don't say anything unless it hurts; you hear me?"

"Yes." I managed to whisper, wondering why I was a nasty girl. Wondering why she climbed across the attic and knocked on my bedroom door. The feeling of her wet tongue on my vagina instantly locked my body. I couldn't move I felt sick, scared and wondered if this is how Brad's stomach was feeling. She kept licking me up and down and around and I kept getting scared. Was I going to pee in her face? Would she drink my pee Like Terra-Lynn or would she punch me?

"Do you like playing house CJ?" She asked me.

I should have kept me eyes closed because when I opened them she was looking right at me smiling with her tongue going in and out of my vagina like a turtle head.

"Are you feeling better?" I couldn't talk I didn't understand what was happening to my stomach. Why was she playing house with me? I don't think I can tell Tasha this, I might get in trouble big time.

"Do you hear me talking to you nasty girl?" She asked now clasping her lips tight around what I learned later to be my clitoris.

"Yes, stop, stop I got to pee!" I cried.

"No hold it right now!" She pulled off her oversized T-shirt and my eyes widened at her naked body. She had boobs like the grown women and a bunch of nappy hair on her cootie cat. She sat up with her legs wide open. My eyes were fixed on her hairy vagina. I didn't want to lick it, I didn't want to touch it, and I just wanted to go home. She pulled my arm forward pulling me off my knees forcing my head to land on her stomach. I felt myself wanting to fight her as she yanked my other hand from under me, before placing her breast in my mouth.

"Suck it like a Popsicle and don't bite it hard." "Suck it!" She screeched unhappy with my inability.

"Suck it like a sucker, firming her grip around my neck. "Yea that's good. Good girl." She clinched my head with one firm hand and my butt cheek with the other.

"Yes, now suck this one." I did the same technique that she said yes to the last time. Hoping that; this playing house would be done soon.

"Good, good- girl." She moaned gripping me around my neck pushing my head down to her vagina again. All the moments before I was scared, now I simply want to cry.

"Come on put your face right in the middle and lick me like I licked you."

"Shawn I don't want to play anymore." I said struggling side to side to get her hand off my neck.

"Well you're not playing fair, and we're not going to stop until your done licking me. And you got me fucked up, If you don't; I'm going to beat your ass for letting me play with you, then you not wanting to play with me and you better not fucking tell or I'm really going to beat your ass."

The lack of oxygen going to my brain was beginning to make me dizzy. And her pushing my neck was making my head hurt. My six year old reasoning just wanted to make it stop. So I opened my mouth and I licked. I licked her slimy stuff; up and down and around, like she did mines. The faster I was going the more she would release pressure from my neck. Gasping from the new found wind I tried to take a deep breath, yet she gripped the top of my head forcing my face back and forth.

"Bite it softly." She whispered firmly thrusting her vagina into my face as her very own punching bag. I wanted to bite it off but I knew she would beat my ass. I attempted to bite it soft.

"Yes, yes, yes there you go. Good girl, now suck it, suck it soft and fast, do it, do it!" Her hunching was making it very hard to do what she said. I just want to be done playing house with her. Suck and bite suck and bite I thought to myself. Until finally her stomach began pumping up and down and she let go of my head after about ten seconds she pushed me over; threw her shirt at my face and opened back up the vent. I sat in silence whipping my face, her pee and my tears. I learned how to cry silently that night because I didn't want to get my ass beat. I didn't want her sweating vagina punching my face. I didn't want her erk and jerk or her blowing her home grown in my face. I thought we would dance to New Edition and crank call people like we normally did while she braided my hair.

"I don't want to smoke." I quivered as I watched her light another joint.

"Didn't nobody say I was smoking with your cry baby ass, and you better not tell!" She inhaled a large cloud of smoke and blew it right in my face.

"If you do tell, I'm-a tell ya' momma you are lying and you were humping my leg when I was sleep."

"No I didn't!" I yelled feeling overwhelmed, destroyed, scared and defeated.

"You hungry?"

"No!"

"Good because I didn't feel like going downstairs anyway." She took another hit of her joint.

"You sure you don't want to hit it, it'll make you feel better." She pretended.

"No I'm sure, my head hurts, and I just want to lie down."

"Suit yourself Nasty girl & don't be peaking through the vent." The last thing she said to me before blowing another cloud of smoke in my face and waltzing into Bradley's room.

"You want to hit this bro?" I heard her say walking into his room. Instantly the tears stopped and I focused on the vent. She just walked into Bradley's room with no clothes on and Terra-Lynn is still in there! I couldn't believe it. I opened the vent slowly, hoping they wouldn't hear me. I watched still semi crying as Brad sat up on the bed moving Terra's semi sleeping head from his leg.

"Damn sis you feeling good tonight?" Bradley smiled as Terra sat up reaching for the joint.

"Damn chill out I just got it." He said smacking her hand away.

"I'm sorry baby, I wanna drag." Terra-Lynn whined.

"You ain't hitting my shit." Shawn laughed positioning her naked body between them, leaning back on her elbows with her right leg arched on the bed.

"Oh I can't hit your shit now, bitch?" Terra-Lynn laughed leaning into Shawn's face close enough to kiss her.

"Yea if I let you hit my shit, you got to lick my shit." She said snatching her joint from Bradley.

"You gone send me like that Shawn-Shawn?" Terra said playfully grabbing a handful of Shawn's breast, force feeding her mouth.

"Yea baby, you know we keep it in the adopted family." Bradley laughed beginning to kiss and suck Shawn's free breast.

"You licking?" Shawn asked passing the joint to Terra-Lynn. "Yes Shawn, I'm licking she said kissing her directly in the mouth.

"Good girl, Good girl." Bradley teased rubbing Terra's head stroking his again growing penis.

It was time for me to go. I just wanted to crawl into my own bed and hope that my mom didn't kill me tomorrow. I rushed to find my clothes, I didn't care about my sleeper or my Barbie heads that I brought over so she could teach me to braid. I just didn't want to be naked; I didn't want to be stuck to the vent. I didn't like Bradley anymore and I definitely hated Shawn. Sitting back down on the bed rushing my feet into my cabbage patch house slippers I looked back at the vent. I couldn't help myself, maybe I am a nasty girl?

I gasped couldn't believe my eyes this has got to be the smoking stuff? They were all on Brad's bed; Terra-Lynn lying on her back and Shawn hunched over her rocking her vagina back and forth in Terra's mouth, while Brad on his knees above her head thrusting his Penis in and out of Shawn's mouth. Everybody was playing house!

I had to go home before they asked me to play. I'm not playing house with her, them ever again. I grabbed my Barbie head on second thought and headed to the attic. I was just going to cross over, climb down into my closet. That way I didn't have to wake up my mom and she wouldn't know that I was playing house, drinking and smoking. I know I'm going to get a whipping.

The next day I woke to the smell of pancakes and bacon. I raced to the shower to clean my nasty little body. Shawn had me believing I was the world's most nastiest little girl. I had to brush her vagina out of my mouth. I heard my dad singing really badly as I excited the shower. They sure sound like they are in happy mode. My brothers already up running around playing batman or whatever stupid game they call themselves playing; tying towels around their neck jumping off the furniture. I wonder if they will be sad when I tell them I want to go stay with my Grandma? I don't want to live here anymore. I don't want Shawn to come to my attic door, I don't want to play house with her, I don't want to see her I just want my Grandma.

§O§

§~Chapter 2~§

Too Much Too Soon

Mom was in a bad mood this morning. I overheard her on the phone with my grandma saying something about our phones being tapped. She said my dad was off on that bullshit; going to get her caught up in some prison time. The thought of my mom going to prison scared me. I sat on the steps eaves-dropping as always; when my brother Son ran down the stairs behind me.

"Nappy neck!" He said running pass me, slapping me hard on the back of my neck.

"Stop stupid!" I yelled mad that he blew my cover.

"Take yawls ass back upstairs!" Mom yelled from the living room of our half double. A loud crash sounding like it was coming from upstairs forced me to run into the living room.

"Shit Ma, I think they're here!" She yelled startled before slamming the receiver down onto the base.

"Hurry up go sit with your brother." She rushed past us, before I could take another step our living room door was kicked in.

"Freeze, Columbus Police Department! Get Down Motha Fucka!" The officers yelled. I was stunned standing in the middle of my living-room with this shot gun pointed in my face. It was like: soon as they kicked the door in; I blinked, when I opened my eyes the officer's gun was in my face.

"Get Down Right Fucking Now!" I dropped to my knees as my mother crawled to cover me. I watched in utter fear as the officer kept his long nose shot gun pointed at my mother's back.

"Thomas Adams show yourself right now, Come out with your hands up!" The angry white officer yelled from behind his large clear plastic shield, as they slowly migrated through the house. By this time one of the officers that proceeded through the house brought both my brothers into the living-room. I crawled, army style towards my mother's wooden end tables, my favorite hiding place. I watched the tears stream down my brothers' face. Son; the second eldest of my biological younger brothers came rushing over to me and we crawled into the end table together.

"C, dad is in the attic." He whispered into my ears in the dark.

"Shut up Son!" I grunted pushing my elbow into his side. We've hid in the wooden end tables before; during games of hide and seek. During spy missions where we fell asleep listening to the adults talk. But this time I'm shaking and afraid for my life. Afraid one of these cops where going to shoot my dad. I hear the dogs barking: Mom's Twin Doberman Pinchers.

"Don't shoot my dogs or I will sue you mutha fuckas!" I heard my mom yell outside of my dark safe box. What is Dominic doing? I wondered as I cried listening to the screams and yells. The shattering of glass scared me so bad; I jumped and hit my head on the ceiling of the end table. For sure my brain was bleeding.

"Keep your head down C"… I laid my head on my brother's shoulder as he opened the door. An army of foot soldiers rushed past us. The one holding my dad on the left arm kicked at the door. We jumped back in unison, before tumbling out to the floor me on top of Son.

"Nooooo! Let my dad Gooooo!" I screamed as the officers lifted my dad off the floor. "Stop dragging my dad."

"Shut up C.J.!" My mom yelled as she held the phone tears racing down her red freckled face.

"Fuck that! I ain't doing no real time Stuff! These mutha fuckas ain't got shit on me. Call Auto Beatty! Call my lawyer."

"Your ass is going to jail today, Mr. Adams. That's for damn sure." The officer walking with his gun in my dad's back smiled & paraded on like he just won the prize ribbon at the state fair, in the best pig contest.

22nd from Long Street down to Mt. Vernon; looked like a serious crime scene. Squad cars, Ambulance, Fire Department, S.W.A.T, Undercover Cops, The News!

"The fucking news Mom!" My mom cried into the receiver, wiping her unstoppable flow of tears. I looked around from the broken frame of what use to be our front door. Now shattered glass and wood debris lay everywhere as a few S.W.A.T Officers still parading across the front of our second level roof; laughed slapping each other high fives.

I watched as they stuffed my father into the Patti- Wagon, banging his head onto the top of the door, before pushing him to the floor.

"Noooo!" I continued to scream, crying, rocking back and forth in the door way. Arms spread gripping the door frame as hard as I could. Imagining I was holding myself back. When everything within me wished that I was 8 feet tall, kicking everybody's ass. I couldn't take anything else this week. My face felt like it was beating up & down; the tears were itching as they soaked the front of my pink and green cabbage patch shirt.

I stepped backwards stepping onto my mother's foot.

"Damn it C.Jay!" She stepped back, dropping the receiver on her shoulder.

"I'm sorry mom". I really didn't want to disappoint her. Or upset her more than she already was. We watched in unison as the news reporters went from filming the now closed patty-wagon to rapping up their stories.

"Get in here & shut the door!" I looked back at my mom, wondering; how I was going to shut the door and the whole wooden part, that use to holster the locks insert was laying on the porch?

Ok CJ lay-low shit is on 1, in my mom's terminology: the shit done hit the fan. I closed the door but of course it didn't lock. Mister Willie our land lord aka my cousin's Grandfather, kicked mom and us out until she paid for all the damages; damn Grandpa that's shady as fuck. But to let the truth be told; my mother and auntie Darlene wasn't Mr. Willies children, he only fathered the last seven of Gan-Gan's children.

While the house was being renovated, we moved down the street to Aunt Aprils aka Star's House. Mr. Willie owned this house too. This wasn't a half double like our house. It was a yellow single family house with a full front porch with a covered roof, right at the alley. Everybody was over Aunty Aprils tonight. Mom, Aunt April's husband Kevin, my Aunt's Lulu, Sissy, Squeaky even Uncle Tim stopped through. It felt good to see my dad's side of the family. We rarely saw them in comparison to my mother's family.

The ever-present weed smoke was in the air, as me and my cousins ran throughout the entire house, playing Freeze Tag.

"Guess who's here?" I heard my Aunt say as the front door slammed closed.
"Is that my dad? Is he here?" I ran out of Shawntay's bedroom so fast. It was my dad. I knew it! Wow he was only in jail for a day and now he's back home. My dad must be Superman. I thought as I ran down the hall, then the steps and finally, wrapping my scrawny little brown arms around my dad's legs as he embraced my mother and little brother Dominic who she held tightly in her arms.
"Chucky!" She cried out of frustration, happiness and anger.
"I know Stuff, I know baby. I know baby, it's over. I promise." He squeezed her tightly, in his attempts to comfort her with a Kiss and a hug. My Uncle Kevin turned up Whodini's "Friends" on the record player.
"Shit I want to send a shout out to my friend Mr. Mutha Fucking Beatty; my favorite mutha fucking lawyer!" My dad yelled raising his bottle of VSOP. The partying continued until a fight broke out like always. Uncle Kevin left earlier after fighting with my Aunt. I heard my mother on the phone with my Great Grandmother trying to work on finding us a new place to stay. When she put us to bed that night she made sure to keep all our shoes, coats and socks together on the chair.

Kevin lost his mind near Halloween every year because his mom passed in October. While drunk he kept telling everyone sitting downstairs watching Freddie Kruger. That he was Jason and he was going to fuck around and make his own Friday the 13th movie tonight. My mom wasn't taking kindly to the niggas threats and forced my dad to act like he was going to take Kevin to get some drinks and instead dropped him off over his sister's house. Uncle Kevin was pissed and regardless of what my mom was saying to him he wanted Aunt April, who refused to get on the phone.

"Bitch I'm tired of your mouth, put April on the mother fucking phone Stuff!" He yelled at my mom through the receiver.
"Listen you crazy motherfucker, I'm not gone be nair-nother bitch for you Kevin. I told you she won't pick up the damn phone, she don't want to talk to your ass. Can't you understand that?"

"I don't give a fuck what she wants to do, I said put her on the phone."
"Listen Bitch I know yawl all plotting against me anyway trying to get me sent back to jail."
"Kevin! April-does-not-want-to-be-with-you!" She sounded out each syllable slowly knowing he still wouldn't comprehend what she was saying.
"April!!!" My mom yelled out in frustration. "April, this nigga keep calling talking about he know you been messing around on him. Come get this mutha-fucking phone April! Don't nobody got time for Kevin's crazy shit but you!" My mom sent us to bed sensing Kevin was just going to keep up his drama. She hung up the phone after realizing he already hung up on her.

-Bam! The sound of the breaking glass window frightened my mother as she stood in my Aunt's kitchen froze watching Kevin as he put his hand through the glass window and unlocked the door. Out of fear my mom asked him for a cigarette; she seen the crazy in his eyes. She had no weapon only the yellow phone receiver she held in her hand. He must've been at the payphone at the corner, she thought as her wide scared eyes scanned the room for weapons.

He turned his back, opened his container of gasoline and threw it on my mom.
All I know is a couple seconds later, my mom was screaming!
"This Motherfucker Poured Gasoline on Me!! CHUCKYYYYY!!"
 On his way up the stairs he poured the gasoline along the steps and hallway before kicking the door to our room; pouring gasoline on his children, my cousins. My father argued and fought with him while gathering us up.
I remember my dad waking us all up rushing us out of the house, talking about he's trying to set April and the house on fire. A lot of yelling, cussing, and fighting, but Kevin kept coming. I think we were escorted away by the police, and I went to spend the night over my great grandmothers.

~§~§~§~§~§~§~

I listened as my mom sat in the living-room talking with Grandma about Aunt April not pressing charges, and that she didn't give my mom the correct court date.

"She's a hateful, doped up, beat up heifer." My grandmother chuckled rolling her blue-grey eyes behind her large gold framed lenses. I watched as they both started to laugh. My mom still with the disappointment and hurt on her face turned to my grandma.

"Grandma sometimes, I swear I think she still holds a grudge, you know Cheryl was her best-friend." I think she's jealous because my children are the finest things to come out that family.

"Whose Chucky's other baby momma, your Aunts ex-husband's people?" Grandma looked shocked at my mom's statement while sipping on her black coffee. I stayed in the dining room, I didn't want to leave, and I was traumatized still.

"Yea my ex-Cousin, but no I'm talking about April."

"Oh hell, those loud, drunk, stanking ass bitches, with them O'l nasty dirty, snotty nosed, nappy head ass kids, of course the bitch is jealous and she beat up." My grandmother sipped her coffee slow, in between chuckles. Grandma never held any punches with anyone, and she dared you to leap frog. She would always tell my dad:

I'll put a whole in your ass the morticians won't be able to close Chucky." She hated my dad; she said he was a sorry, lazy, drunk excuse for a black man.

"Marlene I know you love that nigga, but he can't stay here. I'll keep Chanitha, you and the kids can stay but that nigga will not." She gave my mom some money; she knew she wasn't going to stay without my dad. I kissed my family goodbye and thought about my cousins, Shawn, Gene, and Seven. My grandmother didn't have to talk about them like that; it wasn't their fault they weren't taken care of.

I thought about my mom & Aunt April not being friends anymore, I thought back to a few nights ago they were dancing to Whodini's Friends. Now the song made since to my first grade thinking: Friends! How many of us have them, friends? Ones we can depend on?

We were forced to live with my Annie Ree, Uncle Will & the girls in the trap house with my dad's prostitutes. My mom was not happy at all. I noticed she was always mean to the white lady. Today my parents were arguing in the kitchen; something about a white bitch. I guess my mom was still mad while she was doing the white one's hair and makeup. I watched from the corner door hoping that my mom, would stop hollering, and slapping the white trick.

She carried on for about 10 minutes or until she bruised her face and busted her lip. I sat silently as my dad transported me to go stay back with my Grandmother on the south side. He tried his hardest to apologize to his prize prostitute as she cried to him.

"Dino, please control Madam Stuff! Dino, Daddy her abuse is out of control. She only treats me like that; she doesn't treat Tina or Shelly like this."

I remembered hearing my mom telling my aunt over the phone that my dad was in love with his white whore. This bitch wasn't bringing in the money; like she use to and she didn't know why he wasn't coming down on her.

I stayed with grandma as my parents went from 22nd to Chesterfield to the trap on Livingston Ave. After telling my Grandmother while she was bathing me: "Yea so my dad kissed the white whore when he was bringing me over here, and last night my mom slapped that hoe bitch in her face when my mom was doing her hair."

"What! What? Hold up Chanitha what you say?" My grandma was laughing so hard, her whole face was red. I sat in the bathtub looking at this green, blue eyed, high yellow woman with pink sponge rollers in her black, white and silver hair; turn multiple shades of red and pink. I accidentally rubbed the bubbles in my eye causing a severe burning sensation.

"Shit! Oh I'm Sorry! Oh!" I yelled jumping out the tub grabbing my grandmother's house coat jumping up and down whipping my eyes. I knew shit was a curse word. I didn't know Whore, or Hoe was a curse word. My grandmother wrapped the towel around my wet, shivering skinny brown, knot kneed body and opened the bathroom door.
"Here take these baby dolls put them in that other towel." She motioned toward the sink.

"Little girl you have been exposed to too much." Like usual I didn't understand what my grandmother was talking about, I was just happy to be back with her. I wrapped my three naked baby dolls in the towel and went and sat on my bed.

Like normal she would put some kind of cream in my hair, brush my hair into its pony-tail, on some nights she would tell me stories of her mother having children by the slave owner and her moving to Ohio from South Carolina. I always steered clear of questions and conversations about my Veteran Great Grandfather who died in her arms in her kitchen. We said our prayers as I'd try to catch her taking out her teeth before she turned out the lights.

"I will always love you Grandma." I said squeezing her and her 50" white plush comforter.
"I will always love you too Chanitha, my little beautiful brown doll baby." I relished in her words until the Sandman came.

§O§

§~Chapter 3~§
Lincoln Park

"All, all, all into gather girls never mind the weather girls; January!" I jumped out the double Dutch line as fast as I could. February, March, April, May, June, July by the time we got to august everyone participating was out of the rope.

"I wanna play!" I heard the new girl who just moved into the row of apartments directly behind us yell.

My cousins, friends and I stopped to look at these two little girls, in their matching pink and white halter short set approaching us. I'm assuming their sisters but not twins. I can tell the short thick one is the little sister and the skinny girl looking about the same height as me 4"8 is the older sister.

"Hi my name is Samantha, and this is my little sister Ebony. We just moved into the row back there Sunday. All my friends call me Sam, we're like the same color and size, and we could be sisters." She said reaching her hand out to shake mines.

"Hi Samantha, I don't know about all that but my name is Cernitha everyone calls me CJ. These are my cousins Tasha, Wee-Wee, Bear-Bear, Netta & Scooter. I just moved here last month. If you want to play you have to turn first, that's our rules."

My Cousin Wee-Wee motioned to hand the rope to Samantha.

"Oh, no, I don't want to turn and my sister is double handed."

"Well baby doll if neither one of you want to turn neither one of you are going to jump!" Tasha said standing beside me, with one hand on her hip, placing her right hand thumb back into her mouth.

"Well I guess we can't play Ebony." Samantha hissed.

My cousin Wee-Wee& Scooter began turning again as the two sisters turned to walk away.

"Bitch!"

"Who said that?" Tasha asked looking curiously around at our cousins.

"Who you think said it!" Samantha said rolling her freshly relaxed, pressed, shoulder length black hair, pausing in the small 10 foot field of grass that separated her row of apartments from mines.

"Oh"-

"What"-

"No she didn't." My cousins sang in unison. This little bitch is bold; I thought to myself as her and her bowlegged tom boyish little sister came walking back towards us.

"I said that!" She continued in her new girl bad ass delivery, or whatever it is she thinks she doing. She stood about 3 feet away from Tasha with her hands on both her hips.

"Who do you think you are talking to little girl?" Tasha asked.

"I'm talking to you!" Was the last thing I allowed her to say to my cousin before I walked over and began punching her rapidly, repeatedly in her shit (head and face.)

"Bitch don't you be getting in my cousins face!" I yelled to her as the fury of fist began connecting.

"Ahh!" She screamed as she began throwing punches of her own. Wee-Wee smacked Ebony with the handles of the double-dutch rope and the fight was on!

"Hitter C! Don't let that bitch hit you!" I don't know which cousin was shouting the commands all I know is she hit me in my chest and I turned into the Incredible Hulk. Backed up, kicked her in her stomach while she was bent forward, eyes closed wind milling. When she lifted to clutch her stomach I punched her as hard as my scrawny eight year old arms would allow, square between her forehead and nose. The blow was enough to knock her backwards on the ground.

"C'mon C. You beat that lil' bitch up." My cousin Scooter laughed loudly in my ear as I snatched away from her barely there bear hug.

I began kicking and stomping on Samantha as she was curling herself into fetus style.

"Un-Un mother fucka!!!" Yelled the very skinny brown skin woman who; came bursting out her front door racing toward us.

"Who the fuck; are you calling a motherfucker? You Boney Bitch, I'll beat your mother fucking ass!" I froze instantly when I heard my mother's voice; I dropped Samantha's head on the ground before jumping to my feet.

Mom and Aunt Lisa, her youngest sister; came rushing past us into the face of the lady with the five pink hair rollers in her hair. A dingy ripped pink, yellow and white flower patterned house dress, and some dingy use to be pink Family Dollar house-shoes.

"Now we just moved out here and I see these girls jumping on my daughters." The lady yelled clutching her robe.

"Yea it's for damn sure you just moved out here or you wouldn't have fixed your mother fucking face to open your mouth and call my daughter and my nieces motherfuckers!" My mother barked in the ladies face.

"Now, now ma'am I don't want no problems, these girls aren't being fair they jumped"...

"No we didn't jump nobody! This one with the mouth started everything and CJ beat her up. Wee-Wee fought that one." My cousin Netta pointed towards Ebony who was sitting on the ground with her legs folded breathing like she was having an asthma attack. Netta rehashed looking dead into the face of the lying lady.

I watched my mom still standing face to face with this noticeably smaller, crack head woman.

"Listen my name is Stuff all you need to know about me is: Don't start no shit won't be no shit!" My mom yelled, nose to nose with this shaking lady.

"I was watching these girls play out here; me and my sister, we seen the whole thing."

Aunt Lisa decided to pull my mother slowly away from this lady.

"Your daughter started the whole thing and since she wasn't getting jumped we let her get her ass beat fair and square." The new neighbor recognized the odds of her getting her ass beat was 100% probability. Both these redbone, thick women would have took pleasure in mopping her frail, drug infested, lying ass without a second thought.

"Get your little fast asses in the house, you always starting some shit!" The upset lady yelled obscenities as she hit Samantha across her neck and back repeatedly, while holding her gown together with her spare hand. We all laughed at Billy Bad Ass as she ran in the house crying.

"Stuff my name is Betty. I just got out of the hospital and I'm not trying to start no shit, my oldest daughter Sabetha thinks her shit don't stink with her little frail ass". She looked behind her back watching her daughters go into the apartment.

"Well Betty, it looks like she ran up against the right one today."

"You ain't never lied." Aunt Lisa laughed as she pulled her pack of Newport's from the top of her blue jean shirt.

"Can I please bum one of those?" Betty asked, eyeing the cigarettes.

"Stuff is my nick name, my name is Marlene." Mommy extended her hand to Betty in attempt to make peace.

"These kids are always fighting girl, that's kids, they'll be friends tomorrow. But anyway I'm about to go finish cooking my dinner, once you get settled in come through, we can smoke cigarettes and drink Pepsi." All the women laughed and I stood back against the green laundry pole next to them, wondering did I miss the punch-line to the joke?

Back in the house mom and Aunt Lisa joked about how they would've kicked that little woman's ass if she would have leaped wrong.

"Leap Frog, Roof." My Aunt Lisa laughed making her best big dog impression.

"Girl that little bitch didn't have the chance she thought she had."

"Girl she would have got her little ass folded up and thrown back into her house." They laughed hysterically trading stories of how they would have dogged walked or molly whopped Ms. Betty.

It was summer time so my cousins would normally spend two weeks or so with me, while we got adjusted to the new neighborhood. Mom kept the doors and windows open because the central air kept going out in the apartment. Every day in the living room my cousins and I would turn on our records, Insert our School Days movie and Music Video VHS Tapes and put on for each other. For the past two days the white boy that lived at the end of our row, kept starring in our window. I went in the kitchen to tell my mom that he was starring in the window today, while she was talking to my Uncle Junior.

"Mom that white boy Kenny is staring in our window again today!" I said putting one of my hands on my hip and the other pointing behind me.

"White boy who doing what?" Uncle JR sat his beer down and walked towards our living room.

"Don't beat him up too bad Junie, he's a kid, its broad daylight June everybody can see you!" Mom yelled after my Uncle. Uncle Junior didn't care, he opened the door went right outside and grabbed white boy Kenny by his neck:

"What the fuck you looking at motherfucker; my nieces? Those are babies in there eight and under! Let me catch you out of pocket and I'll beat your ass to death, fucking with my family!" He yanked & slammed Kenny's face into my mom's window, it was summer time so the window was up and his face imprinted on the screen. We all jumped Tasha, Wee-Wee, Shawntay and Bobbi, when he slammed his face into the window the top half hit the glass and the bottom hit the screen. I didn't want my favorite uncle to go to jail was my first thought.

"Nooo!" I screamed for my uncle. Uncle Junior was brave, he was my hero. I wish I had the courage to tell him about what Shawn did to me, so he could go slam her face somewhere.

~§~§~§~§~§~§~
School
~§~§~§~§~§~§~

My first day of 3rd Grade at Lincoln Park was nerve wrecking. I knew a couple of the kids from the neighborhood that I met over the summer. I was in Mrs. Farrell's 3rd grade class with my new friends Autumn & Keyona and things were getting off to a good start. That's until we had to take some mandated test. I was pulled into the hallway and told that I was going to be placed in another class.

I was instantly sad but Mrs. Farrell and the administrator went on about how I scored exceptionally well on the statewide test and I was being put in Mrs. Whilomoski's class with the Gifted & Talented Students. I guess that was great that I would be able to see my friends at recess was my only thought; while these two white ladies smiled impressively in my face.

"So what inspired you to write those essays and where did you learn your math skills?

"It says she's been to five other schools already." They spoke about me like a subject.

"Well..." I interrupted. "My dad makes me study the dictionary, if I know the pages I get the reward."

"And what's the reward?" Mrs. Farrell asked.

"Five or Ten dollars, you know stupid type chump change. So do I get to say good bye to my friends or what?" The ladies laughed and looked at me grasping their chest and pearls as if I was a spectacle. "Hum." I opened the door to the class and went to gather my things myself. Keyonna really wasn't upset about me changing classes because she lived closes to me in the projects. I could see her apartment from my back door. Autumn on the other hand cried like we were never going to see each other again, which made me cry in return.

I noticed the dark-skinned, bushy head black girl Birda who hung out with Autumn on recess sometimes. She waved her hand towards me signaling for me to come and sit in the empty seat beside her.

"Good after noon class we have a new student." The administrator announced to the unconcerned class.

I took the initiative to walk into the front center of the room.

"Hi my name is Cernitha Jean' everyone calls me C.J. I prefer you to call me C.J. too. I hate my name butchered. Apparently I'm smart so now I'm in your class, have a nice day." Some of the kids laughed others made mockery: Oh I'm smart, I'm cute. It didn't matter I sat down next to Roberta who handed me an opened pack of Twizzlers.

"Oh, okay, my kind of girl." I said pulling my king size bag of skittles out handing her the bag. We hit each other's dap as if we just made a drug exchange and for the first time I felt comfortable in this new school.

I was barely through transporting my belongings from my book bag to my new desk when an older white man came to the door.

"OK, Can I have all my GT Students get your things you're going with Mr. Chase today." Mrs. Whilomoski professed over her reading glasses.

"Come on girl; just grab a note book a pencil and a pen." Roberta whispered in my ear as she stood up to go to the front of the class. Oh so she's a GT Student too, how cool is that? We met in the library two to three times weekly for half the school day. I was first introduced to Erica she was a perky red head freckle faced white girl; I was told she was Roberta's best friend. Then Thurman stood to introduce himself. He was a heavy set big-bootied African boy, round all around, round face, stomach and ass. He dressed like a preacher's son every day. Tight button-up dress shirts, with very nice sweater vest, slacks and dress shoes every day.

He was very arrogant something I noticed about all six of the children in this group. Next up was Derrick, the brownish blond heavy set athlete with his pretty blue eyes behind those thick glasses. He told of how many championships he won at this or that. Then Namen stood up; He was skinny, I could tell his parents where into the street life, this little white boy was fly, he had on the newest pair of Nike Cortez the black and white leather ones with some crisp black jeans and a red and black flannel shirt which he had the top two buttons open exposing his necklace.

Who does this boy think he is? I wondered he was cocky, cool and arrogant, outside of Roberta he seemed next most down to earth. Roberta stood up stating she was the only child and spent a lot of time reading hundreds of books. As she continued I realized I was next and I didn't know what made me special like these other kids.

"Uh hello everybody my name is Cernitha Jean as I mentioned earlier I'd like for you all to call me CJ. I've been to about five different schools now and I'm only in the third grade so I've learned to learn fast, I laughed alone. My father has been forcing me to study the dictionary ever since kindergarten and he says I'm going to be a Words Smith, I like music, money and my cousins and that's about it." I sat down looking for reaction.

"Well CJ Welcome to the class, again my name is Mr. Chase a few of my colleagues and myself will be your gifted and talented teachers. You guys continue to test exceptionally high state wide and have been afforded this free program that cultivates, motivates and help execute your genius. Throughout this year you will Learn Art, Politics, The stock Market, Psychology, Chess and many other exciting challenging things. Because of your position you guys are automatically required to participate in various school functions as well as write and read your essays concerning our DARE Program, Drug Abuse Resistance and Education. Furthermore as much as this class challenges you it will also give you immense pleasure, I'm sure you'll be running to this class in the future."

"He's always this cynical." Erica whispered in my ear causing me to laugh out. "We are their smart test dummies, my mother says: she continued, they teach us various things and study us like rats, their amazed at our aptitude being Ghetto babies and all." She flashed her nearly perfect smile and dimples, shaking her bang across her head. This girl must be running for president; I sniggled to myself.

"Oh did I mention in return you get a full scholarship if you complete the program throughout high school."

"You mean a scholarship to college?" I asked her excitedly.

"Yes Honey full ride, how about that?" I raised my hand I didn't know if this girl was gassing me but I wanted confirmation.

"Mr. Chase is it true that this program continues through high school and offers a full scholarship.

"That is correct Miss Miller, thank you Erica for your expedient explanation."

I was geeked I can get out the hood free, just for being smart. This was life. I loved this program learning to play chess and learning how to operate the stock market was a few of my favorite perks outside of getting out of class. The field trips were always fun and the only downside to the program, was the students that didn't qualify for the program that decided to become haters.

School was a new joy, I built a great group of friends and my Mom let me have another Slumber party to introduce my new found friends to my lifelong friends, always known as my Cousin's: We found out that Tiffany was related to my cousin Lanithyia aka Wee-Wee so we instantly became family. She wasn't my family technically through the blood, so she was family through the mud, now my cousin for life. We met via fist fight, I was fighting her cousin and she jumped in so I was blasting both their asses and hence we became friends.

My little sister barely could walk straight but was always trying to tell, with her obnoxious high pitch voice. We all tried to hide the pictures, which made my baby sister even more suspicious.

"Go in the boy's room Poody and don't be snitching!" My friends all laughed as she opened the door sticking her tongue and her middle finger at us.

"She is so cute; she has the perfect round apple head." Autumn said smiling at my bad-ass little sister.

"Yawl give me those damn pictures." I said trying to snatch the picture from Roberta and Tasha.

"Girl Uncle Chucky packing that Ding-Dong." Tasha laughed Frisbeeing the Polaroid at me. I gathered the pictures while my guest laughed and joked about my dad's naked porn pictures. I put the pictures in my brush box, reminding myself to sneak them to my mom somehow later.

"Alright yawl, It's Apollo Time!" I jumped up with both hands in the air, clown style at my friends.

"Oh God, here she go with that shit." Tasha mocked, as my other cousins laughed and my new friends questioned how it went.

"So I'm going to go first. I'm going to do Michael Jackson's PYT." I pushed play on the tape player because I was listening to him on repeat earlier this morning. This song tripped me out, Michael Jackson says some wild freaky stuff real fast in his music, and I loved it. I jumped on top of my dark oak night stand with my dolls hair brush in my hand.

-You know you, you make me feel so good inside, I always wanted a girl just like you, (I shook my hips from side to side) you're such a PYT Pretty Young Thang. OOH.

-Where did you come from baby? And ooh won't you take me there, right away, won't you, me baby, Tender-Roni you've got to be, spark my nature sugar fly with me. Don't you know now, is the perfect time! (Hit the kick)

-We can make it right hit the city lights, (Crotch Rock)

-Then the night ease the lovin' pain, Let me take you to the max!!!

I want your love you "P.Y.T." My Cousins Tasha, Wee-Wee &Bobbi joined in with me as always jumping up to play my Tito, Jermain, & Jacky.

Pretty Young Thing. You need some loving (I pointed at Birdie) "T.L.C" Tender Loving Girl

(I gyrated my hips hula-hoop style, in my best Michael seduction).

-And I'll take you there…, girl ooooo

In my mind Michael Jackson was a bad boy he talked dirty to me. I mean his words was seductive, I'll take you there, yes I will, oooh (where was we going? To Sex, we were going to have sex is what the song meant?)

- Yes I will OOOOOH

-Nothing can stop this burning desire to be with you, gotta get to you baby, Wont you come its emergency, cool my fire yearning honey, comes set me free!

My Cousin Tasha took over because this was her favorite part

-Don't you know now, is the perfect time we can dim the lights just to make it right.

-In the night hit the loving spot, (we all started Crotch Rocking, and hip Dipping)

The whole room screamed

-I GIVE YOU ALL THAT I GOT!!! I WANT YOUR LOVE YOU

I paused in mid performance as I visualized myself as an adult dancing half naked on a stage.

"I'm going to be a strip girl yawl." I announced to my winded party guest, still standing on the night stand, looking at my reflection against the window.

"What you mean you going to be a strip girl?" My new found cousin Tiffany questioned.

"The girls you see on late night cable movies, the girls dancing in their panties and people giving them their money." Trying my best to explain what I thought they were.

"Oh girl you mean stripper hoes." Bird corrected.

"What's a stripper hoe?" Wee-Wee laughed as I started lifting my t-shirt dancing rubbing my stomach until we were all flashing our nubs and flat chest.

Michael said we needed some loving, maybe that's why we wanted boyfriends, to cool our little fires. My slumber parties was the best, I knew how to get and keep the party started. After a few performances of; Kool Moe Dee's Wild-Wild West, and L.L. Cool J's I'm Bad performances I was done with the Jigging.

"So who wants to join our crew?" I asked the entire room?

"Who's the Crew?" Bird Responded.

"Me, my cousin's Tasha, Wee-Wee, Netta, Scooter, Bear-Bear, Bobbi, Nay-Nay, and you Birdie, (because she was my new best friend).

"So that means that means me and Autumn are the only ones that are not in the crew." Tiffany concluded.

"That's about right." Tasha confirmed.

"So how do we get into the crew?"

"Yawl two got to fight!" Wee-Wee yelled out.

"And yawl better fight; if yawl wants to be down and we all protect each other from everybody." Shawntay was always the biggest girl in the room, enforced. Everybody was scared of Shawntay aka Bear-Bear but me, she was big but she didn't know how to fight that good yet, or she just let me beat her up.

"I don't want to fight her, and what if I don't want to be in yawls crew?" Tiffany sassed noticing how she just became a target out of nowhere.

The fight happened so fast Tiffany didn't want to fight but Autumn was already for the challenge. Tiffany kept professing that she wasn't going to fight Autumn and was allowing her to get the best of her until Autumn hit her so hard in the chest that it knocked her into the closet.

"Beat her ass, Un-hun hit her back!" We all coached.

"You got me fucked up bitch!" Tiffany yelled lunging herself from the closet on-top of Autumn hitting her left and right until finally we broke up the fight in fear of my mom coming in whipping everyone's ass.

The next day after my friends left Netta, Scooter & Wee-Wee had to leave too. Wee-Wee was sad that I was no longer living with her over Grandmas. Tasha, Bobbi, Shawntay and I stayed and helped my mom clean up. Then she would let us walk to the neighborhood store lady to buy ice cream cones and candy. You could buy everything in the projects with food stamps. My mom gave me some cash wrapped in a letter to give the store lady and she gave me a brown sandwich bag to give to my mom.

"Ay I wrote yawl a rap song while yawl where gone!" My mom said smiling grabbing the stapled bag from me as soon as we walked in the door. She turned walking in the living room; returning handing each one of us a piece of paper with a different hand written song. My paper said Title: My Way of Life.

CJ's Verse: My name is CJ I'm the smallest of the Bunch, I am here hun I'm not out to lunch and as you see I don't need a man, cause this little girl has a plan. But I don't want to waste your time, so come on cuz and finish this rhyme.

 The hook said: My way of life, un, un, un, my way of life, (repeated)

The Crew and I were super geeked. Ooh, Yup!

"This is Tight Aunty Marlene." Tasha said taking her thumb out her mouth, fanning her paper side to side.

"Right, thanks Totty-wa, now I want yawl to go learn the words and practice the song get it down tight and come show it to me." Mom shooed us off.

"Can we go practice it outside?" I asked my mom, praying she would say yes.

"Go head, don't yawl go too far." I restrained myself from continuing to jump up & down. We ran out the front door and into the field separating us from the last row of apartments.

"Yea, Yea, Yea first we going to learn it, all do are parts and sing the hook together then I'll point to the next one to go until everybody go and we figure out which way sound better."

"Ok cool cuz. We all walked in are imaginary circles or squares. I peeked through the screen to see what my mom was doing and what was in that bag. I noticed she had a whole bunch or plastic bags on the kitchen table. I wonder if she was making us another surprise. My mom was the best when she was in her good moods. I wouldn't trade her for the world, in her good mood.

This song was fun, I was hooked, we- needed to keep this thing going I loved the energy of performing my own song. My mom just gave me my fix, the thing that would find me fixated for years to come.

This was far better than singing the Blue Monday tunes for my buzzing mother & aunts. The Monday night get-togethers, under the blue light listening to their hey-day songs. I would always get called down to sing, Natalie Coles: I'm Catching Hell. I loved the fact that I had to cuss, but why I got to be catching hell living alone?

§~§~§~§~§~§~§
When the world shrinks don't jump
§~§~§~§~§~§~§

Things were going too good. It felt like we were finally settled in. It was our second Christmas in the projects and we had a lot of gifts under the tree, my dad was no longer working for East Side Ambulance, but for the county morgue transporting dead bodies. We play wrestled with my dad in front of the tree as he pretend slammed us and knocked us out, when my mom called him to come get the phone.

"Who think they can take down the big Monsterrr?" My dad yelled at us crouching over us like he was a monster snarling, grabbing at us with his hand claws. My brother Son and I plotted how we would take Dad the Monster down. He would punch or rush him in the stomach and I would grab him by the neck.

"Go!" Son yelled and we executed are attack. All four of us was jumping my dad, even little Poody was trying to hold on to his ankle.

We were so rough with her; we definitely had to make her strong for these streets. We all laugh hysterically.

"Oh yawl little niggas think yawl got me?" My Dad laughed as he body slammed each one of us on the couches one at a time.

"Chucky please come get the phone!" My mom yelled from her bedroom upstairs again.

He grabbed the couch pillow hitting us in the heads two at a time.

"See yawl got cha momma hollering at me." He hit us again as he through the pillows at us. We loved when my dad was happy, he was always bitching about something or another my mom would always say. My Dad ran up the stairs as a knock came on our back door. I went to the back door and was surprised to see my Grandmother Loretta at the door.

"Chucky No!" My mom screamed from upstairs. I froze with my hand on the lock, I heard dad screaming sounding like he was tearing up their room.

"Chucky Stop it, Stop you got kids downstairs!"

-Bam! Bam! Bam! My grandmother banging on the door scared me to my senses. I unlocked the door and stepped to the side as fast as I could. My grandmother rushed up the stairs into my parent's room.

"Grab Him!" She yelled as Dad attempted to climb out their second story window. Something really bad was happening upstairs. I pushed through the metal screen door and stepped into the alley aka our back yard. I looked up as my dad hang on the ledge of their window. What the hell was he trying to do? Break a leg in front of everybody in the projects?

"Dad jump or get in the window!" I was pissed I didn't want nobody thinking my dad was tripping on some kind of dope-trip.

"Dad please get in the house!" Son & I yelled up to my dad as Son began to cry witnessing Dads face full of tears. I needed to know what happen that got my Dad crying, we were just happy. One of the screens from their window lay on the ground, I grabbed the screen and ushered my brother back into the house. Only a couple of the crack hoes whose blood was filled with anti-freeze was on the corner. They stood shivering gathering closer watching my dad make a spectacle of his self, for those with nothing to talk about to keep dredging up.

Mom and Grandma struggled to pull an out of his mind Chucky back into the window. I stuck my middle finger up at Robert; my 13 year old next-door neighbor who was staring at me from his kitchen door. I hated Robert anymore; he used to be cool, now he was my enemy. I think they put a sleeping pill in my dad's beer after what seemed like hours of my mom & grandmother trying to calm him down. I sat downstairs by myself starring at the Christmas-Tree.

"Are you O.K. baby?" Mom asked sitting down beside me.

"No Ma'am, What happen to Dad?"
"Oh I'm sorry baby, your grandfather passed away he suffered complications from Cirrhosis of the liver." I didn't know what all that other stuff was she was saying but I knew passed away meant dead, not coming back. A fit of rage overtook me.

"Mom, Robert stuck his finger inside my cootie cat. He held me down and told me not to tell. I wanted to tell Uncle Junior so he could beat him up. I know he's a kid, but Robert said if I told he was going to throw one of those pipe bombs like you be making into our house!"

I couldn't help myself I had to tell her, I was still haunted by Shawn taking advantage of me, and me still not being able to tell my mom. But I wasn't going to keep letting everybody mess with my private parts.

"Oh Hell NO, When was this!" She yelled jumping to her feet grabbing my arm.

"When you sent me over to Mr. Skeeter's to get some sugar and two Cigarettes. Well Mr. Skeeter wasn't home so I didn't get the cigarettes. Robert told me to go sit on the couch while he went to see if his dad had cigarettes upstairs, then he came sat down beside me on the couch then just jumped on top of me forcing his fingers into my stuff. I hit him really hard in the face, that's how he got that scratch across his face." I said starring at my feet.

"Go get your shoes on!" My mom was undeniably pissed, more so hurt that her daughter had been violated. I ran up the steps stopping to look through my mom's cracked door at my snoring father. I ran into my room and grabbed my Cortez and my pink and blue Charity Newsie Coat. I ran down the steps just in time to see my mom pulling her huge whipping switch out of the pantry. My mom slid half her feet into her folded white girl tennis shoes, she had her leather belt strap and her switch in one hand and her never ending cigarette in the other.

"Open the door." She ordered as I opened our back door turned and knocked on Mr. Skeeter's door. Skeeter was a flamboyant Fag as my mom would say. He tried to live the straight life married a dark skinned sister they had two children and just couldn't take it no more. She found him cheating on her in her bed with another man and left him and their children that same day. Regardless of all that Skeeter was still my mom's good-girl/boyfriend, because he openly swung both ways but preferred a big dick man. They took turns smoking cigarettes doing each other's hair on Thursdays. He always styled my mother better than she could his, because he was a master hair stylist. And my mom ran the kitchen boutique salon.

"Hey Girl, come on in." He said clutching his black and gold silk robe against the cold air intruding his chest. Skeeter's black plush man slippers were nice and he definitely had the best furnished apartment in the projects.

"These hoes ain't fucking with me!" Was a term he used often, and later I would agree he was right.

"So what's going on Marlene?" He asked sipping his mug that was filled with Hennessey and Coffee. The only reason my dad would attempt to act like he was cool with Skeeter was for the free beer and liquor, and he occasionally brought a bag or two off my parents.

"Skeeter, Honey I'm sorry to be at your door this late, but my daughter just told me that Robert held her down and stuck his finger in her Coochie." My mom dropped her head looking as if she was watching her shaking leg. Skeeter dropped his jaw and his hand exposing his very big man penis.

"Oh my God, Miss Marlene!" He clutched his robe again this time speed walking up to his bedroom. He came back down stairs in his v-neck white T-shirt and tan khaki shorts still in his black plush slippers.

An eye rubbing, dark-skinned, big lip, ugly Robert followed behind him rubbing the sleep out of his eyes. Looking like he already knew what was up. We all sat in the living-room me and Mom on the love seat him on the chair and Mr. Skeeter standing up.

"Robert, C.J. told her mom that you held her down and stuck your fingers into her little vagina!" He over emphasized on vagina making me very uncomfortable.

"No I didn't little ass liar!" He looked at me hard as if looks could kill.

"Yes you did liar! You said if I tell you was going to throw a pipe bomb in my mom's house!" I yelled crying instantly. I was scared to death, I was nine years old and Robert was way bigger and stronger than me. I knew my uncles could beat him up. But I wanted to tell my mom first, I was wondering if he was going to attack me when… -WAM! Mr. Skeeter slapped the spit out of Robert's mouth. I ran two the steps which divided the living room from the kitchen.

"I bet you better not jump your black ass up in my face cussing and carrying on motherfucker." Mr. Skeeter took his teeth out and sat them on top of his entertainment stand.

"Bwing yo bwack ass over here if you want nigga." A part of me wanted to laugh at toothless gay Skeeter rocking back and forth with his nipples poking through his shirt ready to fight his ugly son.

"How you want to handle this Marlene?" He looked back at my mom who began to take her coat off.

"Well I want him to strip down to his draws, and I'm going to whip his ass, it's either that or let my brothers come over here and whip your ass." My mom was very calm looking directly at Robert as he tore his face up to cry. She slid her feet out of her tennis shoes, looked at me then back at Robert.

Robert stood up and to my surprise started taking off his clothes. I had seen way too much tonight and I didn't want to see his black naked body in his tighty-whities. Skeeter reached into his pocket and grabbed his cigarette purse, pulled out a square and his lighter and walked to the corner. As soon as Robert stood up from taking his pants off my mom started slicing him with the switch hard, fast repeatedly, moving her arm in different angles to hit him everywhere.

"Oh, Ah, Ha, Ah!" His screaming continued as my mom hit his back over forty slices. I looked at Skeeter who looked up to the ceiling inhaling his cigarette with tears rolling down his now closed eyes. My mom dropped the switch, slapped him across the face with the leather belt strap then across the face with her hand causing him to hit the floor.

"OK Marlene that's good enough!" Skeeter yelled to his son's defense. Mommy slid her feet back into her shoes, picked up the belt, and left the broken switch. We went back next door without saying a word. Was I supposed to say thank you to my mom who just tried to beat the hell out of my attacker? I just wanted to lie down but on my way up the steps my mom stopped me.

"C.J. don't ever be a weak bitch! Don't never try to kill yourself and if somebody bigger than you fuck with you; you pick up anything, I don't give a fuck what it is and you bust'um upside they mother fucking heads or stab they eyes out! I don't give a fuck how you hurt them just get away from them and come and tell me immediately!"
"And C.J." She stopped me at the next step.
"If your world suddenly shrinks on you; don't jump!"
"Yes ma'am." I whispered dropping my head, starting up the stairs.

The very next month after Mr. Skeeter Beat his 16 year old daughter half to death after arriving home early from work and Eve was having her very first threesome in his living room, him and his whorish kids moved away.

Two weeks after he left; this new elderly lady named Ms. Midge moved in. Right off the bat my mom called my Uncle to tell him about the new neighbor and all her grown daughters. That weekend my Uncles where over here like clockwork and so was the sisters. After a lot of sneaking dates and a lot of chasing Uncle Junior bagged Jennifer the small, petite light skinned sister, who also lived not too far from us, in the projects. I knew he had to be seeing her when he stopped bringing his chicks over for my mom to size up.

I sat on the steps listening to my mom on the phone with Gan-Gan telling her that my Cousin Ceretha (Who I'm similarly named after and was always fascinated with) had a miscarriage or self-aborted the baby, and brought the dead bloody fetus in a shoe box and put it on my Dad's friend Nolan's steps and then called him.

"Yeah that Bitch gone in the head." I heard my mom, sounding more concerned than boastful for a change.

"You're right the apple don't fall far from the tree, my mom said in response to whatever my grandmother was saying.

"Yea, yea you right, her momma didn't teach her anything but how to not give a fuck." What in the world is a bloody fetus, I thought to myself? It must be the bloody tampon thing; I concluded before deciding that was some nasty shit to do. But then again if she wanted him to have her bloody puss juice he must've gave her a reason.

I decided to stop eavesdropping and go into the kitchen to find me a snack. I landed on a bag of Doritos as I opened the blinds to look at the neighborhood night shift. Also known as the drug dealers, gang bangers dressed in red, the geek mommas and hoes, of course the pimps and all the weirdo's that came out at night in the projects.

Uncle Junior pulled up with a pregnant Jennifer. She was the prettiest one of Ms. Midges daughter's if you asked me. I knew he was going to get her like he kept saying. She was due around Christmas with their son and my Uncle junior was geeked. They had their problems in the beginning aka him messing with other chicks and her still messing with her other son's father.

Awhile back my Uncle Junior came over limping and scraped up. Reenacting to my parents how he beat up Jennifer's baby dad. He picked up his bike and slammed it on him. Junie went on about him running the man and his bike over and then Jennifer hopping in his car trying to run them both over... My parents and Uncle were in the kitchen howling. I haven't heard them laugh so hard in; ever.

§O§

§~Chapter 4~§
Always Goodbye

Grandma told me last night that my parents got a half-double house on the south eastside of Columbus and that I was going to be moving back in with them. Today I packed my suitcases, I'm leaving my favorite home again; but this time leaving Great-Grand's; felt different. Mom found a half-double on Rich St. She finally left Lincoln Park Projects after 4 years. I was 11 years old at the middle end of my 6th grade year now moving to my 7th school. I wasn't even in 7th grade but had already been to seven schools.

I pulled up to Berry Middle School in tears, for so many reasons. 'Thinking I should write a poem called Todays the saddest day.' Today was the saddest day for me; today was the last day that I would go to Berry Middle School. I prayed that I wouldn't lose touch with Bird, Autumn, Keyonna, Shamika & Tiffany. Outside of my cousins, my LPJ Click was the longest friendships I've ever had. Saying goodbye to what seemed like my lifelong friends, felt like my funeral. This was the end of sixth grade and I've been with this group some before the beginning of 3rd grade. That did it, the tears came rushing down.

Pop's had the tackiest black, white, yellow, pink, orange Toyota Hatchback. Its primary color was black but all the paintball shots made it an even hotter mess. Outside of the fact that it was ridiculous to look at, it back fired loudly like Uncle Buck's. I laid down in the backseat praying no one could see me.

I raised my head slightly when I felt the car backfire for the last time. I knew if no one was outside they would surely hear the seemingly gun shots and look out the window.

"Chucky Look!" Mom laughed in the front seat signaling for my father to witness his embarrassed daughter.

"Nigga why you hiding? You ought to be happy you got a car to ride your scary ass in!" My dad was pissed and maybe ashamed of my embarrassment. Oh well I didn't tell him to buy this shot-up hooptie. I walked into third period, the one class that my whole click & I shared together, Health.

"What up C?" "What's Goodie Blood?" A couple of my friends yelled out.

"I'm here to get my things I'm moving."

"What?" The surprise sunk in, I even seen sadness in the students that didn't like me, but laughed at my jokes. I was always smart and witty; at least that's what my Grandmother said.

The tears began to stream, surprisingly Ms. Cunningham came to hug me first which opened up the flood gates. I loved Ms. Cunningham, my friends and I use to make bets about if she was Gay or Not. In 1991 The LGBT Movement wasn't as powerful and accepted. People including my teacher were still trying their best to come out of the closet; while living closeted lives. I wrapped my arms around Bird & Autumn at the same time. I had a lot of friends come & go because of my constant moving. I was good with "un-attachable" until I met my LPJ's For Life friends. I guess it felt good to finally belong to something.

"Come on CJ we'll walk you to your car." Bird said excusing Autumn, Keyona and herself from class. Ms. Cunningham knew what it was with us. We ate, prank called, fought, and even pissed together. She knew my days of terrorizing Berry Middle School was over and gave over the hall passes.

"Take Care CJ," "Good Luck Champ," "Bye!" My classmates sang in chaos.

"Bye Yawl!" I waved at a few, hugged a couple. gave dap to some, before I was swept off my feet by Marshal. A few months prior Marshal caused me to fracture my tailbone, when he clipped me during a recess basketball game of my girls against his boys. Yea needless to say, he carried me to the office, then to the counselor's car so I could be dropped off over my grandmothers.

"Man I'm going to miss all of yawl!" Especially you's; I pointed to Lil Frank & Michael McGinnis. Frank was mixed, short cute, lil skinny, good curly head nervous dude. I wanted him to be my boyfriend but he was too short. (My friends always said he was a crack baby so I only dated him a little bit on the sneak). He told me I would have me some kind of exotic looking man in the future. Mikey was a chubby, brown-skinned black dude that always came over when my mom fried chicken. I swear he smelt it from his apartment. These were my niggas, we'd fight each other, then fight for each other. Having a history with a group of kids; felt good but the detachment was more than my 11 year old heart thought it could take.

"What the fuck is up with your dad's car yo?" Autumn asked sucking her thumb rubbing the top of her ear.

"You should've told Uncle Chucky to park dat ass down the street!" Bird chimed in as we busted into laughter.

"Hi Aunty Marlene; hi Uncle Chucky!" They all waved. I studied my mom laughing she must've heard them.

"I love yawl I'm going to stay in touch, yawl stay in touch."
"Damn you crying ass nigga, you got me crying and shit, you only moving to the east side, niggas do know how to catch the bus." I laughed at Autumn, she always knew what to say to lighten the mood or turn it up. We hugged & dapped up one last time. I hopped in the backseat and slid down on purpose so they could see me.

"You so crazy girl, ha, ha, ha!" They laughed hysterically.

"Bye Aunty Marlene, Bye Uncle Chucky, Son, Dom, Lil Poody." Everyone waved I'm sure they were happy to be acknowledged.

"I was going to say bye burnt Bart Simpson to your friend." My brother leaned over and whispered in my ear.

"Shut up punk". I jabbed him in his thigh giving him a frog. The rest of the ride to the new house was quite.

Mommy convinced Aunty Darlene to leave her two bedroom town house in Stratford Village, across from Oozy Alley better known as Greenbrier Housing project. I was happy she got a bigger place and my Cousin; Wee-Wee would be right next door. I had my cousin and was happy that my next door neighbor was my favorite roommate and not some strange family.

Mom decided to unpack the next day and not enroll us into school and I couldn't have been any happier. The following day however I would be enrolled in Yorktown Middle School. Same shit different school; at lunch I sat by myself, surveying all the students sitting in their little cliques. As I scanned the lunch room I crossed glances with this light skinned girl named Cheyenne. I could tell she was Ms. Popular she had her short haircut popping her fresh Nikes and daily multi colored sweat suits with the coordinating t-shirt hanging down. She was cute, high yellow; I would have placed her in the pretty girl clique instead of with the big ugly hood chicks terrorizing the school.

It was my 3rd day at this school and finally another girl named Bobbi introduced herself to me right before asking if she could borrow a pencil. We shared two classes together but not the same lunch period. I ate breakfast at home and at school today so I decided to skip the lunch line and head outside. Two little boys dropped their game of basketball in-order to go play football in the field with the students just exiting the lunch room. I shot ball by myself, hoping no one came to play a game.

"Look at this buster." I kept shooting as if that statement didn't apply to me.

"Ay ball check, your game is done, lil dirt." This yellow bitch Cheyenne has got to be out of her mind; I thought holding the ball firmly under my left arm. Stopping to look at this pretty, studly dressed bitch and her big, ogre, nappy head, garbage-pale friend who should've been in high school two years ago, would show them I wasn't moving.

"I don't know why you looking all stupid like you don't know we're talking to you." She wore this stupid overly confident smile as she walked towards me rubbing her hands.

"For one bitch, I'm looking stupid at this stupid ass clown talking shit to me. Number two I'm nobodies buster; bitch and your mouth is the only mouth running bitch. I'd go catch it if I was you." I said while bracing myself. I felt my insides starting to shake, the adrenaline was boiling. She looked back at her friend before walking into my face.

"Give me the ball bitch."

She tried yanking the ball from my arm; I grabbed hold of the ball then palmed it with both hands hitting her in the center of her forehead as hard as I could with the ball. I dropped the ball and began punching her nonstop in the face with my right hand. I planted my foot, grabbed her by the collar of her sweatshirt and slammed her to the ground. On her way down she grabbed a handful of my ponytail and I went down with her. I scrambled to be first to my knees as we both landed on the concrete on our sides.

"Cheyenne you better put in that work! You letting this little dusty bitch handle you." Her ogre friend yelled over top of us. The fear of her jumping in charged me to really beat the shit out of this girl on the ground so I could be on my feet if this big girl attacked. I banged her head on the concrete before being yanked up and held by the gym teacher. I noticed the blood on my Pink t-shirt not knowing whose it was hers or mine, I darted for the bathroom.

"Oh-Oh No you don't! You're going to the office!" The gym teacher yelled in my ear catching me mid sprint.
"Let me go I'm bleeding, let me go!" I yelled, kicked and screamed trying to free myself from his strong suppression.

"Calm down you're not bleeding." He said before softening his yell. He unhanded me and walked me towards the gym.

"Wait I got to get my book bag." I paused.

"Point to it, you stay right here and I'll go get it." I stood there in front of the lunch room doors looking around at all the kids looking, pointing at me. Two Teachers struggled to escort Cheyenne to the office as she was bucking, screaming and cussing about how I had her fucked up, I snuck her and she was going to beat my ass after school.

"Fuck you bitch!" I yelled out towards her, no-longer intimidated by her few inches over me, or her popularity and ogre clique. That bitch was all mouth and her punch wasn't shit! I saw some kids shaking their heads at me giving me the thumbs up.

"Yea so I haven't seen you around here before, you must be new, what's your name?" He opened the doors and handed me my bookbag.

"My name is Cernitha but everyone calls me C.J."

"So where are you from?" He asked appearing genuinely interested in me.

"I'm from everywhere, I just came from living back on the south-side for a while."

"Yea that good O'l Southside; I graduated from South High School myself." He seemed proud of his Alumni." I know I'm stepping out of bounds with this statement, but you appear to be the type of student that could appreciate it."

"I mean spit it out already then." I taunted with a smile as we walked to the Principals Office.

"Well- Miss C.J. I'm glad you stood up to Cheyenne; she uses her cute innocent looks and her friends to dominate most of the other students. But you surely showed her about that dirty south side."

I gave him a little chuckle and a lot of nods of understanding. I was overall pleased, I hate bitches that try to punk and bully people.

"Well she just let her mouth run down the street and I tried to give her a chance to go catch it."

He laughed in agreement as he opened the door to the office. The new male principal stood to greet us and receive my side of the story. Regardless I was giving a three day suspension and not the typical ten for fighting. I guess that bitch was on everybody's nerve in the school. I watched her in the back seat of her White Dad's car, her mother must be black or she's adopted; I conclude as I stayed in my resting bitch face. She stuck her tongue and middle finger at me, before receiving a swift back hand from the front seat. I decided not to laugh and continued to look at her emotionless. Karma is whatever you make it, I was just thankful to God for his sense of humor, allowing me to see my enemy punished.

Aunty Darlene and her family were moving in to the other-side of our half double. That was a pleasant sight to see. This may be one of the best summers yet, I thought to myself pulling up to the house in the backseat of the truancy officer's car. Everyone stopped to look at the

Whiteman bringing me home. Mom didn't have a phone so there was no way to contact her.

"What happened?" My mother rushed off my Aunt's porch toward me as I climbed out of the back seat.

"I'm Ok Mom, this girl Cheyenne a known bully at school tried to jump on me, so I expeditiously whipped that ass and got suspended for only three days."

"Yes ma'am it is normally a ten day suspension, the officer intruded. Because she was attacked and was defending herself and due to protocol we had to still give her an out of school suspension."
Mom turned me around examining me on the curb, before nudging me towards the house.

Turns out Aunty Darlene wouldn't stay in her side of the double for over two weeks. She moved right back to her two-bedroom Townhouse in Stratford and I would be back to trying to figure-out this new life alone.

§O§

§~Chapter 5~§
I Will Fight for Myself!

It was the Christmas Break before my 12th birthday; family gathered over Aunt Darlene & Uncle Charlie's two-bedroom townhouse in Stratford Village. Her little place was packed with their friends and family smashed into the living room, mainly hanging in the kitchen; snug around the bar and the two small card tables where they were playing cards and dominoes.

"You's a cheating motherfucker Chucky!" I heard one of my Uncle Charlies friends say to my dad. The laughter, the music and the partying felt good. But like all good things the party had to come to an end. My aunt's friend's husband for some reason decided to beat up his wife in my aunt's upstairs bathroom. He beat her up really good knocked her and the shower curtain into the tub, my aunt of all people broke it up.

I sat on the downstairs couch with my legs folded waiting for everyone to leave so that I could pull out the let out bed. My Aunts 5 children and my mom's youngest three all slept upstairs in the kids bunk beds and I slept down stairs on the pullout bed with my parents for the most part. Our pipes had busted a couple days ago and the house was frozen and flooded. My grandmother kept saying we should be thankful that we were over Aunty Darlene's and not there sleep in the middle of the night when it happened.

As the crowd left and everyone went to bed, my mother came down with a sever migraine headache. She always got those headaches when she was under a lot of stress. I decided not to go to the crazy hospital with her; she could get her Orudis Shot alone. The last time we went some crazy wild haired black lady was calling me and my mom a witch, more so my mother. It freaked me all the way out; I decided not to go back.

I woke up to my father telling me that he had to go pick up a body and if mom called here looking for him to tell her that he had a run to make and to put her code in his pager.

"Yes Sir, I'll tell her dad." With that I laid back down, what seemed like an hour went past when I heard the phone ring. Damn I cursed to myself, upset to be awakened from my sleep. I crawled in the dark to the end of the couch bed to grab the phone off the stand.

"Hey is this Chachi?"

"Yes Dad." I growled into the phone.

"Did your momma call Chach?"

"No Sir."

"You cool?"

"Yes Sir."

"Oh aiight, let cha momma know that I called."

I hung up the phone and lay back on the couch bed. For some odd reason I started thinking about my old History Teacher telling us during Black History Month Black People should exercise their power and existence by refraining from participating in White America.

"Don't buy their products, don't watch their shows, be segregated, segregation was good!" The bald black man ranted.

"Who here loves Looney Toon's?" The class looked weirdly at him an around at one another.

"No go on, lift your hands up its ok to be in Middle School and still watch cartoons, they're supposed to be the purest enjoyment, its ok." The class started to raise their hands.

"Good!" He continued. "Who has ever seen the Tasmanian Devil? Who likes it?" More of the class raised their hands. I remembered looking around in amazement at all these kids wasting their brains watching stupid cartoons.

My brother and I fought all the time over the TV. He always wanted to watch cartoons and I wanted to watch the videos; he always won.

"OK how many of you students ever read the Encyclopedia Britannica?" Myself and couple other students and I raised our hands. "Interesting enough, The Tasmanian devil story derives from the Caucasian making fun of their massacred conquering of the Tasmanian People (or Tribe) which later led to their extinction. These savages pillaged, destroyed the people viciously destroying everything in their way and they laugh in mockery in our face with the cartoon that we all love so much and the history behind it, that we know nothing about." -Damn that was deep.

I opened my eyes slowly as I felt the presence of a strong body lying on top of me. At first I thought it was my dad drunk, crawling into the bed, until I realized that he was trying to stick his fingers into my night pants and panties.

"Stop!" I screamed out, before he smashed his hand over my face. Instantly I realized it was Uncle Montreal, well my cousin's uncle. "Ahh get off me!" I screamed into his hand trying to bite at his palm that was covering my nose and my mouth, as he dug his other finger into my vagina. The tears begin to rush down my face as I was fighting to breathe.

"C'mon keep your little ass still, I know you like me, you've always had a crush on me." He plunged his fingers deeper into my vagina sending sharp pains up my side and through my spine.

"Please." I cried into his hand. I squirmed from side to side, attempting to release some of this pressure from his heavy body on my chest, and hoping to pull his hand out of my vagina and the other off my mouth.

"Be still this little pussy getting wet, be quite before you wake up your Aunty' nem." He lifted his body weight off me as he tried to position himself to pull my jogging pants off.

"No!" I yelled pulling my knee up into the back of his balls as hard as I could. Causing him to grab his growing, jump off the bed and run into the kitchen. I laid there holding my sore vagina, and my broken mind, too mentally paralyzed to move. I took a loud deep breath coming to my senses, realizing I needed to go wake up Aunty Darlene & tell Uncle Charlie before my parents got home.

Quietly I lifted my head off the bed and slowly turned seeing his geeked eyes beaming at me through the bars through the dark. It wasn't hard to miss his crispy black ass in those tight bright yellow booty shorts; with the cut out pockets that his dick hang out of when he spread his legs open.

"Shit!" I shrieked to myself; dropping my head back onto the lumpy hard couch-bed. Mad at him and myself for being too scared to get up and walk past him sitting on the steps. I took a deep breath as I imagined what might be a big fight to get passed him.

I held my hands clinched together squeezing, stretching my t-shirt in-between my legs.

"Dear God I'm so scared, please send my dad and my mom here right now, please." I pleaded inside my head. God please give me the strength to fight him if he grabs me on the steps because I want to get out of this dark living room away from him." I tilted my head to the side to wipe some of the streaming tears that were saturating my itching face. The burning sensation of anger and hurt perused through my veins like venom. The adrenaline began to make me feel like the Incredible Hulk. Oh my God, I could just feel him staring at me, contemplating if he should come back over or if he should watch me cry myself to sleep and deal with the after math in the morning.

"Ooh fuck it." I jumped to my feet and darted up the stairs past Montreal who was sitting in a daze overlooking me on the fourth step.

I felt as if he was reaching to grab me, as I reached the fifth step, I kicked him in his back forcing him to stumble down the steps.

I ran the rest of the flight busting into my aunts room jumping in the space in-between my Aunt and Uncle's passed out bodies.

"Aunty Darlene." I cried lowly shaking her, watching as my tears dropped to her face and she began twitching & whipping in her sleep. Surprisingly Uncle Charlie didn't budge.

"What the hell?" She questioned shaking herself out of her sleep. "Cernitha?" She looked baffled as she tried to focus into consciousness.

"Aunty Darlene please get up, I want to talk to you in the bathroom." I heard the toilet flush knowing it was Montreal eavesdropping. What if he attacked me? The fear didn't stop the tears and this nonstop shaking feeling in my stomach. I plunged my head down hard on her soft bed.

"Ok Cernitha damn, go to the bathroom, I'm going to get some clothes on, and I'll be in there."

"Please hurry up Aunty, I'm scared, I'm scared to go in there by myself." She looked very concerned at my face full of tears.

"Ok baby go get in the bed with Wee-Wee nem. Let me get a cigarette and I'll come get you."

I looked at my hung over Aunt, as she held her comforter to her naked breast. I climbed backwards on my knees off the bed wondering why Uncle Charlie who still lay face down, didn't move to help me? With my hands clinched onto the bottom of my T-shirt I ran as fast as I could down the short hall to the kids' room. Montreal had already left the bathroom, and the fear of seeing him was causing my heart to beat out of my chest.

I opened the door to my Cousin's room as I tripped over the shoe skate that Wee-Wee and I shared alike from Grandma.

"Ahh…" I wailed allowing the defeated and wounded feeling to overtake me, I made my way through the clutter to the twin bed where my cousin and two other bodies lay at the opposite end. Her ripping the covers off her face and down to her knees out of nowhere sent me into panic.

"Oh my God, Wee you scared me!" For the first time I thought to wipe the tears from streaming down my face.

"Come here cuz." She opened her arms to me signaling for a hug. I fell into her arms as if they were going to protect me from the monster downstairs.

"Did Uncle Montreal do some nasty things to you?" Her question shocked me, as if she seen what had happened.

"Yes I woke up because he was on top of me covering my nose and my mouth with his hand and he was mashing his other fingers into my cootie-cat, then he was trying to take my pants off." I started to cry hard again.

"I thought he was going to come in here and stick his fingers in my stuff again. Whenever he put on them nasty yellow shorts and let his nasty thang hang out he always be trying to touch me; and play with his thang." She hugged me tighter as if her comfort was for the both of us.

"I'm about to tell your mom, I don't know what's taking her so long." I wondered as I stared at the closed door.

"You're not afraid of what he's going to do to you after you tell on him? What if they whip you?"

"Who?" I asked pushing from her embrace.

"No I'm not scared, I want my dad to kick his ass and while he's kicking his ass, I'm going to jump in and hit him as hard as I can too." I wiped my face again, finding strength in my momentary resolve to have his ass beat.

"Don't say nothing to my mom about me, I have to live here and yawl will be moving soon, and I will be stuck here with him by myself like before yawl moved in." I watched the tears well up in her eyes as she relieved his abuse in the movie of her mind. I jumped to my feet as I heard the door open. I sighed with relief as her mom's yellow hands and flawless red fingernails gripped the door.

"Don't worry I got you." I looked back at her with guarantee, this motherfucker was about to get dealt with. I sat on the tub as my Aunt sat on the toilet lighting another cigarette. Her pink foam rollers reminded me of Grandma's. I wish I was over Grandma's right now instead of crying and shaking in this small, cold, smoky bathroom. I relived the story three times to my aunt as she kept asking me the same questions.

"Are you sure you wasn't dreaming?" She asked.

"Dreaming about what Aunty?" She rubbed her eyes an inhaled her cigarette.

"Didn't you say you had a bad dream?" For some reason that really pissed me off.

"No Aunty I didn't say anything, Montreal was on top of me when I woke up with his hand over my nose and mouth, digging into my cootie-cat with his other hand. He was trying to slide my pants off with his body, and he said that I know I wanted it and I didn't." The tear flow returned without warning.

"Aw shit." She shook her head realizing the problems that lay ahead. "I mean are you sure that's what happened CJ?"

"Yes I'm sure Aunty why do you keep saying that?"

"I don't know ladybug I'm still trying to wake up and wrap my mind around this shit. So is your mom still at the hospital?"

"Yes ma'am my dad called I talked to him and when I went back to sleep that's when Montreal got on top of me." I was already growing tired of the line of questions. I sensed that Aunty Darlene was stuck inside her head and my best option was to wait until my parents got back to take action.

"Aunty I'm-a just go lay-down with Wee-Wee and wait for my parents to come." She sat on the toilet starring at the wall smoking her cigarette as I walked back into my kid's bedroom.

"So what she say?" Wee-Wee asked popping back out of the cover. I now realized why she always stayed so tucked in her bed.

"She just kept asking me was I sure, was I dreaming. No he woke me from my dream, I'm sure I was awoke."

God where is my parents. I hope my mom got enough migraine shot to deal with this drama when she comes back. I felt a tinge of sadness for my parents. I knew they would both be exhausted an out of their minds.

My Aunt knocked on the door about an hour later. "CJ your mom is here."

I jumped up and ran downstairs to where she stood in-front of the fridge downing her left-over bottle of Pepsi. I hugged her tight as if this was my first time seeing her in years.

"What you doing up so late Lady Bug?" She took a deep breath looked at me and jerked her head. "What's a matter with you CJ, have you been crying?" I didn't want to make my mom sick but I had to tell her, as my dad walked into the kitchen, I blurted out my announcement in fear.

"Uncle Montreal held me down, climbed on top of me and was sticking his fingers into my cootie-cat." Both their mouths dropped open at my confession. By that time, Uncle Charlie, Aunty Darlene and Wee-Wee joined us in the kitchen. Uncle Charlie went straight to his small freezer behind his bar and grabbed two beers.

"So somebody tell me what the hell is going on around here?" Uncle Charlie asked popping his can downing his beer.

"That's what the fuck I'm trying to figure out, what's really going on?"

I looked at my mom who was holding her head shaking. "Montreal climbed on top of me, held me down and stuck his fingers in my cootie-cat."

"What-the-fuck-you-just-say Chach?" My dad slammed down his can of beer as my mom walked over and grabbed him. I stood beside the refrigerator looking at everyone seemingly lost in the fucking sauce. I mean it wasn't rocket science. The grown ass motherfucker climbed on-top of me held me down and stuck his nasty crack headed fingers in my cootie-cat...

"MONTREAL!!!" Uncle Charlie screamed into the living-room at a fake sleeping Montreal.

"MONTREAL wake up! Get in here; you're being accused of molesting a kid!"

"He digs in my stuff all the time too!" Wee-wee yelled into the atmosphere. That was the feeling of the second bomb dropping, everyone was already shocked by my confession but her confession just made this motherfucker a repeat offender a certified pedophile.

"I didn't touch those kids, man them my nieces, I've known those kids before they knew their own mother fucking selves." I heard Montreal pleading his case as he slowly joined us from the living room.

"Oh no motherfucker, my daughter ain't none of your kin, neither is my niece for-real and you gone end up dead, touching mines motherfucker." The calmness of my mom's voice silenced the kitchen as she slowly grabbed one of the steak knives from the wooden rack.

"No Stuff." My dad scrambled from behind the bar towards my mother as she was slowly moving towards Montreal. She must've had way too much Orudis because she was moving in super slow motion. The whole scene made me break out into a loud wail.

"You did touch me! You did hold me down! You did stick your fingers in my stuff!"

"Your fast ass must have been dreaming that." I couldn't believe he said that standing there holding the wall. I looked at my dad who seemed to only want to hold my drugged up mother. Uncle Charlie, Aunt Darlene pleaded with him, each other, my dad and Wee-Wee.

"So ain't nobody going to do shit, to this child molester?

How many mother fucking times are yawl going to ask me what happen and I say this motherfucker did this to me and everybody still standing here stuck on stupid.

"Ahh!" I felt myself fall out of love and into disgust with my parents. I charged towards Montreal, I was going to hit him so hard in his dick, just like I seen on TV, drop down and punch as hard as you can while leaning into the drop down.

"Ugh!" I gasped for air as my dad grabbed me around my neck mid drop.

"C'mon C, C'mon we bout to get some shit together over here!"

"Fuck That!" My mom went back for the knife rack. It was Chaos but through all the confusion nobody was whipping Montreal's ass. Is this some kind of alternate fucking universe? Why ain't my dad or Uncle Charlie whipping his ass? Well of course he was Uncle Charlie's grown ass younger brother so he wasn't going to help. But what was my dad's problem? His o'l keeping the peace, body snatching, weak ass didn't swing so I snapped; snapped right into Irate.

I tried to run up on him again, before my aunt grabbed me and folded me into her bosom.

"That's alright bitch, I'm going to call my Uncle Jr, My Uncle Reggie, my Uncle Timmy, Uncle Kendal and Uncle Tony and I'm going to have them fuck you up! I hate you motherfucker!" I yelled.

"Cernitha; watch your mouth!" My mom yelled snatching me into her arms.

"No!!! No!!!" I cried into her shaking chest as she held onto me for dear life.

I must've lost my mind that night, because I can't remember what happened next, I was enrolled into Eastmoor Middle School. Home at my aunties' six kids slept in the set of bunk beds, Wee-wee and I shared the twin bed occasionally inviting one of our little sisters. The 3 boys slept on the top bunk and the three girls slept on the bottom. Baby Charlie slept in the room with Aunty Darlene.

I just remember waking up daily into this life that I hated. Everyday Montreal's creepy ass would smile at me, smirking at my demise. I hated my weak ass father; if I was my dad I would have killed that motherfucker. Put him in the body bag and took him to one of my friends. Of course he would have gone to jail because of Uncle Charlie who would have had to help his brother.

"Damn Fuck I hate the world!" I screamed at the early brisk May morning.

"Yea fuck the world girl!" My red head friend Melissa laughed as she walked up to the bus stop behind me.

"Another hard day at the farm?" She smiled sipping on her orange juice box.

I wiped my eye and the slow tear that sporadically kept escaping my right eye all morning.

"I just wished that I could go live back with my grandmother." I fought back the tingling in my nose as I felt the emotions gather and my tears surface.

"You're not going to do this today CJ you are stronger than this." I said to myself hoping my words would block these building emotions.

I melted in her unexpected embrace.

"It's ok CJ I know what you're going through. My Uncle molested me too, and my mom is still cool with him today, and I feel like she's been even harder on me since it happened. Which is real fucked up, I'm just doing this school shit because that's what we're supposed to do, then as soon as I turn 16 I'm going to find me a man girl and he's going to take me away from my fucking mom, and I'm going to go to school and do my life with him at his crib girl. Shyyyt I'm too pretty to be in foster care, you too pretty to be in Juvie girl."

We laughed and hugged and laughed some more as the other students approached the bus stop.

~§~§~§~§~§~§~

School

~§~§~§~§~§~§~

School was the same boring ass rigmarole; they didn't have the GT Program so I had to catch a bus twice a month to the program down town. I hated this fucking life. My aunt moved my Grandmother out of the house that everybody grew up in, three generations. It was pretty cool my aunt Karen took over the place for a little while. I was happy my cousin Tasha got to move back to Columbus. I never ever understood for the life of me why her and her brother had to move to Alabama with my Aunts' Husband's mother, who wasn't any kin to us, while he my Aunt and their new son stayed here in Ohio.

My cousin called me one night crying: saying that she hated her mom, and that her and her brother was sleeping in the broom closet. Through the tears she told me that Uncle Hallen was molesting her when their mom left for bingo. I couldn't believe this shit, these fucking women in this family was crazy. And they hooked up with a family of brothers who was crazy, crack-heads, child molesters and fags. Why did Karen send Tasha to Alabama? Why couldn't she stay here? Why was she getting molested and not doing anything about it? Why was Wee-Wee and I getting molested by the other brother here and no one was doing shit about it?

I shared what happened to me and Wee-Wee and told her that I was going to start robbing them all when they got drunk and high, So we could save enough money to all move back in with Grandma and to keep her house. Hell all a twelve year old could do was dream and scheme. This boy Andy or Anthony Dixon decided to be my boyfriend. He was cute light brown skinned with pretty hazel eyes. He told me when he grew up he was going straight to the army. We could get married and I could go to law school from the army base.

I loved it, another plan of escape. He was working out and I was hoping he could kick Montreal's ass before we moved. I hated school my cousin Tyunn was super popular at this school and I figured that he didn't really bring me into his circle because I was bummy. We lost everything when the pipes busted. We were only able to salvage a few things, including my clarinet which my aunt & grandmother brought me. Band and Track was the only life I had outside of Misery.

There were a few bitches at the school trying to give me the blues as usual, my mind stayed constant on other shit. I didn't give them the time I only just gave them the "jump if you want, resting bitch face." Melissa and I were going to meet Wesley and Andy behind her park to go walk to the other neighborhoods together. I arrive to Melissa's house on Lil' Charlie's bike as she rushed her bike around to the front.

"Girl hurry up lets go, Ms. Diane's ass tripping again today, she missed her meds." She laughed scurrying onto her bike.

"Your mom?" I was puzzled.

"Yes!" She laughed pushing past me on her bike. As I caught up to her I heard her mom yelling out the front door.

"Melissa you think your ass is funny, you're going to clean the whole house when you get your red headed, fast, yellow ass back here! You Hear Me?

"Ah!" Her mom was a trip. She had the cleanest apartment I have ever seen. All her furniture was still in the plastic. Melissa had to do toothbrush detail sometimes, and I always wondered why the hell did she have to clean a spotless house so much?

We rode the two building distance between her house and the row of apartments before my Aunts. She pulled up behind Mandy's apartment where Mandy, Erin and her twin sister stood laughing. Melissa parked her bike and hoped off. I pushed up the hill hoping not to get my hanging jean jumper strap caught in the spokes. I pulled up to the conversation as Wesley and Andy turned the corner. I got off my bike and pushed the kick stand.

"Erin I know you were talking about me, Regina told me on the bus, and you supposed to be beating my ass?" Melissa was about five inches taller than all of us, she was the same height as Andy, who she grew up with and hated the fact that we were dating.

"He's such a buster CJ." She would always say laughing at him. But today this heifer could have told me that some shit was going to pop off, but with us time was always of the essence. I smiled as I seen Andy riding closer he was so cute.

"Nobody said I wanted to fight you, I said I was going to beat CJ's ass." I snapped my head back to their conversation right as Erin was walking up to me.

"Oh hell naw!" I yelled as she pushed me down on the bike and I went crashing to the ground. I struggled to my feet from the bike, looking at an utterly shocked Andy and a smiling Wesley. Erin stood there smiling right before I rushed to my feet, ran up and socked her square in the mouth.

"Oh Shit!" Mandy yelled; I'm sure they weren't expecting that, or the fury of blows I socked to her, backing her up to the rail pillar. The last blow caved her, forcing her harder against the pillar.

"Erin hit that bitch back!" Her sister yelled beside us. Tussling; as we locked hands on each other's hair.

"I bet you bitches better not jump in!"

"Shut up Melissa you always instigating some shit!" Wesley jokingly taunted his hyped girlfriend.

Her wild monkey punch stunned me, knocking my fake cap loose. I was overly conscious of my front tooth which was constantly being repaired since my biking accident. I bent over holding my face, securing my tooth back on the mount. The crowd fell quiet not knowing if Erin hurt me, if I lost my tooth or what happened. All they knew was as soon as I stood up (secured my tooth) I grabbed her hair with my left hand and punched her repeatedly all over her face with my right.

"AHHH!" I shrieked pulling her head toward the pillar.

"Bitch!" I punched one more good time through her failed block attempts.

"You got me fucked up!" I yanked and yanked until I pulled her head through the weak cast iron pillar. I kicked my foot back at her approaching sister as I began to hit her captured head. Andy grabbed me dragging me down into a squatting position on the ground.

"Damn Bae, Stop! What you trying to do, Kill the bitch?" I busted out laughing at his concerned face after a few seconds. He pulled me to my feet as I rubbed my instantly hurting wrist. I looked at the girls helping Erin's crying head out the flimsy cast iron, low income pillar. I was proud of myself, I felt good for a change. Andy handed me my bike and we rode off toward the entrance. I looked back at the three light skinned girls, Mandy who was officially now my ex friend and the two twins who tried the wrong bitch today!

Hum; I snorted feeling alive for the first time, rushing to adventure and high off my victory.

~§~§~§~§~§~§~

This was going to be one of the best Friday's of my life. Mom said Aunty Karen had just got back from picking up Tasha and Larry and they were going to come over for a-while. We kicked it hard, the adults all went out to the bar up the street and returned in small groups to collect their kids. Tash, Wee-Wee & I caught up, joked, laughed, cried, mainly about the shared stories of molestation. What the fuck is going on? How come the guys in this family are molesting me & my cousins and these blind shallow ass women we call our mothers aren't doing anything about it? I watched as Tasha fought back the tears from dropping down her face as she told me how they had to sleep in something like a closet, and he would molest her late at night. We gossiped and hugged so much, like we were soldiers coming back from war. Aunt K came back for Tasha, she and her husband dropping off Montreal.

"Damn!" I ran upstairs to tell Wee-Wee that he just got dropped off and our parents weren't back yet.

"Get your stockings on Girl." I whispered as I ran into the room. History told me that he only got in the molesting spirit when he was drunk or high on his dope. When he was sober he tried to be the black player or the Holy Roller. This bastard was fucked, but we were ready for his ass if he tried some shit tonight.

We kept our weapons beside us and under the bed in-case he ever decided to come back into the room. We tied the shoe skate to the door to alert us to anyone coming in the room.

"He put his yellow shorts on C." Wee-wee said running into the bedroom. She jumped in the bed and we said the same prayers every night that we use to say together at grandmas. It wasn't even 45 minutes later when this bastard came strolling into the room; It didn't matter he wasn't digging today. We had thick tight stockings over our panties under our sweats. I took it a step further putting on my body suit. I hated showing my body at all; this bastard would have to dig through my neck to touch my Coochie tonight. I felt Wee-Wee nudge me in the side as he felt up the course of my leg. I nudged her back one quick time.

"Not today Mother-fucker!" I yelled pulling the cover off me, hitting him in the head with the shoe skate I was clutching.

"YAH!" Wee-Wee followed up hitting him on the top of the head with her Easy Bake Oven. I kicked him in the stomach causing him to double over as we continuously beat him with the skate and oven. I kept looking in-between ducks, kicks and swings. If she was up I was down beating this motherfucker everywhere. Son sat up asking 'what was going on?

"Just hit this motherfucker!" I yelled as he smacked me down to the floor. I dropped the skate that was hurting my hand & picked up one of the boy's plastic & metal red fire trucks, this motherfucker was trying to flip my cousin off his back; so I kicked him in the dick. Scurried to my feet, hauled back and hit him across his face as hard as I could, with the metal part of the fire truck.

We continued to kick and hit him as he ran out the door.

"So I guess yawl wasn't lying." Son huffed trying to catch his breath. That fight was every bit of two minutes but seemed like a life time. I couldn't wait for my fucking parents to get home so I stood at the top of the steps listening watching him put his pants over those tight ass yellow shorts. I guess he was getting dressed to leave, I'm sure he couldn't explain away that ass beaten we just gave him.

"Oh God, why? Why won't they hurry up and get here?"

§O§

§~Chapter 6~§
Heavy & the Vydoc

Here we go a-fucking-gain. We hadn't even moved all the way in the half double, literally and my dad was in the front yard grilling. Yea everyone knows it's the first of the month, we BBQing and moving in at the same damn time. Shit I'm sure my parents were happy to no longer be sleeping on Aunty Darlene's & Uncle Charlie's couch bed. Hell I know I was tired of it; it was the summer before eighth grade. And whatever school I was about to attend would officially be school #9 and I'm not even in the 9th grade yet.

I sat on the concrete slab considered a front porch with my box of shit for my bedroom. I looked up and down Sidney Street in disgust. Why are these stupid motherfuckers at the end of the block huddled up like a football team, blasting that loud ass music? I wonder how fucking long we're going to be here?

"Hey Lil Momma what's happening?"

I looked at the black Nissan Maxima and this huge light skinned, hazel eyed, wild nappy head nigga in the passenger seat. The crazy; who the fuck are you? Expression on my face and my dancing eyebrows caused the two big niggas in their small ass box car to bust out in laughter. I watched my mom look at the car behind her U-Haul and back up at me in my peripheral.

"Fuck nigga, do I look like I care to talk to strangers?"
"Ooh Fuck Nigga!" The apparent bigger light skinned driver yelled!

"Fuck you nigga." The hazel eyed passenger said play punching the driver in the body before turning his attention back to me.

"Alright attitude I'll see you around." The driver turned up his stereo very loud as the passenger hung out the window waving his black and white scarf at my mother.

"Wrong Set Nigga!" Mom snapped at the two rude light-skinned wild hair fat boys. "And you watch your fucking mouth." She mugged before smiling at me leaning against the corner of the U-Haul lighting her cigarette. I wondered what a 'Set' was, as I looked at my mom and back down the street at the car now parking down the street with the rest of the loud cars. My mother had on a red and white scarf a red spaghetti strapped tank top, herself-made blue jean shorts and her white girl tennis shoes. She looked much better today than in days recently passed. She had her episodes more when she was stuck in stressful situations. She was alive, alert and bossy as fuck today, her usual self. When she would have a migraine episode she would do whatever it took to get to the doctor, to get that shot or pill that gold balance for her body.

I know she smoked a joint earlier with my dad. My mom got high but I knew it was more of my dad's thing. I dropped the box on my little sister's mattress and leaned over my bed and opened the window.

"So this is your new place Marlene? I knew that voice. That was my Gan-Gan, in traditional terms: My Grandmother. I stuck my head out the window and looked toward the street. Yes that was Grandpa Harvey's car so I knew they were dropping off Tasha. I ducked back into the window as fast as I could, racing towards the bedroom door, which so strangely reminded me of Shawn's & my old bedroom on 22nd. Yea I lived on both sides of the property.

"Where you at pimp?" Tasha yelled!

"I'm coming player!" I yelled out towards her voice as I raced down the dark staircase. We both laughed and braced ourselves from smashing head first into one another. What up Boss, What's up Killer, we thought we were hard with our made up hand shake.

We walked back outside "Hi Gan-Gan, hi Grandpa Harvey." I waved to him as I walked down to hug my grandmother. I didn't have anything personal against Harvey. Even though he wore that big creepy thick mustache always smiled and talked very slow he was cool with me. I heard stories throughout the family how all of Gan-Gan's younger children tied him up one drunk night and beat the shit out of him with toys, tennis rackets and shit.

"So you know that Ollie is taking us to Dayton next weekend to get in the studio with Kenny Logan and some other industry people. I heard him telling Gan-Gan yesterday, has he talked to your mom?" Tash questioned.

"No, not that I know of." We grabbed two more medium boxes and headed back to my room. I stepped over, then kicked the box in the dining room on my way upstairs.

"Ay grab that box right there cuz." Using my foot to point at the box containing my vinyl record collection; "So did they say when we were going down there?"

"Nah but I'm thinking this weekend. Maybe Ollie couldn't get in touch with your mom because yawl was in transition. But I thought we should wear our Tan Dickie outfits, I'm wearing my grey sports-bra and Boxer set." She said looking at her reflection in wall mirror against my wall.

"That's cool but since you wearing Tan & Grey I'm going to wear Grey & Tan. I got these cute colorful Looney-Toon Boxers, I got them before we packed up, I'm-a look for the fit first thing."

~§~§~§~§~§~§~

"Girl you won't believe this shit." I said as soon as Tasha came to the phone.

"Girl I come home and this chick sitting in my living-room with an outfit just like mine, I'm like oh hey I'm CJ, I got an outfit just like that."

The chick like "oh hey I'm Kisa were moving in next door and we were meeting with the landlord and I started my period in my jump suit so your mom let me borrow your outfit. Her and my mom went to the store; they should be on their way back soon."

"What girl? So she just sitting up there in your shit! Bwahaha!" Tasha busted out laughing.

"Right, my mom always picking up strays bringing them into her stray family." We both laughed as I thought about all the extended lifelong family members my mother created over the years.

~§~§~§~§~§~§~

The ride to Dayton was fun, Uncle Ollie & Bobbi sat up front, while Tasha, Kisa & I sat in the back. We decided to add Kisa to the group since she could dance really good. She kind of looked like the odd chick; Bobbi, Tasha & I where wearing our Dickies, while Kisa wore jeans and a jersey. Cute but odd, none the less.

The producers introduced us to their three all male rap-group Named 3Deep: CJ, Travis, and Kevin this is CJ, Bobbi, Tasha & Kisa 3Deep meet Next-N-Line. We stood in the foyer shaking hands and reintroducing ourselves, Instantly CJ pulled me to the side.

"I see you share a few things in common with me, we're both named CJ, We both the oldest and we both the leader." He smiled self-impressed.

"Not to mention we both look good and I think you want to look good with me." I looked him up and down twisting up my lips."

"Oh you're something else aren't you Miss CJ? He laughed rubbing the sides of his chin with his right hand.

"I like you already." He smiled. I looked at him as if I was sizing him up.

"You should." I smiled before walking back to Tasha. We flirted and recorded the same song over and over and over all night. By the end of the night it was official: CJ was my boyfriend, Kevin was Tasha's boyfriend and Travis was Kisa's boyfriend. Bobbi said she didn't like any of them, after heavy flirting that lead to nowhere.

~§~§~§~§~§~§~

As Protocol mommy told me about the slumber party to help us unpack. My cousins were all coming through. Uncle Ollie gave my mom these two huge speakers at our last party on Rich St. We planned to shake the neighborhood. It was way more teenagers and kids my age here on the North-side. The crew and I took turns on the front porch choreographing our new Hip Hop Pop (twerk) dance to Daz Efx, when a mob of neighborhood girls came walking down the middle of my street, stopping in-front of my porch.

"Hey is CJ up there?" One of the girls from the crowd yelled. Oh my God I thought, surveying the number of girls verses the number of me & my cousins.

"I'm CJ." I said stepping in front of Bobbi on the porch; leaping off the concrete slab and down the steps to the side walk.

"I'm Marnika, This is Leni, Tina, Jasmin, Shawntay, LaPina, Brandy with a Y and Brandi with an I. We heard that you be dancing and doing music and we wanted to see what's up, if you wanted to have a dance competition or if you wanted to make a group."

"Oh, Ok that's tight, that's what's up." Tasha nodded her head back and forth. This was the first time a group of new girls came for us for a dance competition, I loved it.

"Ok, OK we can do a dance competition and then we can make a group." Scooter said slapping fives with her sister Netta.

"Alright so give us like a half an hour. Oh and I'm CJ, This is Tasha, Wee-Wee, Scooter, Netta, Bobbi, Bear-Bear or Shawntay, us three have a rap group and my other cousins dance for us from time to time, but anyway. We are working on this routine to Das Efx yawl make up yawl version and we'll do ours." I smiled pulling my grey jogging pants up by the knees.

-BOOM the crackling of the thunder and lightning scared us all. We laughed, slapped and shook hands as they made their way down the street to practice. We ran up the steps into my house geeked.

"We popping off, its' going down!"

"So yawl about to have a dance completion hun?" My mom asked with the widest of smiles on her face. "Move the dining room table and practice in here, so they can't see any of yawls moves."

"That's right Aunty Marlene!" Wee-Wee co-signed, this was going to be fun, she was our secret weapon the youngest smallest one but could flip down into your Chinese splits, Scooter could out Shake everybody and we knew we had it in the bag. Mom helped us choreograph the quick routine and the knock on the door meant it was 'Go Time'.

Because they called for the competition we made them go first and their dance was tight. These chicks had a whole different style; they were dancing hardcore but sexy, Coochie and back popping. Leni went up to Netta and started popping but Scooter ran in front of the challenge. This shit was live, and so the heavens must've thought as they decided to send down the pouring rain.

"Damn-it, we're still going to do our routine yawl. Mom rewind the song!" For some reason the song wasn't working and my mom put on Slam and it was over, we were slamming, popping, shaking, flipping in the rain. A lot of the neighbors stood on their porches and in their doorways cheering us all on. That night I made a whole neighborhood full of friends. The multitude of slumber parties, talent shows and performances grew like wild fire.

Me & K'dog (Tasha) was popping, our name was spreading, more local artist wanted to do features with us. Our managers T.E.O.S (The Element of Surprise) Sonny, Gi'Ant, Ron, & Rick; were really grinding for us, we were getting exposed everywhere big and small. Sonny believed we found the right chemistry with the group with just Tasha & I. I wrote the raps on every song for each girl anyway. Being conscious of four different styles for four individual girls and considering my cousin's unique voice was hard work for a fourteen year old.

Three was better than four: Bobbi aka Misdemeanor; was pulled out of the group because of her Joe Jackson father Uncle Ollie. No one wanted to work with him which meant we couldn't work with her. Then Kisa got kicked out because her mother tried to make us clean up and do all sorts of other wild shit when we were supposed to be at her house practicing.

Unlike Kim, Ollie would practice us to death and back. He said he looked like Howard Hewitt back in the day and he had all the ladies. I guess it was true because he had My Aunt Darlene, My Aunt Lue, Aunt Roz and Wendy. Shit either he was pimping or getting seriously passed around at any rate he had dreams of being a star and it showed how he pushed us, but really how he pushed Bobbi. I felt like he pushed her into using that overly aggressive voice, but at the end of the day she's a Mic killer none the less.

My friends from the Doc would tell me different things she and her dad would say about me when they saw them, they said that she was now going by the name Mystery and she was signed to Columbus Mob. That was all well and good she was still my cousin regardless. The problem came in when they said she was still using my rhymes and not just the ones I wrote for her but the ones I wrote for myself too.

"Dayyum Cuz; now that's crossing the fucking line." Tasha said to me in response to Lenny & Tina's confession. Uncle Ollie had stopped coming around for a while, he was pissed that all the mothers voted him off, the management team. In spite he wouldn't let Bobbi be in the group anymore.

"Damn he cold." I exaggerated as we all laughed, shaking our heads. This music shit to say the least was an added entertainment in my life.

I stayed in-touch with Travis and C.J my 1st male rap buddies. Even though they lived in Dayton, It felt good to have somebody to share my music news with. Most of my friends couldn't be happy about what they couldn't understand and for the most part they probably didn't care out of jealousy. But we popping, fuck'um pass they momma the blunt.

~§~§~§~§~§~§~

The police arrived pushing everyone back to the curb, I watched as they took pictures, questioned the Lesbians and next door neighbors. Tommy's cousin cried frantically putting on like her soul had just been snatched out of her. It's funny she had her head down and was rocking on the steps of the porch, smoking her cigarettes before the police pulled up. As soon as they arrived she became the grieved, answers demanding Cousin-in-law. I was fixated; I've always been afraid of death; crazy considering my father worked in the afterlife business. My mother at times would do the hair or makeup of the deceased only for the families she cared about or that couldn't afford it.

My brothers, my mother and all the neighbors were now standing on the sidewalks and in the street, checking out the crime scene. I sat on the oversized elevated concrete slab we called our front porch; kicking my legs in a daze. Entranced by Tommy's dead beaten bloody white head laying out the side window, looking directly at me. The police assigned two officers to keep the growing crowd back. But today death was in my face, death was staring at me for an hour through Mr. Tommy. Poor Tommy; he told my dad, he felt something was going to happen to him and he was right. One of them chicks smashed his nose bone up into his brain with a hammer.

We watched in amazement as Tommy's head hang dead out the side window. I imagined how the rest of his body looked inside the house. His dead eyes staring into death, wasn't ready for that blow to the head; looking directly at us his eyes said he was traumatized before he departed. Tommy was a frail, West Coast Valley boy, in his late twenties, trying the Midwest drug & job supply. Tommy was 5ft 8 blond haired, blue eyes not ugly but not handsome; Tommy lived across the street in a 2 bedroom half double, with the two fat black Lesbians. One was his mean, overweight oddy- body cousin. The other woman was and his cousin's wife.

Tommy would get drunk with my dad and Uncles telling stories of them Dikes Robbing him, fucking with his blow and other shit as he would say while nearly falling out the chair holding his beer mug.

"Chucky I swear man!" He slurred, If any mu-fucking thing happen to me, (he continued in his drunken slur) tells the police them Dikes did it, these bitches don't know I got me a new place, I'm about to move in and leave them nasty, ungodly hoes here. You hear me Chuck?"

"Yea, I hear you Tommy." My dad shook his head and drunk his beer.

"Good." Nodded a semi coherent Tommy.

"But man, if you felt like those bitches might hurt you, why don't you leave now?" Dad expressed a genuine concern patting Tommy on the shoulder, more so sitting him up in his chair.

"Chuck I fear for my life, with this settlement coming; I don't know Chuck."

I heard my mom telling my aunt that he believed it was his cousin's wife 'the Big Stud' convincing her to do something to him. I would be scared too, that stud stood about 6'2", 300lbs, Sloppy woman-man. She wore the low-Fro or fade, dressed in saggy jeans, jogging pants and wife beaters. She wanted all the niggas in the hood to know she was a Lesbian Stud. Mish short for Michele thought she was a certified dick slinger in these streets. She treated her ugly frumpy, long breasted wife like a Queen, which was cool in my book.

These two Lesbians were sick thou, forcing their lifestyle on the neighborhood. When they first moved in they had all the lights on in the house, their loud R & B music blasting, and no curtains up to the widows. Windows wide open, ass naked painting the walls and each other's body.

My dad was called by his employer John Forney Sr. Owner of the body snatcher company my father worked for. A more official title would be Deceased Body Transportation or Mortuary Retrieval Services. I'd laugh at the different job titles my dad would tell people that were curious about his profession. The good thing about my dad working for Forney instead of the Ambulance or the other body snatchers was the vehicle upgrade. The trucks Forney used didn't look like a meat wagon, but an all blacked stretched extended body, Chevy passenger cab with tented windows.

It was easy to transport dope in the meat wagon. The police surely didn't expect the Morgue service to be transporting dead bodies and dope. But that's a whole other story. I watched my mom's attention shift to my dad when his work phone rang.

"Damn!" Shaking her head; throwing her cigarette to the ground before walking up to the porch towards us.

"Was that your job Chucky, do you have to go get Tommy's body?" She looked at him sympathetically knowing he should have told Forney that this particular retrieval was a conflict of interest because he knew and had a personal relationship with the body.

"Fuck it Stuff, Mother-fuckers die every day all day, it's my job." He stood to his feet beside me, downing the remainder of his 40oz. I figured while he sat beside me in silence watching from the porch, instead of up-close with everyone else; that he was mentally preparing himself to say goodbye to his friend and take him in that black bag to the cutting slab.

"Are you Ok C.J.?" Mom questioned; fearful for her, transfixed daughter and her emotionless husband. I watched her rub my dad's shoulders as he fought back the tears.

"I'm good Stuff; it's nothing to talk about." He took the last swig before going in the house to wash his face. His normal routine; wash his hands, neck and face, spray his cologne, brush his teeth and pop in his gum. Same ritual after each beer and before each body retrieval. My brothers ran up to the porch hitting one another excited that the news station had just pulled up.

"Can we go across the street to be on the news mom?" My brother Son questioned smiling stupidly like she was going to tell him yes.

"Boy, sit yawl stupid asses down on this porch, yawl ain't going no damn where!" She must've been nervous because she fired up another cigarette after just throwing the other one down. The news Camera man and the skinny, white, frail, overly made up white lady from Channel six came across the street towards us.

"Good evening ma'am." The Lady smiled as the news crew approached us.

"Good evening my ass, we didn't hear anything, we didn't see nothing and I don't want my children on your damn cameras." My mom stopped the lady before she could even start.

"Thank you." She said stepping backwards off the steps turning to go back across the street in front of Tommy's house.

My brother smacked his teeth, angry that my mom stole his chance to be on the news, Son always wanted to be on TV.

"She always tripping." He huffed barely above a mumble.

"Stinky Lady..." He mouthed in silence which made us both laugh.

"SON KILLED TOMMY!!!"

"What Nigga?" Slipped from Son's mouth before he could catch himself; we looked at one another stunned as my youngest brothers' outburst.

"What the Fuck?" my mother uttered slapping my brother Dominic on the back of his head.

The news reporter turned around at the sound of my little brother and his rude, dangerous, hilarious outburst. My brother Son and I fell out laughing, Dominic was a little slow from having Grandma Seizures since birth, so his elevator only went so far.

"Matter of fact get yo silly ass in the house." My mother slapped him again. My dad pulled the truck from our backyard and was pulling up in-front of the house. I was praying he parked on Tommy's side and not our side, I didn't want the body any closer to me than he already was.

"What's up CJ?"

"Hey Ms. Marlene!" Tina and Lenny sang, my dancing friends from down the street.

"Hey baby." Mom replied watching my dad, take the stretcher out the back of the truck.

"Dang, Mr. Chucky is going to get that guys body?" Tina asked in amazement sitting down beside me on the porch.

"Yea he's going to transport the body to the morgue for its autopsy." My mom answered with her eyes locked on my dad.

"Eugh I bet he pick up all types off shit… Oops I mean bodies." We all laughed at Lenny's slip up in-front of my mom; as she bugged her eyes and held her mouth in embarrassment. Anything to lighten the mood was a blessing.

"Girl babies, shot up, burned up, stabbed to death, head blown off, he's seen it all." Mom replied, dropping her cigarette to the dirt mashing it with her ugly white-girl tennis shoes.

We never imagined that a few years later my dad would be transporting Lenny & Tina's father after he suffered a heart attack at home. I was told that my dad being the one picking him up made it that much easier for my friends and their family. My dad had a really rough job.

~§~§~§~§~§~§~

Two weeks later the dikes were nowhere to be found. Jim, Amy their son and three daughters were shook for days. They were some funny Hill-Billy ass characters, during a fight between his daughters and my sister: Jim gave his daughter a purse full of rocks to hit my little sister with. I was so proud of Poody 8 years old in the middle of the street banging with these two white girls. I was begging for the oldest sister to come out and fight me, not because I was beefing with her, but because I was pumped up and needed an outlet. When my mom noticed Jim putting rocks in the purse, from our porch across the street. She quietly went into the house grabbed her tan trench coat and the sawed off shot gun she was keeping for Uncle Tony.

"Jim I bet I blow a mother fucking hole through your fat ass stomach, you gave that girl that bag of rocks to hit my daughter with!" Everyone in the street turned their attention to my mom as she yelled across the street; leaning against the wall positioning herself to shoot Jim in front of everybody.

"No, no Mrs. Marlene, these here is kids fighting we don't got to get no guns!"

"Right motherfucker!" She said moving her coat over further, "It was kids fighting until you gave your daughter them rocks. Since you're getting into a kids fight I'm getting into your ass."

Fat Joe ran who was three doors away from Jim's house ran off the porch of the trap and up to my mother.

"You got a problem Ma, you want me to handle your problem Ma?" My mother stood silently, barely nodding her head yes. Joe ran up onto Jim's porch while wrapping his scarf around his hand and knocked Jim cold the fuck out and off the porch. Amy his wife came out screaming saying she was going to call the police.

"Yea Bitch if you call the police Ms. Marlene gone beat your ass and I'm-a comeback and beat your sons ass and your weak ass husbands ass again."

"Don't be stupid!" Mom yelled to Amy across the street.

Fat Joe, Ray, Bishop and Lil Bill ran up in Jim's house a couple nights later. I sat on the porch, chewing my Bazooka, excited about what June and this new neighborhood had to offer.

"You good lil momma?" Fat Joe asked bent over out of breath after running over to me.

"Yea I'm good, but why did you just go beat Jim and his son up?" I looked at him disgusted.

"Why you the police little nigga?" He smiled at me completely ignoring my question.

"No asshole, but I'm sure they're not far away."

"Why you keep that attitude Shorty?" He said stepping his foot in between mines leaning over into my face.

I continued to chew my gum, not uttering another word to him.

"Aiight Shorty, I'm-a see you and your attitude later, tell your mom Jim is tight, but it's all good." He grabbed my chin, blowing me an air kiss.

Yanking my head from his grasp; "Right...bye." I didn't know what to think of this crazy dude, but one thing for sure; he was good at knocking niggas out. I might have to be nice to him, in-case I need him to knock out a nigga or two somewhere down the line, I smiled to myself.

The very next day the white people moved out. Not even a week later Mrs. Johnny Mae moved into Jim's old house and Ms.V, Tierra and her two brothers moved into Tommy's old house.

~§~§~§~§~§~§~
The fight Life
~§~§~§~§~§~§~

"Be still Shorty." Fat Joe rubbed the witch hazel Moe's Grandma gave him on my eye.

"I hope you got some punches in the way your eye looking lil' girl." Moe's grandmother said to me in mockery, rolling blunts to my surprise.

"No C.J. beat that girl down Mom." Moe said in my defense. Her nose broke and everything."

"I'm-a break your nose." Pee-Wee said to Moe jumping up play fighting her.

"Then I'm-a shoot yo black narrow ass." Moe's grandma ended his play domestic violence on a serious note. I wondered if she knew he use to hit Moe on the school bus?

I thought about the girls nose being broke and instantly thought I was going to get an ass whipping from my mom.

"Nah she good ma." Joe interjected, trying to lighten the apparent mood change in the room.

"As a matter of fact Shorty that's what I was just saying to you. Don't be ashamed of your bruise Ma, you earned it like a champ. And you won. You raw as fuck, like you go hard. Tia was much taller than you, had a longer reach, and she had something in her hand. Misha gave it to her I saw her. But anyway you beat Tia ass. You got form; you wasn't pulling hair or no girly shit like that. But when she hit you in the eye; I saw you charge up, like I be charging up. You put that beast on Shorty. I'm still trying to figure out how you were punching her then flipped her on the ground over your back!"

"Man!" He was getting amped up just talking about the fight. He hit his friend Terry in the chest trying to get his attention for his demonstration.

"Nigga you almost made me spill the weed." Terry said looking up annoyed at his animated friend.

"Shorty flipped Tia over her shoulder. Mow, bitch dropped to the ground! Shorty jumped on top that hoe, mop, mop, mop punching left to right, rocking shorty dome! Then she start slamming her head, bow, bow, bow that's when I tried to grab you Shorty!" He said pointing to me with his open hand, proudly resting his other hand across his chest pledge style.

"I'm like alright, alright Shorty you got that. Shorty like let me go. Roaaar started stomping Tia Head in! Bow, Bow, Bow on BOS that was one of the trillest girl fights I ever seen! I mean outside of my sisters you know they fight like straight niggas. But on the strength lil momma I can teach you how to perfect them sleepers."

"Ya Mean?" He continued.

"I mean nothing nigga" Terry interrupted, "clearly narrating ass nigga we was all there, we all seen the same shit." Terry threw me the blunt.

"Blaze up!" He nodded before starting to play box with Fat Joe. They called themselves brothers because they both had hazel eyes.

"Nigga that's my girl, she don't want your narrating, oh soft eye rubbing ass."

"Both yawl niggas get out my house with that shit!" Moe's grandma yelled at them; turned around and without a word threw her lighter at me. It dropped to the floor as I tried my best to see it with my one good eye. I looked around squinting, nervous that I was about to smoke in-front of Moe's grandma. I lit the blunt still squinting and looked at Moe. The mockery face she was making at me squinting her eye, contorting her lips made me laugh hard. Moe was cool I really fucked with her. Of all the chicks in the hood beside Tee, Moe was my Rollie.

As I got up to walk the blunt to Moe, I heard Terry say: "Shorty

Gone be my chick, why you rubbing her eyes and shit Casanova ass nigga." They both started laughing as Joe put him in a head lock.

"Stop playing nigga!" He said pushing him back jogging up the stairs. "I'm about to smoke."

I wore that black eye like a badge of honor. I was so embarrassed when my mother called my Gan's to have Pa-Harvey take us to the emergency room. The whole hood seemed to be on the corner as we drove past. Grandpa Harvey's ass always drove and talked so slow. "Hey… U h… Look'-a- Dear Mar… That boy got his….pants hang… ing off his butt, that's not how we dressed back in our day hun Mar?"

I took a deep breath pissed that rolling my eye made it hurt, as we drove funeral procession slow past all my new on looking friends. I felt my mom frustrated with me, having to go to the emergency room (which we didn't) and my grandpa's slow ass conversation. Why the hell did she call him anyway?

"Oh my God can we drive a little faster?" At the sound of my humiliation my mother busted out laughing. I watched Harvey looking confused like he missed the punch-line of the joke. Oh My God, this whole situation is getting on my nerves!!!! I yelled (inside my head). "You pissed hun?" My mom continued laughing.

"Well your pissed ass should've thought about that while you were out there trying to play Billy bad ass." Instantaneously I broke out singing.

"Billy Jean is not my lover; she's just a girl that thinks that I am the one." I never heard my grandpa laugh so hard in my life. The look on my mother's face was priceless.

"Yea well Billy Bad ass and Cernitha Jean both got a black eye, now sit you funny ass back, making me have to go to the hospital." I knew not to say anything so I repeatedly insulted her in my mind. Yo ass live at the hospital what you mean, I got you going I said I didn't want to go.

"What you say back there smart ass?" I whipped my head to look at my mom. I know I didn't say that out loud, did I say that out loud? I questioned myself.

"I know you back there talking shit to yourself?" Ah this woman was crazy, was she reading my fucking mind?

I was on punishment for the next week which I didn't mind. I had hella rehearsal time with Tasha for the upcoming Dana Dane and Doug-E Fresh Shows. I didn't mind my eye healing up either. I was forced to be in my front door five minutes after my busses drop off time, and mom wasn't playing at all.

"C.J.--Slick!" Dad yelled up the steps. "You got company lil nigga, Fat Joe down here to see you!"

What? I was shocked I leaped to my feet, grabbing my all black Cortez and my grey Ohio State hoodie. He stood at my door eyes beaming, with that cunning smile he always wore; the one that masked his soft side.

"What up Shorty can we sit on the porch or something?" I looked at my dad, who looked as if he wasn't trying to pay attention.

I stepped beside Joe and opened the door. We sat down on the edge of the porch as he took out a black & mild and started freaking it.

"Yo Shorty I've been thinking a lot about you, and the late night phone conversations we've been having. I've been beefing with my mom, but I put that all aside to get her input about you."

"That's tight, I guess, good for yawl."

"True but I couldn't sleep the other night after you told me about you being molested all those times and the fuck nigga that molested you right before you moved over here. That's why I had to come see you. I mean your dad he aight but your dad smoke crack, I know he got a little job or what not, but each check we seeing at-least $125 for a ball."

I dropped my head in disappointment and shame.

"Damn that's what it is?" I knew my dad smoked weed and bragged about doing and selling every drug back in the day, so surprised no, disgraced at the most.

"Him, Ms. V and Ms. Terry are very loyal they even smoke together from time to time. I told Eddie Kane that I was going to let him serve your dad from now on. See I want to fuck with you like that and I don't want to be responsible for problems in your household type shit."

"I can respect that." I said feeling the need to hit his black & mild.

"Like I want to protect you for real Shorty, and as a matter of fact I'm going to start calling you Star, because God sent you, my Star from Heaven. And Ma I really believe you gone blow up with this rap shit, you got skills for real. But ya pops fucked up in the game and you out here in the wilderness by your damn self, trying to get it." He jumped up to his feet punching his palm with his fist.

"Man Star if I would have known you and you called me and told me your step-uncle or whoever the fuck he was held you down and finger fucked you and tried to climb on top of you I would have pulled up in 10 flat and beat that nigga to death!"

"That's real, I wish I would have known you too, but on everything he be around, maybe those cards are still in the future." I passed back his nasty black & mild, I really don't see how anybody smokes that heavy shit.

"I want to bring you into my family Star, shit fucked up! Out here in the hood we got to stick together. Our parents doped up, coked out, or brain-dead slaves and we got to raise the next generation of dope babies, you feel me Ma?" He smiled pushing my shoulder.

"Yea I feel you Joe, that's real talk."

"You damn right, but my family is not a gang, we're an organization. I mean we got Doctors, Lawyers, Government Officials down with our shit, we like a different strand of the Black Panther Party Movement. I mean for real Folks, it's a lot to learn and its different levels to this shit, but we going to spend a lot of time together Star, I'm-a teach you everything I know and how to really get it in these streets so no other motherfucker will ever take advantage of you." He grabbed my face and leaned in for a kiss.

"You hear me?" He questioned before kissing my lips and melting my heart.

He stood up and grabbed the brown paper bag beside him, "Come on lets go down to your Aunties and drop this shit off to your moms, I called and talked to your mom earlier and she knew I was coming to get you to take you out."

"Really?" I was shocked and impressed. "So what's in the bag?"

"Two packs of Newport 100's a 2liter of Pepsi a box of Motrin and two packs of Double mint Gum."

"Oh the care package..." I laughed. My mom is a trip, but the trip tonight was Joe, he was saying things that were changing my life my concepts and opinions. The way he was handling my parents was respectable, he was down for me. I never had anyone take me under their wing before, besides my Grandma I guess, this was real, this is what I wanted my life to feel like. He was my boyfriend and we were going to ride together.

~§~§~§~§~§~§~
Born In
~§~§~§~§~§~§~

I was scared as fuck; I didn't know what to expect walking into Eddie Kane's garage. All the Lit he was forcing down my throat and rules, regulations and codes had me noid. It was dark and it seemed like every nigga from the neighborhood was in the garage. I'm sure the scent in the air was weed and mildew. Why did they have mask over their face? Why were the covered in those black scarves? Oh My God these motherfuckers about to gang rape me. Oh no the fuck they not. Why did I listen to Fat Joe? Why did I listen to Moe? I keep hearing Tierra's voice in my head: "Tell me what happen's C. I might do it next!"

What the fuck, I hate my 'want to be brave ass' sometimes; writing checks with my mouth that my ass was forced to cash.

"Come into the middle of the floor CJ. Just relax and be born again." I heard Joe's voice say.

"Be born again! What the fuck is this yawl bout to kill me, baptize me?"

The uproar of laughter in the room shook my already shaken soul. *Born again Jesus Christ, what these niggas about to do to me? I'm not taking off my clothes; I'm not smoking no fucking crack. Sorry Lord, I didn't mean to cuss,* I trembled inside myself.

"Drop to your left knee and put your pitch folks in the air, like this."

I dropped to the floor like a wet rag. My dad would call it copping to a misdemeanor. I felt everyone assemble closer around me as they begin to cover me in their black flags. I had flags over my face my shoulders my arms. They begin chanting which sent me into hysteria.

"Darrel are yawl about to sacrifice me?" This time there was no laughter. I felt the presence of Joe seeming to be preaching some sermon over me, the words were hazy as I was only listening for trigger words until he said repeat after me.

.... The Prayer continued.

I felt multiple touches to my body but not sexual. I was going to hit the door the first time somebody tried to molest me. Directly after the ceremony was a blur. We got into Big Booty Johns car for my official Smoke-out. I only smoked twice before last month at the East High School Talent Show. I leaned over to tell Joe. My eyes had already begin to burn. Only the G's were in the car dropping what they said was knowledge on me. They younger dudes from the hood surrounded the car begging to hit the weed. After about fifteen minutes in the hotbox I couldn't breathe and I couldn't see. I felt my heart change beating patterns and it scared the shit out of me. My vision was being distorted from the smoke both inside and out.

Eddie Kane & Bishop went on about how I could tell everyone at school tomorrow how I'm now affiliated with some real gangstas...

"Please let me out of this car Joe." I tried to whisper.

"Hell Naw she gone let all the smoke out, you suppose to stay in here until the session is blow'd out!" Big Booty John yelled at me.

"Look John I don't care about all that, my eyes is burning."

Eddie Kane, Bishop & Darrel Started laughing: "My eyes are burning, let me out and shit." They chocked, laughed & taunted.

"Man just let her out John, she don't even smoke for real." Joe asked still laughing at his niggas mockery.

"Nigga I don't give a fuck I came all the way over here for the ceremony." Big Booty yelled.

"Man fuck the ceremony my chick want the fuck out, unlock these fucking Child Lock Shits!" Joe pushed up Big Booty's seat and I thought a fight was about to break out in the car. John hit the locks and the both of them jumped out. The barrage of fresh air caused me to choke from the smoke I was still trying to escape. I bent over gagging and hacking up phlegm as the two big hefty guys argued in the background. I surely wasn't trying to cause a fight but at least the nigga is riding for me like he said he would.

I walked up to Joe put my arms around him and pulled him in my direction. "C'mon baby, walk me home; Alright Folks Tomorrow!" I yelled to my new gang family, throwing up the sign I just perfected in the garage.

"7-4- til the world blow Gangstress." Whatever that meant? What Eddie Kane said brought a smile to Joe's face. I guess I could add that shit in my next rap if I can remember this shit tomorrow.

~§~§~§~§~§~§~

When I got home from school Ant, my manager was parked out front of my house. I picked up my pace because I knew that Blue BMW from anywhere.

"What's up Ant?" I asked winded leaning in his passenger window.

"Get in ToPazz homicidal manic killer." He laughed opening the passenger door from the inside.

"They all mad, mother fucka's I'm the real Daddy Mack." I recited Tasha's line of the song in response to his.

"What they know about the P-A Double Z."

"They know she spit hot fire, he responded before pulling off."

"Wait I didn't tell my mom."

"Nigga please I already talked to Stuff, I'll be dropping you off tonight." He turned on his radio and headed to the east side.

We swooped Tasha off Courtright and headed to the studio in East Haven, a predominately blood ran community on the east side of Columbus, Ohio. As soon as we hit the lab, everyone broke out the trees and pre-rolled's. After 5 minutes or so we were ready for the get down.

"So what's Goodie?" K.Dog asked as I began to choke on my blunt.

"OK lil niggas calm down, Stop smoking Paz, I'm trying to tell yawl that we got yawl a show at The Vets' Memorial." Ant said snatching the blunt from me leaving us hanging in suspense.

"For real?" When? Who are we performing with?" I taunted him for answers.

"Nigga-aaa Sayyy somethingggg!" I whined.

He laughed choking on his smoke. "Some reps from Def Jam are going to be down here with the concert, performing on the same stage as yawl: Dana Dane, The Human Beat Box Biz Markie & the Crowned King Dougie Fresh!" He inhaled his blunt with an air of pride as we went hysterical. I mean these guys were a lot older than us, but their names still rang bells. Hell we were happy performing at the African Gold, The Skating Rinks and the Boys and Girls Clubs. But The Vets Memorial Right after we just did the Columbus Convention Center was Big. We thought Alphonso's East High School Talent Show was big which it was, but this was huge. 94 & 95 AftaShock was popping.

I asked my girls in the hood first Lenny, Tina, Tierra, & Moe if they wanted to do the event, and everybody was geeked. We practiced in the street and in front of my mom's porch. At their house, at the park, everywhere we could. At an instant my managers turned all my friends against me by saying they couldn't perform and that they picked up two professional sisters who was going to do our routine with us.

"What you mean you picked us out some dancers? Since when did you ever pick us out some dancers?" Tasha –Kdog asked stuffing her chips down her pissed off face.

"Since we didn't place high enough at the East High School Talent Show and the group of dancers won, it seemed like the best business move to get yawl some professional dancers. Your home girls are cool but can wait until we shoot a video." Ant was arrogant as fuck.

"But Ant we've been practicing on this fucking dance for the past week, they going to be mad at me: like I was lying the whole time or some shit." I was pissed I can't believe how he just trumped my whole existence in one fail swoop. We had two more weeks until the show so it gave me enough time to get my life.

"ToPazz this is the business side of music and you're the artist not your friends. You need to learn now how to separate the two, if its pleasure it's not business. If it's cultivating your talent and your finances then its business, everything else is BS and barging-chips." He looked at us both as if he was searching for his words to be mistaken, before adding: "Blessed Be the Name of Allah". Most of our team was Muslim and Ron I think was Christian, either way I hated when he tried to lecture us then put a righteous spin on it. I know one thing for certain, he made sure we didn't have to go to school and stayed home to watch the million man march, they all caravanned from Ohio to D.C. Good times.

We substituted our friends performance at the Vet' Memorial with our promo show for the drunks at the Cabaret. My friends still got to perform, their friends and family was still able to come and see them and my team didn't let me suffer social suicide making me into a liar. The Cabaret shows were always little to no money but it was fun to sneak and drink and laugh at the older crowd. Our crazy gangsta lyrics always got rise out the younger men who couldn't believe some of the heartless raunchy shit we were saying. We swore we were going to be the younger female NWA.

The day of the Vets Show was nerve wrecking. This would probably be the second biggest crowd I've performed for, if the turnout is bigger than the convention center. Our Black White and Grey Camo Fatigues Beaters, Sports bras and Berea's, & our Black Buckled Combat boots were popping. We were straight street soldiers, that and Dickies with boxers and half shirts was our look.

Gi'Ant picked us both up, took us out to eat then back to his place for a blunt and a big lecture, His fiancé Michelle was home unexpectedly today and seen him smoking weed with us on the hill in the back of their house. They made sure we stayed outside during their argument. Meanwhile he was crying the whole way downtown to the venue.

"Ant what happened, did Michelle call off the wedding?" K'Dog asked from the back seat, in her nosey as fuck manner.

"No she just very disappointed in me, she accused me of having sex with ToPazz."

"WHAT!!!" We both yelled out.

"There is no fucking way, and that is the truth, we never thought about nor tried to have sexual relations." If they thought about it or even talked about it was never brought to my attention and anyways Ant knew Fat Joe would kick his ass.

"Oh hell-naw Ant you got to call her and I'll tell her that nothing has ever happened between us, I'll swear to God the whole nine." I was pissed, her thinking that must means she thinks I'm some little sneaky, conniving hoe. I knew she treated me and Tasha differently I always told Ant that I thought she didn't like me, and to think this nigga had the nerve to tell me I was tripping or sipping paranoia.

"Fuck outta here. Is she coming to the show Ant?" His forced silent sobs and tears were pissing me off.

"Nigga quit crying, Damn." I sighed falling back in frustration.

"Fuck it Cer, you ain't guilty don't let that shit even sit with you, we bout to pop off, in a minute." With that she shuffled to the side stuck her thumb in her mouth and continued to stare at the window.

Backstage our manager hugged us telling us how proud he was and how we've come a-long way in such a short period of time. He encouraged us to do our best have fun, pop off like we always do but keep in the back of our minds that the label execs where watching. After our hugs and prayers and the quick run through with the dancers (who turned out to be stylist and lifelong friends) we were next for the stage.

I was over Ant's drama & pissed that Joe and the hood didn't show up, or at least not to my knowledge. I wanted everybody there to see us go in; especially the niggas in the hood that always said I was lying about doing this or that.

We decided to run on to the stage while our dancers where lying on their stomach to begin the show. Midway through the song, I begin to hear a lot of rooting and yelling. They were actually supporting us, we dropped to our pops as our dancers ripped off their button up skirts exposing their boy shorts; and again the crowd went wild. I heard my hood chanting and yelling different Gang-lit.

I looked back pissed and happy at the same time to see Joe and G'man snuck on stage and was dancing and throwing gang-signs up on stage behind us.

"Oh Shit." I thought this is not going to go over well with Ant that was not a good look. Like always the show went good, we turned up, they yelled our names. Dana Dane invited us up on the stage for encouragement and fellowship with his last song of his set. I'm sure that made T.E.O.S happy considering Ant went nuts on us back stage almost causing him and Joe to get into a fight. I was excited to meet Dana Dane I remembered him mostly from my Aunt Lisa playing his Cinderfella Dana Dane song on repeat when she lived with us.

"Yo you actually came; What's up G'Man?" I said to Looney's friend while giving him dap.

"Where is Big?" I asked. Hoping there wouldn't be any drama.

"Keep your ghetto ass hood niggas in the hood ToPazz." Ant fussed as I came off the stage.

"Who the fuck you calling a Ghetto Hood Nigga!" Joe said walking up behind Ant.

"Look yawl we not going to run that shit right now!" I yelled mainly at Joe because he would be the one to take the shit to the next level in a millisecond.

"These execs are here looking at us and I don't need this drama out the gate." I smacked my hand as I turned to look at Ant.

"We're about to go holler at these people, take a few pictures and we ret- ta go." Joe picked me up off my feet and kissed me in-front of everyone.

"I love you on BOS, Bitch!" Wow I couldn't believe he called me a bitch.

"That's because I am Boss Bitch, I kissed him. I love you too Fat Ass Punk now put me down." I pinched at his arm laughing as Big John walked up the same time as my Mom, Gan-Gan & Nem.

"Damn I hope the shit don't hit the fan in my yard." Tasha whispered to me as John fell back on instinct signaling for Joe & G'Man to come over to him. This night felt like a break through, everyone got along, the women stayed cool and we kicked it hard considering we were 15 & 13, we thought we were going hard.

~§~§~§~§~§~§~

"Man fuck you talking bout? My bitch go hard in the paint, her show was lit as fuck, ain't non-yawl rapping ass niggas performing at the Vets Memorial!" Oh God! I thought to myself walking into Fat Joe's conversation with Bishop and some other niggas I've never seen. He was still on his high from crashing our show at the Vets'. If this nigga don't stop having me battle rap, and Johnny on the spot for all these random niggas I don't know what I'm going to do. My head was pounding from the studio session and the arguments I was having with Gi'Ant about leaving my hood nigga alone.

"Star, Queen we was just talking about you my nigga. I told this O'l Duxberry ass nigga that you the hottest, you can go off the top on any topic." He smiled passing me the blunt.

"Yea babe, that's what's up." I recognized he was in stunner mode and to appease he's need for idolatry I handed him the package of coke he asked me to grab for him in Easthaven. My lil blood homie that liked me always gave me a sweet price that they would have never given Folks. His kool-aid smile & kiss on the forehead indicated that he was proud of my flossing.

"Oh yawl get down like that Looney?" The guy in the two toned blue Cadillac parked illegally caddy corner on the corner of Sidney & Shoemaker laughed at our broad daylight transaction. I passed Fat Joe the blunt before acting like I was about to leave to go down to Tee's house.

"So she gone spit or what? The tall light skinned guy standing next to Joe in his white T & black shorts swinging his fist & palm together repeatedly questioned.

"What, fuck you talking? Star spit to these niggas about how you ride for me." He insisted with a head nod & his crooked stunner smile. This Gemini I thought, pulling my gum out my mouth, walking up closer to the group of 5 guys.

Umm- *Better ride, better drive, better die with me / I build the bread, Betty Crocker share the pie with me / We in the earth we in the air, split the sky with me/ light years from the bum shit we high on them sky beams / love is blind tell me how we counting these stacks / I see the future in the matrix catch me running it back/ I make it clap, reign the rounds get applause right back/ kitty rubbing against the chair getting off on the Nasdaq / Dow Jones hard bone from the back jaw sex/ gymnastics on the mattress on fleek when she flex that/ we gone tumble I'm on fire baby hose that/ hot as the dessert but its wetter than haboobs be/ slow down for me baby beast the Coochie/ cause we gone suck it and fuck it/ and we gone kiss it and lick it/ and we gone keep it real loyal /gone divide up the difference and ain't no stopping our pimping/ I'm gone keep it hundred for you baby/ ride this unicorn yea I'm so amazing/ behind closed doors or in the front yard/ this our world it's our stage we can play it all / any time any place I Bonnie your Clyde non other/ kiss the crown of your mother/ show how much you really love us /we gone stick it to the script and ain't gone let nothing come before us/ it's death before dishonor with their life they'll pay us homage /amen.*

I licked my bottom lip before giving him a kiss to the sounds of his friend's approval, if anybody loved to stunt more than me, it was definitely Joe and I couldn't get enough. His hazel eyes twinkled with fascination, admiration, pride and ownership.

"That's what's up Shorty, you go in; that was hard as fuck?" Joe's stranger friend in the white-T said reaching to give me dap. Surprisingly I dapped up with him and he was GD.

"Hell No!" He laughed as I locked G's with him.

"Shorty 7-4?"

"Til the world blow nigga, I told you I fuck with the realest!" Joe spit matter-of-factly before pulling me toward him to do our special handshake that took us an entire hour to create and perfect.

"I'm about to go meet Tee, Big Daddy, I have rehearsal tomorrow." I said as he squeezed me in his huge bear-hug.

"I want you to come through tonight and play Chief's & Indian's Ma." He gave that obnoxious laugh I hated to love so much. He was really feeling his self.

"Page me babe, I replied flipping my shoulder length box braid ponytail before walking the block. I was excited, he always made me feel good whenever I turned up for him, I love that shit. In my departure I heard him tell one of the niggas to run him his money. Mental note, I had to remind that nigga to run me my money when I got to his moms later, always betting on me, pay me in cash or pay me in kisses.

§O§

§~Chapter 7~§
No Fucks to Give

Today just felt like one of those days. I decided to skip rehearsal today, I just didn't have the energy after I got dressed and headed down to the kitchen. It was the middle of the month so I knew not to expect a selection of food. We barely ever had two things that matched after the second week of the month. My Dad, Kim my mom's adopted neighbor- sister and Montreal the molester was partying all night.

I hated to hear drunks up loud talking, especially on the weekdays. My mom kept it down to a minimum on the weekdays, she didn't drink or at-least not in-front of us, if she did. My dad on the other hand drank& smoked for breakfast, lunch and dinner. What the fuck is this? I thought to myself, feeling myself mute the words but my lips actually moving. Oh these motherfuckers done took disrespect to a whole another level. I thought as I looked in my mother's living room and there with both the love seat and sofa pulled together sleeping like one big happy family was my dad, Aunt Kim and Montreal.

Where was my mother? She must have been still sleeping. I couldn't believe this shit! Why didn't they go home last night and why the fuck was my dad sleeping with them on the pulled together couches? I fought back the urge to say anything as I watched over these three drunken idiots, mouths hanging wide open, legs &arms thrown everywhere. I felt myself about to cry, I know nothing good was going to come from this episode. I decided to chuck my feelings and go into the kitchen to grab me something to eat. My mom is going to be pissed when she wakes up and see's this, I thought as I opened the empty refrigerator.

Instantly my blood started to boil as I looked at the empty pack of bologna, the brand new Colt 45, a nearly empty bag of sugar and a gallon of purified water. This sorry motherfucker; I said through clinched quivering lips as I grabbed his Beer from the middle rack of the empty fridge.

"How the fuck is there brand new fucking beer in here and nothing for your kids to eat?" I grunted as I opened the back door and pitched his beer as hard and fast as I could at the tree, shattering it instantly.

"Yea fuck your buzz idiot." I laughed to myself as I sprinted back up the steps to my room. I slowly opened the door to my bedroom hoping not to wake my nosey little sister who thankfully was still sleeping. I climbed into my closet reaching to the back shelf to retrieve my oversized stuffed white teddy bear.

I grabbed what looked like an eighth, the remainder of my personal sack, $120 worth of dimes and twenties. Stuck the other zip-locks back down into the legs of my teddy bear, reached into the center of my bears head where I kept my cash. Examined my folded rubber band bankroll. It seemed to all still be here. I peeled off the top four twenties, and placed the rest back in the bear. Fastened the ten safety pins that I used to hold the cut together; placed the animal back onto the shelf behind all the other stuffed animals my sister and I collected over the years.

Secretly wishing I would've been the little sister, sleeping like she had not a care in the world. I reached in my pocket for the daily $5 I operated on and placed it under her hand. Crept out of the door and slowly made my way into my mom's room. My mom didn't drink and was truly a light sleeper when she didn't have a headache. I wondered where I was going to slide this forty. I couldn't leave it in her purse, my dad would probably steal it, or it would be lost in all that unnecessary paper she keeps cluttered. I'm just going to try to slide it in her shirt. She keeps all her cash in her bra. I'm sure my dad would steal that too if he could. I slid the money softly down the center of her cleavage as she lay on her side.

"Chucky what are you doing?" She said shacking herself side to side awakening from her sleep.

"No it's just me mom. I wanted to give you a hug and tell you I'm going across the street over Tee's house." I said as I firmly embraced her.

"Dad's sleep down on the couch with Montreal and Kim."

"What?" My mom shouted sitting up wiping the slobber she must have felt from her mouth. Her hair was wild on the right-side and smashed on the left. "It doesn't look so good, is all I'm saying mom, I'm out of here, Oh' There's nothing to eat down there." I said looking back at her watching her pull the money from her breast. I didn't stay for a thank you but decided to jet out the back door and walk around the house. I didn't want to be the one to awaken the losers on my mommas couch.

Dear God give my mother the strength to deal with her house today. Give her the sense to finally put my dad out, put him on child-support, learn how to drive and find a better man. Oh and please don't let me get caught by the police today. In Jesus name: Amen.

Tee must've been waiting at the front door because before I could knock she was rushing out the door, pushing me away as if I was trying to rush up in her house.

"What's wrong with you?" I asked her looking down at her hand still pressed in my stomach.

"Uh" she smacked her teeth together.

"This fucking bitch in there ass naked passed out on the couch with some fucking white trick. Both the motherfuckers high as fuck." I watched as she pulled out what looked like a broken piece of antenna. Her body language told me we weren't going to eat breakfast in her house today. One thing is for sure. Ms. V may have done her dope but unlike my father her children always had food.

"Did you grab your Swisher? I'm out." I asked Tee as she continued to push me off the square slab she called her porch.

"Oh Shit, hold on I'm going to go in the back door, stay right here!" Whatever was going on in her living-room had to be as fucked up as what was laying in my own house. Why can't these people get their shit together? I thought as I sat on the slab reaching into my oversized Cargo Pants pulling out my personal. I broke down a few choice buds attempting to busy myself. I looked up the Street watching the church goers and their respectable clothing make their way to the house of the Lord. I watched a few of the scattered crack heads picking cigarette butts from the sidewalk.

"C'mon girl you ready?" She handed me the Cigar as we made our way to the McDonalds that was barely standing on our street corner. I was looking out my window one night when I saw a group of neighborhood boys all dressed in black running from the McDonalds as if they just robbed the place. Later I found I was right. But most times I am.

I gave Tee the crisp twenty dollar bill I had in my pocket to order our breakfast. I proceeded to the bathroom to roll up the blunt in the stall. I rolled up as fast as I could. I wanted to get over to Milo with Joe so I could off some of these sacks. I needed some money bad. I was tired of going to sleep with no food in my fridge. It seemed like I was spending more money on food than anything else.

"C' I'm ready to go this nigga done pissed me off again!" I looked up at her, pausing the video game. Joe's ass snatched the blunt from my mouth as I turned my frustrated attention to Tierra.

"What happened now?"

"Nigga not trying to lick, I ain't trying to let him hit." She hissed reaching for the blunt.

"Oh hell naw! Ray! Ray!" Looney shouted grabbing his Sagging pants with one hand balancing to not fall into the wall with the other, as he ran to the next room to torment his friend.

"You eating pussy lil nigga? Hun?" He questioned throwing soft jabs into the body of his much smaller unsuspecting homeboy.

"Get the fuck outta here nigga." Ray laughed bobbing back throwing his own set of jabs and defense slaps.

"Nigga I beat the pussy I never eat the pussy. Matter of fact the only pussy I ever ate was my momma's cuz I wasn't a C section, nigga." They both laughed and continued to slap box. I fucked with Ray, he was Looney's best-friend and my best-friends boyfriend. I told Looney of all the family we called Folks Ray was really his nigga regardless of how many other niggas he put in position. Ray rode and he rode hard, Betty Lou's Chopper dropper.

I heard the knock on the door, grabbed Joe's 9mm and peeked through the peep-hole.
"Who is it?"

"It's Stan, Eddie Kane's Cousin, is Bat Mike here?" Bat Mike was the chick that stayed in the apartment; I opened the door cautiously with the pistol pointed toward the ceiling resting against the door.

"Nah she not here Stan but I'll tell Looney to let her know you came by."

"Oh Fat Joe here? Ask him can I get a twenty bag." I motioned for him to come in the house.

"Who at the door Star?" Joe yelled from the back room.

"I got it!"

"It's me Stan man, I was looking for Bat Mike."

I reached in my pocket and pulled out two twenty bags. I held my hand open in-front of Stan before he gave his money to Joe.

"Oh Ok. Good looking lil CJ." He placed the folded twenty on top of the bag to the right and pocketed the bag that was on the left of my palm. I maneuvered the twenty with my thumb to check for legitimacy before sticking the cash and sac into my pocket. I opened the door after handing him one of my tear off papers with my pager number on it.

"If you're around the 4 corners of the hood I'll deliver for anything over twenty."

"Ok lil momma I'll remember that." He smiled shaking his head as he stuffed my number into the pocket of his extra tight button up shirt.

Tee & I decided to call it a day at the trap with Looney and the boys around 4pm. While walking back to the Doc from Milo, I saw my mom, two brothers and little sister, walking up 5th Avenue.

"Come on Tee that's my mom & nem; let's catch up with her, she never walks far, I wonder where the hell she going?" I began a light jog which turned sprint when the light from the freeway ramp turned green. No cars where coming so I took it.

"Mom!" "MOOOOOOMMM!" I continued to yell until my little sister recognized me. I was about a block away from them, when she pointed me out to my mom. My mom looked disappointed, from where I was I could tell she was crying I caught up with them at the gas station at 5th Ave & the on Ramp. I reached in my pocket and grabbed a ten dollar bill.

"Get mommy a sprite and some Gum."

"Make it a Pepsi." She corrected. And yawl get yawl whatever yawl want, split it equally." I handed the money to my oldest little brother Son.

"Split it equally." I said." Trying to give him the: I mean-business stare.

"Shut up punk." He snatched the money and ran toward the gas station.

"Un-Un Hold up Son wait; for your sister and your brother." Mommy should have known he was not thinking about them. I stepped in front of my mom's eyesight as Tee caught up to us.

"Why have you been crying, what happened, where are you going?" I questioned her.

"I'm going to the shelter." She broke down crying grabbing me for comfort. I snapped my head back in shock.

"You're going where, Mom?"

"I'm going to the Shelter." She cried loudly, not given two fucks that we were standing on the corner of 5th at the freeway and everybody and they crack babies could see us.

"Wait I paid Mr. Thorton the rest of the rent?" She looked at me puzzled like: what the fuck are you talking about? I squeezed and shook both her hands with both my hands.

"Mom what did he say?"

"Who?"

"Mr. Thorton?"

"He didn't say nothing!" She continued to sob.

"So Mom why are you talking about your going to the shelter?" I was getting mad with this entire scenario.

"Your Dad; Your Dad and Montreal and Kim. She said in between uncontrollable quivers.

"On The Bed Couch!" My statement stopped her in her track. I reached in my pocket turned my back to my mom and pulled her out a twenty dollar bill.

"Here; mom." I motioned her money. I looked at my friend as she stood there holding each end of her flag that she had resting around her neck. Her face said handle that, at least that's what I thought I read. "Go get you some cigarettes damn it, and take the kids across the street to Wendy's get yawl something to eat. Where is my dad?" My mom was still looking at the money in her hand.

"CJ where the hell are you getting all this money? I've been noticing you always have money here and there. You quit acting like you were going to go get the money from Joe a long time ago."

"Mommy I told you; Tee and I work at Milo Center. They pay us thirty dollars a day I just stack it up." She knew I was lying.

"Ay C. CJ!" We all turned our attention to the gas station, It was Tony, Kenyetties brother calling me, this old dude always be sweating me, I thought. I lifted up the front of my shirt unsnapped my fanny pack and gave it to Tee.

"Tee can you go check on my brothers and sister? Make sure they get the Pepsi and the Gum?' I widened my eyes and nodded towards Tony, I knew he wanted some weed but I didn't need for him to blow up my spot with my already dysfunctional mother.

"Mommy!" I called her name real fast; to take her attention away from the apparent grown man hollering at her 14 year old daughter.

"Mommy where not moving, I'm tired of moving. We have it pretty good out here right now. You know we're stable and Mr. Thorton is cool. We're being courted by these record labels mom; and now is not the time to move. I want to stay close to my job so I can keep helping you when you need me to." I didn't like lying to my mom, but I knew my truths would hurt her much more.

"Where is my dad?"

"His drunk ass was over next door with ya Cousin KC Nem'. CJ this ain't your business, they over there drinking and shit."

"But mom it is my business, and they always everywhere drinking, my mom standing out here on 5th Avenue crying, walking my brothers and sister to God knows what shelter? I don't want to move mom, so I'm just going to ask him to move, simple as that." I scratched my braids, trying to remain calm with my mom, she was pushing my nerves.

"Go down to Aunty Darlene's for a little while after you get your food." She looked wildly at the cars as she lit her cigarette from the fresh pack.

"Cernitha don't go upsetting your dad."

"How are you standing here crying and worried about his drunk-ass feelings?" (oops) I grabbed my mouth instantly.

"I'm sorry mom, we're not moving." I watched as Tee held my sisters hand and they walked towards us. I pressed the button on the pole, hoping they light could change as they came so my mom wouldn't have time for more questions.

"Ok yawl grab hands yawl about to run across the street to Wendy's."
"Yes!" They sung. My brother kicked me sideways on my butt as he ran pass me.

"Thanks Turd!"

"Ooh your welcome toilet bowl!" I yelled after him. Son was and will always be my favorite brother he's been with me the longest. We show our love through our dysfunctional abuse.

I kissed my mom on the cheek. "I love you mom, I ain't tripping and we ain't moving, enjoy your food." Tee handed her the Pepsi and gum ass my brothers and sister ran across the street with their bags of junk.

"Bye Aunty Marlene." Tee waved.

"Man that's some fucked up shit your dad did."
"Yea I got something for his ass though, I'm sick of his sorry shit."
"I thought you loved your dad, and he was your best friend and all that shit?" The sarcasm was thick in her voice; I still didn't give a fuck.
"Yea I do love the sorry motherfucker but right is right and wrong is just that, I'm tired of his drunk- shit I open the fridge today and ain't shit in there but a brand new 40. I pitched that shit at the tree, so fast." She busted out laughing knowing I wasn't lying. I grabbed the fanny pack from her as we crossed the street. I took out my pre-rolled from the back zip section.

"You got your lighter?" Yea she said handing me her pink lighter. "I got pink so wouldn't nobody take my shit." We chuckled for a second.

"So Tony brought a dime told me to tell you to come sell him an ounce later."

I hit the blunt a couple times to get it burning.
"Here I muffled passing her the blunt. Blow me a shotgun, a big one."
I chocked on the mouthful that just invaded my lungs. She hit the blunt out in the open like she didn't give a fuck about 50, her momma, or anything else. I stood up from my damn near having a heart attack as she tried to blow my head back.
"Let me hit that." I asked snatching her Grape Faygo. Man we swore by this Grape Faygo in the hood.
"C can I get twenty so I can grab my brothers something to eat?" I

reached in my pocket and gave her the money without a word.
"Look Tee I'm about to run into my house and into my dad's face. If I go to DH or if something happens to me, At the head of my little sisters bed a small slit cut into the middle of the mattress is a letter, get the letter don't read it, and give it to my mom.
"CJ For Real Paz, Topaz maybe CJ is not with us at the moment; don't do nothing crazy, please. What the fuck you got so much stuff coming up next month. And next month your sorry ass dad, still gone be your sorry ass dad." She turned up her lips and then hit the blunt.

Tee was my nigga, I felt where she was coming from just like I felt my face getting warm with sadness, anger and escaping tears. My mind skimmed through the work/dirt that we did together in such a short amount of time.

"Don't cry my nigga G's up! Ain't that what you taught me?" I wiped my running nose with the back of my hand and whipped my hands on my tan Dickies. Inhaled the blunt & G'd her up, we did our favorite hand shake that took us three days to perfect.

"I got you"- "I got you" we repeated to one another. I drunk another swig of her pop snapped my fanny pack and took my normal sprint pace home. I looked back when I got to the freeways intersection. Tee was taking her time slow walking enjoying her blunt. My Uncle Charlie walking into my Cousin KC's house, who now lived on the other side of our double; caught my attention.

"OH MY GOD!!" I yelled to myself, I really respected Uncle Charlie, he takes care of my Aunt and her kids, but he's my dad's number one rider, I still never forgot that he didn't help with Montreal. I really hope he don't get in the way. My mind started racing frantically.

I was getting real comfortable with snapping over the past few months and I felt that same sensation building as I entered my key to open my front door. I couldn't take it. We were not moving no fucking where else. I refuse to get molested again, and here this motherfucker laid up with that motherfucker and his drunk ass chick. Livid felt good, it felt better than hunger pain, it felt better than sharing a bed with fifty other kids.

"I've been selling this mother fucking shit to help with the bills so we don't have to fucking move again… and my dad just can't keep his sorry ass shit together.

"Ahh!" I screamed as I busted into my parents' bedroom. Looking around frantically like the mad woman I was. I couldn't find a weapon in sight.

"Ahh!" I screamed again just thinking about confronting my dad. What happened to my fucking dad, the stand-up guy? This drunk stuck on stupid motherfucker was breaking my heart for the last time.

I saw his can of Right Guard Deodorant sitting on top of the dresser and that was it. I was going to light a fire under his ass. I grabbed the can and checked for the lighter in my pocket. If my momma didn't want to set this nigga straight I sure was going to. I ran down the steps, heart beating like a lion was chasing. I looked at the living room furniture all put back in place like that ignorant shit didn't just happen this morning. I was so sick of his dumb drunk ass stunts. I opened my Cousin KC's door without knocking.

I heard Tee calling for me as I opened the door. I wasn't stopping I had to feed this raging monster that was fed up to the top of my box braids with my dad.

"CJ!" I could hear her voice running closer; I heard my dad and the fam' in the basement. I know they were smoking some fire because the entire upstairs was lit. I took the steps slowly trying to regulate my heart beat, my face my neck was beating with anger. I felt the adrenaline piercing through my system like a runaway freight train. As I turned the corner seeing him sitting on the barstool smoking the joint with a full 40oz in his hand I wanted to attack.

"So you just sitting down here laughing and drinking like you ain't just fuck your family up again being the drunk ass buster that you are!" The lighter and the deodorant clink together behind my back as my hands shook in fear.

"What the fuck you just say nigga?" My dad paused staring at me like he was pondering if he should hit me or not.

"Oh ok hold up C!" Uncle Charlie chimed in like clock-work rising slowly to his feet.

"Don't none of you motherfuckers touch me!" I screamed flicking the lighter, spraying the deodorant creating my very first torch.

"Hell No!" My Cousin KC busted out laughing trying to grab my dad who damn near leaped over the bar.

"No!" I blazed the torch again purposely missing my dad, as my Uncle Charlie approached me.

-WOOSH the flame expanded as I turned up the lighter. I saw Tee approach the room from the corner of my eye, with the fear of God on her face.

"CJ c'mon stop, let's go girl."

I lost the flame as my lighter went out and I backed up as Uncle Charlie rushed me grabbing me around my arms in a bear hug. I lit the torch towards the concrete hoping it would force him to let me go. I hated the feeling of hot burning tears saturating my face. I hated being restrained by motherfuckers that should have been protecting me. I bucked hitting Charlie's mouth with the back of my head as he released the grip I through the can and the lighter on the floor.

My Cousin KC laughed still holding my dad in his own bear-hug.

"Ay lil' cuz, Topazz, you snapped. Ha ha ha ha Ay I'm-a put that can and shit in a frame, I'm gone memorialize this shit, this shit funny as fuck." His laughter was like a slap in my face.

"No ass holes, Chucky grab that shit and set yourself on fire! Go To Hell!" I yelled running up the stairs with Tee pacing slowly behind me. I ran back to the trap as fast as my legs could carry me. I needed a feeling I needed Joe to make me feel better, to protect me incase my dad called himself coming for me.

"Ooh, come get me motherfucker." I screamed running through the traffic at the corner of 5th Ave. & Sidney.

"Go Home Tee!" I yelled back to Tierra. I didn't want to hear common sense I didn't want to hear anything. I just didn't want to feel this pain anymore and I'd rather feel him.

~§~§~§~§~§~§~
School
~§~§~§~§~§~§~

This week has been crazy. I found myself on the bus on the way to school fighting back tears out of nowhere. It was Thursday and my dad was still mad at me about what happened Sunday over my Cousin KC's house. Damn! I hate when my dad is mad at me. But I hate him more for his selfish, sorry ass reasoning. I felt the animosity building up, but decided to shift my focus.

School was becoming more like work. Every day I was watching my back and the door, my nerves was shot to hell. I was happy Peanue was still working in the office. He always overheard when the police was going to round up all the suspecting drug dealers; for their stings, the war on drugs was some bullshit. I was nervous because I had a few customers complaining about the acid I was selling. Fuck I never took no acid, I don't know what's good from the bad, and they asses the ones that brought it from me.

The feeling sat in my stomach that something was going to happen today.

Lord please whatever happens today, please don't let me get suspended or go to jail. Mr. Thorton is meeting me today to get the rest of my mom's rent money. I have to re-up with Big and I promise if you see me through this I will never sell any acid again.

The tardy bell rung snapping me back to reality as Molly raced in the door with her big bouquet of Roses. Molly was my dog; that down ass white chick with that ghetto bitch mentality. She repped the North side too, that's what made us click the first day of 9th grade.

Derrick was always our 5th period art class entertainment. He hated the fact that Molly as he called it: Acted Black. He hated that she dated black baller's. He hated she openly confessed to getting piped down by black dick. Molly was about 5"10 bright blue green wide almond shaped eyes with blonde red hair. She had the biggest pair of titties that I've seen this far in the 9th grade.

She sashayed around the over large wooden square table we shared with four other students including Derrick.

"CJ Look what my boo got me." She smiled straddling over her saddle chair, placing the bouquet to my nose.

"Aren't you all chummy and shit today?" I asked her looking up from my marijuana drawing I was going to mask as something else for my teacher.

Did she not know she was helping me sell this fucked up acid? I didn't like her clientele; I stayed away from the hard dope heads at school. I never knew how many kids were strung out on some kind of drug one form or another until I started selling weed at school. Weed, coke, psychotic pills, their parent's pain and nerve pills, acid, shrooms, inhalants the list never ends.

"So what did you have to do to get those flowers; Hoeing Perhaps?" Derrick's snared with is hate filled venom. I watched Molly flip her Blonde hair directly in his face ignoring his bullshit with flair.

"Like I was saying C' before that mark ass busters interruption!" She leaned over the table stretching her back in the direction of Derrick and her frustrated face towards me.

"Ahh!" I gasped as Derrick snatched her bouquet from behind her and started ripping the flowers apart. The laughter and amazement caused the art room to go up in an uproar.

"Hell no you didn't motherfucker!" Was the last word from Molly's mouth as the stiffest hardest jab she could muster up landed square in Derrick's mouth, knocking him backwards off his saddle stool.

"That is no way to conduct yourselves in my class room." Mr. Shaw the art teacher yelled back at Molly as he pulled Derrick to his shaking knees.

"I'll take her to the office Mr. Shaw, and wait for the 190." I pulled on my book bag, pushed my pager down into my Pocket, grabbed Molly's purse, books and her arm.

"Come on crazy ass girl, you off the fucking hook, as if we not already hot enough." A couple of the homies had to dap her for finally giving Derrick's jealous hating ass exactly what he deserved, what he'd been begging for. I know he had to feel stupid as fuck. She kept telling him she was going to hit him in his yapping ass mouth. Like most sucka's shit don't get real until they wake up on the floor from that blow to the mouth.

"Molly we got a much bigger problem." I strained to whisper to her through clenched teeth. People are getting fucked up behind that acid. Mother fuckas is talking. My locker was raided, but you know I never store shit in their property. Anyway how much of that shit did you sell?"

She looked at me a little nervous. "I sold all of it! We cool C the mother fuckas brought it, ok, shit happens like that with the dope." "Did you see o'l girl getting taken out of here by the ambulance today?" I really wanted to smoke my nerves were shot at this point. "You know the one long dark haired Weirdo, the Elvira looking bitch, well she took all that shit, I was meeting white boy J to sell him the rest, when o'l girl was on the stretcher being taken out. She kept screaming she felt like a Bear and her fur was growing. Bitch I just hope she don't tell anyone I sold her that shit."

"Chill out sis, the police here know you sell weed, they maybe suspect you of selling powder but they not going to suspect you for that shit, maybe me thou." The expression on her face as we walked into the office let me know that the reality of the shit I was saying to her just kicked in.

"Damn Homie."

"Dam is right." I replied. I walked her into the office, dapped her up and decided to run outside to hit my blunt real quick. I kept a big bottle of that cheap as Exclamation perfume that you get from Family Dollar. That shit was loud enough to mask anything. I threw the half of blunt in the grass and decided to head up to Mr. Trinnis's Class for my next period.

This day seemed like it was never going to end. I kept hearing rumors that the police was going to search me again, and that I was supposed to be getting jumped. Looney wasn't answering none of my pages and my stomachs been in knots since the police ran my locker earlier. I pulled my hoodie over my head and laid my head on top of my folded arms. Where was Mr. Trinnis? I felt myself dozing off when I began to hear desk moving around me. I figured class was about to change. Next thing I know I hear…

"Bitch you think you can steal my man and it's all good?" I lifted my head to pull my hoodie back to see the action. Instead I felt someone hit me on the back of neck hard as fuck. My first instinct was to back hand whoever was behind me. I swung like a mad woman hitting her in the middle of her throat with the side of my fist. I snatched my hoodie off and as I was pulling it over my head, this bitch began to hit me with a fury of punches. I had no choice but to eat the punches, while my head and arms were still in my hoodie.

I threw the hoodie to the floor pulled my hanging flag off my head wrapped it around my fist and start throwing three pieced combinations at her; left cheek, right cheek, in the mouth. She stumbled into the desk and as she tried to stand up I kicked her in the center of her stomach, causing her to crash to the floor.

"Un-Un Kia get up don't let her do you like that!" I turned my attention to her bitch ass friend Trina. "Oh so you the one that was supposed to jump me, I began walking toward her in my fighting stance when Rikkia called herself going to rush me from behind. I stepped to the side catching her in her right jaw. I grabbed her by her shirt and slammed her over the desk. The screaming and hollering from the class room had people in the hall way staring into our class rooting the fight on.

I grabbed her by her right arm that I caught mid swing and her throat and slammed her onto the desk. I held her pinned to the desk with my left hand on her throat, repeatedly pounding in her face.

"Bitch don't you ever come at me again, bitch, bitch, with every bitch I tried to hit her harder. Stupid bitch! I can't steal no big ass man he didn't want you bitch!" I grabbed her hair kneed her in her pussy and started banging her head against the desk. Stupid bitch!

I felt Mr. Trinnis grab me with my arms crossed above my head. I began kicking wildly so she didn't try to run up on me while he had my hands pinned.

"Justin get Rikkia out of here, take her to the office, right now!" He yelled to my classmate for assistance.

"CJ what were you thinking about, I thought we talked about you staying focused for your scholarship sake?"

"We did talk about it Mr. Trinnis, I was sitting here with my head down and she came in here hitting me first. I heard I was gonna get jumped; so if you want it bitch!" I screamed trying to walk towards her scared, pretty, petty ass friend. Who was slowly walking backwards out the class. My heart was beating out of my chest and my mouth was dryer than slave feet. I wanted to hit that bitch in the mouth while she swirled her weave around sipping her Capri juice pouch.

"Yea bitch that's what I thought!" I had a habit of grabbing my pants repeatedly at the sides of the knee when I was charged up.

"I swear to God, let another bitch try me! Who the fuck supposed to be jumping me? I'm ready bitches!"

"No CJ you're ready to go to the office. Dewayne walk CJ down to the office, I'll bring the 190 down myself." I grabbed my book-bag pulled the scarf off my hand and used it as a ponytail holder for my box braids.

"Ay C, you fuck that Slob ass bitch up for-real, bitch wasn't ready for lil scrappy doo, she thought being bigger than you gave her an advantage."

"Man fuck that rat bitch, she ain't shit, I got that bitch in the hood, she better not ever bring her blind ass to my hood again. Bitch what she thought, you wear mother fucking bifocals how you gone fight with your glasses off, stupid ass tramp." I jogged down the long staircase.

"Ay before we get to the office you got a $5 blunt for sale you never met me for lunch?" I stopped at the bottom of the stairs, dropped my book-bag to the floor opened my side-compartment where I kept the Nicks and gave him one, via dap: we made the exchange.

"You know you really don't have to walk me all the way to the office."

"Oh yes I do, you in my care and if you get jumped I'm-a have to fuck with Fat Joe's ass, I'm straight lil nigga you going to the office." We both laughed mildly, neither one of us wanted any problems, period.

I walked into the office taking my usual far right seat closes to the secretary. Secretly hoping that I would get our female Vice Principal, Ms. V for Vice is what I called her. She was cool about 5'5 frumpy white lady, her graying shoulder length bob cut, looked brittle and wiry She really could use some conditioner. She was married but I believed to another woman. She just gave me that stud vibe. I Knew it. I thought as I seen her door open.

"CJ!" She peeped out her door signaling me with her two fingers to come. I put my book bag slowly over my back, sniffing to see if I smelt the aroma of Marijuana.

"Have a seat CJ."VP was in the wrong field, she needs to be a choir director or airplane guide all these fingers she's giving me. I laughed to myself as she waved her three fingers signaling for me to sit down.

"CJ I find myself very much worried about you as of lately. You're one of our schools scholar students yet you're trading the chess club for beat-boxing? Mrs. Author told me she took you and three other girls to the modeling agency after school and they said they would love to work with you once you removed your nose ring. Furthermore Mrs. Author said: you decided not to pursue it."

"Ms. V. I didn't decide not to pursue it; my family just couldn't afford it. I can't afford to spend hundreds of dollars on pictures when there are bills to pay."

"You speak CJ as if you're paying rent and utilities."

"I never said that I wasn't." I appreciate Mrs. Author and when I can afford it, I'll take up the offer. As far as the chess team, I just grew tired of it, it takes up too much time and nobody supports it like a contact sport."

"OK so why did you quit the basketball team Cernitha?"

"Mrs. V I'm barely five-two and those chicks' legs are ten times longer than mines. I was tired of running twice as hard. Besides I don't have NBA Baller ambitions."

"Is she in there with the Vice Principal?" I heard my mom's voice over everyone's.

VP Nodded her head signaling for me to head to the door. I threw my book bag on my back and opened the door.

"Don't worry Mrs. V I got my priorities straight. I'm focused on maintaining my Grade Point Average to keep my Scholarship. UCLA is still my destination, Hello California, Goodbye Ohio."

"Good Cernitha, Now and at least now I can stop worrying about you."

"Yea you should never worry, it's the opposite of faith, just lift me in prayer." I walked out and smiled, Mrs. V was like butter when she wasn't menopausing.

Looney, Mom and half the niggas from the hood was hanging around the principal's office.

"Did it really take all yawl to come get me?"
"Shit that's what I was wondering." Mom said, before rolling her eyes at the secretary for her language slipup.

~§~§~§~§~§~§~

"Baby, Star lay back." Joe insisted as I kicked off my Timberlands scooting backwards in his bed until I was against the head board.

"No baby lay flat on your back" He pulled my feet toward him then slowly began to unbutton my pants.

"Are you going to turn the light off?" I asked nervous about my naked body exposed.

"How many times do I have to tell you that you have a beautiful body Star? It's the most beautiful little body that I've ever seen." He smiled then stood up to go turn off the lights. I decided to rush my clothes off and get under the sheets. His laughter only made me smile as he pulled the sheets off exposing my naked 15 year old body. I watched as he removed his black t-shirt and kneeled down in front of me. Again pulling my legs towards him until my ass was at the edge of the bed.

"Just drop your legs to the side and relax." He whispered slowly massaging my thighs. I felt awkward to say the least with my naked pussy in his face. He rubbed his hands up and down my vagina as I lay with my eyes covered. He licked from the bottom of my vagina to the top of my clitoris, and then slowly circled the underbelly of his tongue around my growing clitoris. I tried to relax but the waves of emotions caused me to twitch. This licking was feeling really good.

"I like when you do that baby." I whispered in my Smokey voice.

"You mean this?" He flicked his tongue up and down real fast on each side of my clitoris.

"Yes baby that, Ooh…" I moaned as the nervousness became pleasure and awkward was being replaced with throbs of ecstasy. He stuck his hard pointed tongue in my vagina, tongue fucking me up and down sucking and pulling the clitoris with him each time he came up.

"I'm sure, oh my God, Babe, I think I'm, Ooh." Of all the times we've had sex and the different small sensations I've felt it never felt like this.

"Ooh, oh Joe."

"Yes baby, rub Daddy's head, and call me Daddy."

"Yes Daddy, please don't stop, please." I begged crying in this new pleasure. I couldn't escape this feeling in my stomach it felt great, I felt strong and weak at the same time. I wanted more. Ooh the twitching turned to shaking and for the first time I was coming. The pleasure was taken over, the sensation too extreme. I tried to push his head to stop, as he shook side to side with his lips gripped around my clit. I tensed up as he took the moisture from my vagina and rubbed it around my ass hole.

"What are you doing baby, I –I mean Daddy?"

"I'm taking us to the next level Star, I want all of you and I want you to have all of me. Baby just lay back." I felt like my body froze and melted at the same time, the first time he plunged his tongue into my ass.

"Ahh!" I shrieked from too many emotions to explain. He spread my but cheeks further apart, kissed, licked and sucked on every part of me. After I was damn near ready to pass out I felt him begin to slide his brick hard dick firm but slowly into my butt hole.

"Ooh No, that hurts, stop Joe!" I tried to crawl away but his 300+lbs outweighed my strength.

"C'mon baby, it's only going to hurt for a little while. Baby c'mon enjoy me." He moaned with a look of ecstasy on his face I've never seen. I wanted to keep him in this new ecstasy but…

"Ooh no babe it hurts for real, take it out, it feels like I'm about to pee on myself!"

"No, no baby it's the pressure. He chuckled; Big said it's going to be pressure for a little while, c'mon babe him and stinky already Rumping." He said finally thrusting the rest of his penis deep into my rectum.

I was confused, Tasha never told me about her having anal sex before.

"Ahh baby, it's still burning." The lubrication on his penis was slowly loosening my virginal walls, but the pleasure factor was nowhere in sight.

"Oh, Joe take it out, I'm about to pee on myself!" I tried gripping the sheets, biting the pillow even pumping back, but it still hurt like hell.

He began to pound harder and faster. "Damn Star your ass is tight as fuck, this feel super good, if you gone piss…ooh… just piss I told you it's…uhh… He moaned "-Just the pressure?" I relaxed until what felt like an eruption happened and I pissed all down my legs and on to his bed. I snatched his sheet with me as we both jumped off the bed.

"I told your nasty ass I had to piss!" My embarrassment was at a whole new height.

"Damn Star yo pissy ass couldn't wait?" Pointing, laughing hard at my embarrassment. I stared at him resentful pulling on his oversized t-shirt to go upstairs to the bathroom. By the time I came back down he was already in his boxers & beater, changed the bed and was smoking his mild.

"Sit down baby." He patted beside him on the bed. He kissed me on the lips and smiled soft and genuinely with his dancing eyes. 'I really need you to know that I love you Star and I'm going to ask your mom, if she will allow me to marry you when you turn 16."

"Wow!" I didn't know what to say.

"Star in this short period of time, we've ran through a lot, and you down as fuck, you'll fight beside me, get money beside me and that shit mean a lot to a Gangster, feel me?" I nodded my head, pushing back to fold my legs Indian style so I could roll a blunt.

"Queen, I know I ain't the best nigga, I may not be the best nigga for you, shit when you finish school and go off to college you might leave a nigga in the hood." Stunned; I sat the tray down leaned on his back and wrapped my arms around him.

"You're my nigga, my King, my Daddy, right? Why would I leave you anywhere? We've been holding each other down from Go and because I don't want to live & die in the hood don't mean that college is going to change who I am or who I love, we riding till the casket drop, right?" I questioned him with a kiss.

"Star, you know my love is true, a nigga real to you, but on the strength of the life we live it's going to come a point in time where as my Queen you are going to be required to do more than move these little packs, more than the little gang fights. Like the shit you're exposed to right now; this shit is nothing and I want to know on life that you down for me till the casket, through jail, heaven or hell."

"What you mean it ain't shit Looney? I've done a lot of shit and I've been in a lot of trouble behind fucking with you; and I'm still here, just like today, fighting bitches because of you."

"Yea I hear all that but do you love me?" He questioned.

-"Shhh I interrupted him, I think I hear your mom calling you."

Apparently someone was here to see him. Eddie Kane & DOG came and they had a private conversation in the separate part of the basement. I lit the half blunt in the ashtray and began to flick through his mother's countless channels. In between stations I kept hearing them say gotta go on BOS, this on BOS, that on BOS. I knew whenever they were putting something on BOS some drama was sure to follow.

"Star I need to talk to you." I watched him nervously as he walked back into the room, handing me a full bottle of Remy.

"What's up Bae? Looney you know I don't like to drink, what's this for?" I questioned as he shoved the bottle at me. "

We going to put in some work tonight Star and I need to make sure that your head is 100 in the game."

"Don't you think if you wanted me at my best I should be sober?"

"Nah babe, not for this." I watched him in fear as he pulled as hard as he could on the blunt. He looked over at me with those: fire red hazel eyes, as if he seen right through my soul.

"Drink up Star, take that shit to the head Ma." I took the hint and swallowed the Remy down about five big gulps before I reached the middle of the bottle.

"Alright lil nigga that's enough." He laughed snatching the bottle from me.

"Here smoke up." I laughed as I climbed on-top of him in my sports bra and boy short underwear.

"Blow me a shot gun big daddy." I looked up at his wild nappy ass mat fro as I inhaled all the smoke through my nostrils. I wish he'd keep this nappy ass shit braided, I don't know why he love this Wildman look, I thought to myself. I began to choke as the smoke from the dank hit my lungs.

"Yea choke that shit up." He kissed me on the forehead before effortlessly lifting me off him, placing me back on the bed. I still wanted to touch him. I wanted him to kiss my pussy the way he was doing before we were rudely interrupted.

"Baby!" I called out to him, trying to arch my back and look sexy in my Tommy Hilfiger Sports Set.

"I told you to call me Daddy, Big Daddy Ma, remember?" Oh Yea his lack of response deflated my sex-appeal and the forced arch in my back.

"Listen Ma I need you to focus. When we get back home, I'm-a fuck the shit out of yo lil ass, like I know you want me to. I'm-a eat that little juicy box until you cum again. I felt you coming for the first time like that." His sentimental smile was brief.

"I mean when we fucking I can feel it get wetter through the condom but I didn't know you came like that."

"Uh baby, Daddy, Big Daddy do we have to go out tonight?" I whined hoping he would change his mind, stay in and give me oral sex again.

"Look we gone fuck and suck all night Queen; but first you got some more stripes to earn. Daddy made you feel good like I promised you I would. Ma you had a rough couple days, I know. But tonight I need my Soldier, not Wifey but Star. I need Star on deck tonight you feel me?"

"Star--Folks you on auto-pilot?" He waved his hand in my face.

"No nigga I'm coherent I was just thinking." I smirked, smacking his hand away.

"Thinking what?" He belched before drinking the rest of the Remy straight down.

"I was thinking how whenever you call me Folks or Queen or requesting Star then some o'l crazy shit attached to it, like some random fight or some shit you call putting in work. Work for whom for what?"

"There you go with that clueless shit again. You know the oath you took. You know the work is for the Fort our Fort. Quit tripping Ma. Do a nigga always got to pump you up to ride out? You talk all that wild-girl shit in your raps Buck, Buck and all that shit but you get jelly hands when I hand you the pistol."

"Whatever nigga; Jelly hands my ass! You always trying to get me to do your dirty work, I should have more stripes than yo ass by now." I relit the Dobie as he laughed hysterically.

"Oh that's real funny to you hun?" I wanted to slap him.

"Ma you can live three more lifetimes and still not put in the amount of work I have. That was cute, now get up and get dressed Ma. Put ya Black hoodie on in the closet. I gotta run to Eddie Kane's and grab something real quick. You get dressed, roll us a couple more L's and be ready when I get back. Oh take this couple hundred to Mom and go grab her other bottle of Remy."

Uh my little 15 year old mind was spinning. I drank too much of that liquor too fast. I stood in his full size mirror admiring my defined four pack abs in my blue, white and red underwear ensemble. 5'2 108 I was skinny, but I was ripped and my little tits were perfect torpedoes. I slid on my black stone washed jeans my black and white Jordan's, my black beater, black-T and then my hoodie. I decided against the coat I most likely was about to be in some kind of fight or altercation. I gathered my black shoulder length box braids into a French braid going down the center of my back, grabbed the money and headed upstairs to his mother's room.

"Come In!" She yelled after my second knock.

"What's up honey, what you need?" She quizzed.

"Looney, I mean Joe told me to give this to you and grab your other bottle of Remy." I stood there nervous as she rushed the three hundred dollar bills back and forth in her hand.

"Yea he better had given me some money drinking both my bottles." She laid back on her sitting pillows rubbing her feet together.

"The Remy is in my closet on the floor to the right honey & don't you look like a little version of Joseph." She laughed; as I glanced at myself in her dresser mirror. I continued to the closet and grabbed the liquor. "

"Grab that purse beside the liquor honey. Un-hun reach in there and get out my stash of refer. Can you roll me up two of the blunt things real quick? They seem to last longer than the joints."

"Yes Ma'am I'm going to roll it in the kitchen."

"No you can roll it right here."

"Oh, Ok well I'll be right back I'm going to get Joe's sac I have to roll him some too, before he gets back." The sound of her laugh took me by Surprise. Was she laughing because she checked me about her weed? Or because her and her son thought I was the anytime blunt roller? I really didn't care for the answer; I was just really annoyed and still nervous at this point. I took the steps up by two. I didn't want Looney to come back to my job undone.

I laid one of the swishers on his mother's chest size deep freezer beside the trashcan. Licked and split the first one with my finger nail, emptied the tobacco and repeated the steps for the second. I opened the packed grinder and filled both swisher sweets to the brim. I rolled them both and left them on the kitchen table to dry. I glanced out the kitchen window, before proceeding back to his mother's room. I tapped on the door slowly; silently hopping she wouldn't jump at every opportunity to clown me.

"Come in honey, its open." I slowly entered her bedroom, I figured I'd just roll her blunts real quick, maybe try to figure out what's up with Looney, or Heavy as he's now trying to call himself. I grabbed her sack and both of the still wrapped swishers towards the corner end of her dresser; opened the bottle of Remy and took a big swig. With the moisture from the liquor I licked a straight line down the center of both shells, busted down and rolled her blunts.

"Here you go Mom." Sitting both Stogies on her nightstand beside her bed.

"That was fast Girlie, shit you did that like a pro." We both shared a laugh.

"Show me how to do it from the beginning." I grabbed another one of her cigars, removed it from the plastic. Took another swig of the Remy, licked a center line, down the base, pressed my thumb nail pressed it along the moistened tobacco leaf and busted it open. I dumped the shredded tobacco into her trash can and laid the shell on her dinner tray beside her bed. Took out one big nugget bud and broke it down into the shell. After removing a few sticks and evening the fillings I clasped the leaf defining the pouch. Licked the interior of the blunt and folded over again until it was a stuffed cylinder. I dried it quickly with the lighter from her table and handed her the blunt.

"Light it up" She said.

"For sure." I replied happy to be calming my nerves.

"When's your birthday CJ."

"January 18th".

"Oh that makes you a Capricorn, I'm a Capricorn too. No wonder why I like you!" I was shocked. I never thought the lady liked me, let alone thought anymore about the likes of me when I wasn't in her presence.

"So you're the end of the sign and I'm the beginning of the sign December 22nd. So our union will be like an Alpha-Omega situation." I decided not to even explore the comment but to inhale as much of this weed as I could.

"Yea hit that again baby girl, you're going to need to hold your head."

"So what happened? I asked her, what's going on? Where are we going?"

"Here pour you a cup of that Remy." She pulled two small Styrofoam cups from the hidden sliding drawer of her wood & mirror King-Sized wrap around bed. Passing me the cup she sat up straight against her pillows inhaled slowly while her hazel eyes pierced through my soul. What was she about to share with me?

"You know Loyalty is thicker than blood?"

"Uh, yes Ma'am."

"And you know that sometimes to prove your loyalty you have to do things you don't like to do in order to help your family or whomever your proving your loyalty too."

OK. I was really lost as to what she was really saying.

"CJ I know your part of the Gangster Disciples. I don't know why you allowed yourself to swear into something you didn't know about and why my sons drug you into it. I feel more comfortable knowing that you are a Capricorn, a natural leader a go-getter ambitious. That's the only reason I've given my son my blessings with you, I know you are going to be my daughter."

I began choking off the smoke and the shock. In my ignorance I uttered: "Uh is this a psychic reading?"

"Bwahaha woo girl!" We both began laughing very hard. The way she laughed herself to tears made me laugh into my own hysteria.

"Yes and no." She finally said pulling herself together.

"We are going to be family yes. I see how Joseph looks at you, I know he doesn't really know what love is but believes that he loves you. I also know that you sneak over here from time to time cutting school. I don't know if anyone has told you but that's a recipe for pregnancy or disaster. I'm going to leave you with this while you wait for Joseph. You only get one life little girl. Boys/Men come and go. Remember to stand for something or fall for everything."

"Enjoy the rest of your drink dear and remember what I told you. Shut the door all the way behind you." She shewed me off with her hand as she grabbed for the remote to turn back up the volume on her recorded Montell Williams show featuring Renowned Psychic Sylvia Brown.

As I closed her bedroom door the front door open suddenly causing me to spill a little of the Remy on her plastic runner.

"You got the bottle Star?" He questioned wiping his shoes.

"Yea what's left of it Bae, your mom and I started drinking it." I motioned the bottle in the air so he could see the damage. I gave your mom the money too and we shared a drink and a blunt.

"Really?" He smiled at me. "I knew my mom would love you, she say you always act so damn scary when you come around. Where is your flag?" He asked looking me up and down as I stood there clutching the liquor bottle?"

"I put your L's on the kitchen table." I pointed aimlessly.

–"Where is your flag?" He interrupted.

"It's downstairs on the table."

"Ay go get it and the latex gloves out the top dresser drawer under the TV." I did as I was told; turning off the light in the bedroom after grabbing my Black Flag off the table. I paused wondering if I would go to Jail tonight. Fucking around with Looney I've seen the cops more on the daily then I did my entire life. I also wondered if he was going to lick my friend as I liked to call her. Lick my pussy, eat my pussy was just too vulgar to me; even asking him to do it made me shy and awkward.

"Star, let's ride!" He screamed from upstairs. As usual I took the steps by two.

"Are you going to tell me where we're going? I slid into the car getting angrier by the minute.

"You know our favorite game right?"

"You mean your favorite game." I rolled my eyes.

"Why you acting all stank, Star, seems like you got an attitude for no reason?"

"No Looney; It's definitely a reason why I have an attitude." I said firmly slamming the door to his mother's four door blue ford escort."

"Damn don't break the door." He laughed puffing on his black & mild.

"You know I love you, right Star?"

"Yea I guess so Joe, like what's up, really you only get like this when something bad has happened. What happened?"

"A lot of shit has happened Star and honestly I didn't want to get you involved but love and duty calls for your help ma."

"And what does that supposed to mean Joe?" I grabbed one of the two blunts he placed in the ashtray as he turned onto Cleveland Avenue. "Eddie Kane got word on the niggas we beefing wit, where they trapping at. We bout to ride thru the Terrace to pick up this rental; and all we got to do tonight is send these pussy niggas a message, feel me Ma?"

"And what's the message Daddy?"

"The message is not to fuck with the Vydoc on BOS or niggas will feel the heat." We pulled off Windsor and pulled up behind a black Nissan. "Put ya gloves on Star and grab your flag."

"What up Folks?" Eddie Kane nodded, dapping me up.

"Shit; you tell me?"

"Shit all I know is you're going for the crown tonight."

"Word, that's what you know?" I shook my head in disgust.

"Yea nigga G's up." He pulled me in for a hug and rubbed the G across my back. "Keep ya eyes open lil sis."

Looney looked to be in the zone, the music was down normally he would have it blasting. We pulled behind some garages off Joyce Ave when he slightly turned the music up. Oh My God he was playing Brown Stones: If You Love Me!

"Looney were not about to play that game tonight are we?"

"Nah ma, matter fact ain't shit about tonight a game. I saw the niggas on the porch when we rode past; but them niggas on your side of the street."

"Huh?" I replied. I watched as he pulled the burner out from the pouch of his hoodie wrapped in his flag, opening it with his flag.

"Open ya flag, Star." I opened my neatly folded flag that was sitting flat across my lap. My legs instantly began to shake as he sat the black 9mm on my left leg.

"Wrap this part around the handle and this part on the trigger." I pulled my right glove tight as I silently begin to cry.

"Grab the burner Star, Grab The Burner Star!" He yelled at me before turning the car back on.

"But Bae!" I felt the tears well up in my eyes.

-"But Bae nothing". He interrupted me.

"I didn't say but Star last month when you needed the money for your rap-shit, or your new hair for yawls pictures, you knew I just Re-Upped. So I had to get at a nigga to get the bread for you. So, so what I don't hold you down no more?"

"Nah you done fucking with me like that?" I hated when he flipped shit around like this, and got all loud with his high signing shit.

"Bae, I didn't say that."

"-Good!" He interrupted me again this time pulling from the alley onto the street.

"The niggas bout three houses down on your side." He lit his black & mild, I could tell he was nervous, which made me that much more scared. He creped slowly down the street; stopping diagonal from a porch full of dudes laughing & shit talking.

"You better bust Star! That's all the fuck I know!"

I pleaded nervous with the pistol sitting on my lap; trying not to grip it so he couldn't see how bad my hands were shaking.

"Scared my mother fucking ass, on BOS, you bust, on BOS you bust! ON BOS!!"

My body and soul shook! The hell in his voice was the trigger in my ear. The fear as the bullet left the chamber the first time was all the power of hell I could stand to gain.

"BOS!!"

I pulled the trigger again. This time trying to aim through the blur of the tears that filled my squinting, blood shot red, traumatized eyes. I didn't know who I was shooting at. I didn't know why. I just knew I loved him; I had to prove to him I loved him. Brownstones "If you Love Me" played on repeat for the hundredth time.

The fear, anxiety and sorrow that engulfed my body was now hate, a beast's snarl of protection: As I imagined my targets harming Looney. Life without Looney was the catalyst behind my trigger finger. If you love me the song questioned and I was letting off the 6th bullet. The engine revving stopped. The jerk from us skirting off was worse than the kickback in my wrist from the Nine. The same Black Nine that would later change my life forever.

"Babe I love you! You hear me? You hear me Star? I love you! Wipe your face." He said hitting the corner damn near on two wheels, then taking his rugged right hand in a quick effort to rub my tears away. We played the "Prove You Love Me" Game all the time; this time was the worst of all. If mom found out about this, it would be more than her extension cord on my soaking wet body. An ass whipping for this stunt would be far worse than her throwing the lit packet of firecrackers on me while I was damn near naked.

"You think you popping? Oh I got some pop for that ass." She said as she took the firecrackers and the lighter out of her pocket. I guess her splicing my skin 35 times with her switch wasn't enough.

"Baby ain't shit ever gone come between us." Looney said snapping me back into reality. "You down to ride out ride for me on life. Fuck the tears Star you're that bitch, your that Boss Bitch! I'll bust for you. You busted for me, we bonded for life Star. Wipe your tears, I got you Ma; you gone be my wife."

I tried not to think about just ruining my entire life on our high-speed drive back to the hood. I can't wrap my mind around what just happened. But this on BOS would be much worse than prison.

Lord I love him, Let him protect me and love me forever and ever and eva.

I can't remember how many times I came that night, how many blunts we smoked, how many shot guns we gave one another, nor how many bottles of Remy we drank. All I remember is I became addicted to his oral sex. I never wanted him to stop; it was the only thing that could clear my mind.

~§~§~§~§~§~§~

I paged Looney over and over, I wanted to go to the studio, I couldn't stop thinking about the other night. I smoked so much weed my dad said he was going to take me and drop me off to the rehab. I assume this was my first bout with depression. My mother trimmed her upstairs bathroom in Black Paint. I had the genius idea to take the rest and paint my entire bedroom black. My baby sister was scared shitless when she came in.

"AWWW CJ! I'M TELLING MOMMY!" She slammed the door and ran back downstairs to tell my mom, which she already knew. I blew Looney's Pager up. 219 /410 /911

I was getting pissed; I figured if I go into the lab, zone out to a hot beat, I could come up with something that could take my mind off this reoccurring dream. What if I hit somebody? Did I hit somebody? My head felt sick, my stomach felt worse. I'm about to page him again, I thought to myself sitting nervously on my twin bed.

"CJayyyyyyy!" My mom yelled from down stairs

"Yes Ma'am!"

"Joe's down here to take you to the studio!"

"Yes!" I jumped up, grabbed a couple sacs out of my bear, some Philly Blunts, my backpack, flag and I was ready to go. For some reason when I entered the living-room my mom's Newport's didn't smell like death to me, instead I wanted to ask her for one, but I knew better.

"Is your little ball head manager bringing you home tonight?" She asked me, pausing her played out Sonic the Hedge Hog Game.

"Yes Ma'am."

"Well tell him or Joe to buy me a pack of cigarettes."

"Yes Ma'am."

"What's wrong with you? Is your ass knocked up?"

I sucked my teeth as hard as I could. "No Mom, I just got a lot on my mind." I slung my head back so she could sense I was ready to run out the door.

"Suck ya teeth all you want too, have your ass back here by a decent time tonight. Before your daddy bring his drunk ass home and start questioning." She un-paused her game, meaning the conversation was over.

I walked out the door and into Joe's Jaguar Geek Rental.

"I see you caught Mr. Rental Car first today?" I laughed throwing my backpack in the backseat; after shutting my door I grabbed his Newport's.

"You Tripping Ma, when did you start smoking?" I waited until he hit the alley before I lit the cigarette.

"Today, I've been stressing about the other night, Looney, that shit wasn't right at all, and I can't talk to nobody about it."

"Who the fuck you wanna talk to Oprah? Star on some real shit, you talk to me about it, talk to yourself about it, baby you don't share that G shit with nobody. Fuck you thinking bout Babe?"

"What you mean, fuck I'm thinking about, that's the shit I'm thinking about, like for-real you could have really talked to me first, like you should have-"

"Star quit tripping with that should'a, could'a, would'a shit, A mutha fucking Star was born, aiight, feel me, motherfuckers can't tell you how to feel, motherfuckers never lived your life. Bitches ain't walked in your Nike's. Star you really need to forget the whole shit ever happened, we never left the bed. I stayed kissing your friend, all night; you stayed kissing my friend all night. We ate, we drank, we smoked-out. The rest of that shit we put it on G, It's in Gangsta heaven."

"Gangsta Heaven? Joseph why you fucking with my head? I can't talk to yo stupid ass nigga, I don't process like you."

"Well you need too! And stop with all this crybaby ass shit Star, You a mother fucking G. VGD Vydoc Folks Gangster Disciple till the day you die, you were born again, you gone die with this shit Star. You take that shit to the grave."

I wanted to cry, I wanted to reach back and punch him as hard as I could in his shit. I wanted to shoot his ass. Fat ass evil motherfucker. Yet his driving 75mph on the freeway reminded me to sit tight. We were to the eastside in no time. He dropped me off in East Haven, at my producer's house.

"Mommy Sell me a forty sac. I'm bout' to go post up over sis' off Champion til you call me; less I get a sting, but hit me up before you're ready." I dug in my book bag and pulled him out two twenty sacs. I gave him a fat sac and a skimpy one; he really was pissing me off. I snatched the money from his hand before giving him the sacs. I slammed the door and walked around the car into the street.

"Lil nigga I don't care if you got no attitude, you're lil ass always got an attitude. Put your mean ass eyebrow down and come and give your gangster a kiss." He got on my nerves but he knew what to say. He pulled me by my arm into the window again while I struggled positioning my book bag.

"Dang Looney!" I laughed kissing him again. He reached out the window and smacked my ass.

"And I see that skimpy ass sack, you gone pay for it later, Daddy gone tax that little ass."

He flashed the most adorable straight teeth smile. It made the handsome monster; human.

"Is that right?" I gave him my normal sass.

"Yea nigga that's right. Give me another kiss and quit playing." I bent over into the window tongued and kissed his mouth with passion, trading turns sucking each other's tongues then lips.

"I'm sorry I had to be so rough with ya mental ma, soldiers can't wallow in the aftermath." He grabbed my chin and gave me a soft still kiss on my forehead. I love you Star with your Big Ass Forehead too."

"Shut up Nigga I love you with your big ass body!" We both laughed, did our signature hand shake locked at G and I went into the studio.

"Ron already down stairs, he was making some beats I didn't know you were coming over today." Sunny the main owner of TEOS Records said to me as I walked to the basement door.

"Yea thanks Sunny, no today's not my scheduled day. I just had some things on my mind."

"-Say no more; he interrupted. Ay before you go you got any trees on you?"

"What you need?" I responded.

"Oh just a little dime a little tension he laughed making his thumb & index finger into the small sign." I liked Sunny, he was cool, but mean, stern when it came to the music, the shows and the business, he would make us all compete against each other for the best events and opportunities. I reached in my bag and gave him my last skimpy twenty sac, hell he should be grateful.

"Damn Paz, when ya dimes get so big?"

"They never did, that's not a dime sac." I grabbed the money and put it in my pocket. I never flashed my wad in-front of any nigga but my nigga. especially if I couldn't beat the nigga.

I grabbed an apple juice out the fridge and headed to the lab.

"What up Mayo-naise" I said to my favorite producer Ron Mayo, giving him dap. He was in the zone, he'd always push his tongue to the left bottom corner of his mouth when he felt like he was making some hot shit; and hot it was.

"It kind of sound like that drop from that Young Lay feat Mac Mall & Ray Luv: Fetti I've been vibing real hard to this song lately."

"Yea I got you lil sis, you told me at the last session, check this out." He pushed some button and the beat dropped to a sick tick, symbol & horn pattern.

"Ewww that's nasty Fam, I like that." I said pulling my Pre Rolled's. I lit the first blunt and gave it to Ron.

"My Little Nigga, aye did you see Sunny he was looking for some?"

"Yea I got him right." I lit my blunt sat on the couch and pulled out my note book and pen, exhaled and tried to get lost in the beat.

"Ay sis, I'm going to loop this beat for you, I'm going to the store to grab me a beer you want something?" He put out his blunt and then decided to light back up. He grabbed $10 out his pocket and dropped it on the couch beside me.

"You got me?" He asked looking skeptical at me.

"Nigga of course I do, I got the shells too."

"Oh cool."

" Here." I handed him a five dollar bill.

"Can you get me some Strawberry Hill Boones Farm, Double Mint and a small bag of Dorito's?" I reached in my book bag and got out a dime sack & dropped it on the table.

"You want me to roll you up or you good?" I'm good he said putting the sack in his pocket.

"Now you know what you got to do if you want to record right?" "I'll wait for you." I continued nodding my head to the beat trying to think of some happy or party shit, because in reality I was feeling like prison or death was around the corner.

"God why did I do that? Please forgive me, give me the opportunity to make it right if at all possible. Please give me a sound mind and help me to stop thinking about the other night. Help me to believe it never existed like Looney Said." I took a deep breath. Amen!

I began to write the first thing that came to my mind:

Intro: *Welcome to me ladies & gentlemen*

Vs.1 Look Cuz baby girl she the queen so fly / you see I got the killas all standing in a line Looking for a ride/ I'm-a take you on an expedition let's get it funky pump the base turn up your volume. Your girls a go getter heavy hand she a cold splitter / to the left with the rest when I'm the pick of the litter/ These niggas after me like a got a super on my chest / but I'm drove on a mission benz on my head rest/ Get you high like Cess / Escalate me to success / I keep me manned up / see the look I express/ I ain't on no play haters/ haters back it up. I'm feeling real good so I'm gonna shake my butt.

Hook:
And we gone kick it kick it and we gone keep it funky and we gone pop and dip it. Around the world honey, we Midwest two step it, we hair and weave prep it. We drop it cause it's hot, we Midwest soldiers hun? We rap and swing them things, you know I stack them G's don't hate me once if you a hater feel free. Cause I'm gone kick it kick it and I'm gone keep it funky and I'm gone pop and dip it.

Vs2... Look. Look. Look. See I'm gone do my thing your thing I will not do, cause I do what I want real bitches do them too/ Haters do what they must/ We body bag them mutts / it's one life to live here and so we live it up/ I'm in my zone homie, I twist like hurricanes /I keep it big pimping no time for little thang/ can't roll no wack wheels I got to spin on Chrome/ I'm holding down the fort/ fuck what a nigga want/ My bitches on they grind/ we tear the floor up- we aint playing here/ we off that drank cuz-/ Stress we left it at the door / I did my thing real good buy me some more / but since I do me I'm gona buy you a drink and we gone

Hook:

I couldn't shake the torment, I decided to go upstairs to the kitchen and use the phone. I grabbed the black plastic phone hanging from the wall and decided to call my Great Grandmother.

"Hello" I smiled at the sound of her voice

"Hey my favorite pretty lady, how are you doing this evening?"

"Oh Chanitha, is that you?"

"Yes ma'am and I couldn't stop thinking about you, how you doing Grandma?"

"Well to tell you the truth half the damn time I can't remember who the hell I am, let alone how I'm doing. Let me look around, well the house still clean and standing, I guess I'm doing good."

I busted out laughing even thou I knew she was telling the truth. Grandma's memory was slowly fading and mentally she jumped in and out of different phases of her life as if she was living in that very moment.

"I tell you what Chanitha I'm standing in the kitchen looking out at the yard and Denise's damn dog Ashley done ruined my fucking garden. He ate the cabbage, tore up my onions my small bushel of Greens. I think I want to have that damn dog put to sleep."

I laughed because I knew she was throwing a punch-line, however I was brought to tears by the state of my Grandmothers mental health. Ashley tore up the garden years ago, and she decided not to replant it.

"Well Grandma if you like I can stop by tonight to see you for a quick minute and bring you some seeds. Then I can come over tomorrow and help you plant a new garden." I wiped the tears streaming from my eyes and switched the receiver to the other ear/shoulder routine.

"Oh that would be nice Chanitha, can you bring me some Coffee too, you know Folgers my only brand."

"Oh I know Grandma, I said with a smile. I'll see you in a couple hours. I love you!"

"I love you too Chanitha." With that I hung up the phone wiped my face and picked back up the phone to page Joe. I went back down to the lab put on the headphones, armed the track and pressed record. Midway through my first hook Ron came back.

"I just want to run through this song, I don't want to format it right now, no structure just let me flow."

"You got it lil sis Ron said putting on his ear phones then busting down his shell."

After about an hour my pager was blowing, Joe was outside.

"Alright Mayo-naise I'm out of here, see you for our regular session."

"Yep and try to get some more of those trees that you had last week." He said inhaling his badly rolled blunt.

"I got you my nigga." We hit hands three times and hugged as I bounced on my book bag.

"Hey babe can you take me to Kroger's real quick so I can grab some stuff for my Grandma. We can go to the one on Refugee then Hit the 104 to the South Side." I asked Looney as I crossed the street to his car.

"I know where I'm at lil nigga (he laughed jokingly) I got you ma, sit back relax, hit this, ay Star try this tea, this shit good for real." I couldn't wait to see my Grandma, I grabbed a few packs of cabbage and green seeds, some onions and some tomatoes. This should be enough seeds for her to play with I thought smiling. I grabbed a cheap colorful bouquet of flowers, a large tin can of Folgers and headed to the register. On the way to the car, I noticed Joe leaning his back against the car and some random hood rat looking bitch smiling to close too his face.

"Does this look like congregation hour, Pastor?" I said walking up beside him opening the back door.

"What did you say? He laughed and looked at me crazy. Star this is Tracy, Tracy this is my Fiancé Star."

"Fiancé?" She looked baffled

"Yea that's what he said the 1st time." Her side eye look showed she was salty. I slammed the back door and proceeded around the car. Opening my door I leaned over the hood of the car: Joe say goodbye to your little friend so we can go over Grandmas. Goodbye Tracy!" The chick looked at me like she was ready to fight. I snarled my lips, and then twisted them to the side, like bitch you really don't want this problem.

"Quit tripping Star; -Yea she always on it, I'll catch up to you later Shorty, He said hitting her dap.

"Oh no you won't either nigga, we said goodbye to Tracy not catch you later, ass nigga."

He started laughing and got in the car. "Man Star you Hell For Real, ain't nobody fucking with that girl, she buy work"

"-Nigga you a work ass lie, the bitches shoes too bummie to be getting money, the fuck you think I'm stupid, I seen yawl ass all teeth keeking with the bitch. Keep fucking around with these ducks you know Andre right around the corner, right?"

"Yea you better hold ya mouth Star talking crazy! Don't get you and that nigga fucked up!" He was instant pissed and I liked it.

"Yea ain't nobody say anything about beating on your rat. You better find some more respect for me nigga, don't be gumming up in these bitches faces in front of me if ain't no money being exchanged."

He turned his body sideways in his seat and starred me directly in my eyes. "You a fucking trip, I love the fuck out of your little short woman complex having ass."-

"Will you stop saying that I told you I don't have no short woman complex." I waved off his criticism.

"Ay but I'm-a fuck the shit out of your little slick talking ass tonight. We not going to be over your grandma's long are we?"

"Aww the baby ready for dick time, he don't want to play in the dirt with Grandma." I joked and kissed him passionately on the lips before falling into my seatbelt.

"Don't be out here fucking with these bitches for real Joe, if you really love me."

"I do love you baby, he kissed me again, and I ain't out here fucking with these hoes, I don't treat these hoes."

Yea whatever, I thought to myself but decided to fall back from the game of lies tonight.

"I want you to fuck the shit out of me and stay out those dirty bitches panty-grounds."

"You just couldn't help yourself, could you?" He looked at me sympathetically before his final kiss.

"You know me so well don't you?"

§O§
§~Chapter 8~§
Welcome to the Fast Lane

Tasha Mac, aka K'Dog, bka Spicy; my nigga is coming over this weekend. Gan-Gan has been tripping lately about letting her come over; but it's all good. Cuzzo coming thru this weekend and we going full throttle; all the way turned up. As you already know Tasha is two years younger than me and Weezy is three years younger. However we grew up together thick as thieves.

Cuz had her eye on the pretty nigga Terry after he walked up and slobbed her down at the bus stop on Cleveland and Leona; right in front of Cheesy.

"Damn Cheesy; how you gone let that nigga stick his tongue down your girl's throat like that?" Joe couldn't help but taunt his mouth dropped homie.

Cheesy stood looking stupid as fuck while Tee, Tywan, Looney and I laughed our ass off. Tasha wrapped her arms around Terry and kissed him back. I couldn't explain the feeling of respect and admiration that came over me as she sunned the nigga she didn't really like. Our bus pulled up just in time. I kissed Looney on the lips.

"Don't take forever to come either nigga. And don't be getting sidetracked with these neighborhood bitches." I flinched at him as I held his chin in my hand.

"Calm down lil nigga! After I finish my pack I'll be through the Folks." He smiled smacking me on my little ass.

"Yawl better hurry yawls little fast asses up if you catching this bus." The bus driver yelled through the opened door.

I swiped the bus pass that I got off this Fein for a dime sac. He needed some weed to come down off his trip and now I'm riding Cousin-Cota free the rest of this month. I couldn't believe Terry's ass just tongue fucked my cousin in front of her dudes lame ass. I mean on everything

Cheesy my nigga, he put in work. He standup strong beside my nigga and he definitely put in work.

I watched Looney and Terry Dap up the greeting through the window as I plopped down in my seat. Looney appeared happy that he sunned Cheesy like that. I guess him and Terry was closer. I remember them two arguing back in the day; over whose girlfriend I was going to be. These niggas, I watched Tash as she waved the pitch at both her wiling niggas while taking her seat.

"You crazy cuz!" I said reaching over the back of her seat to push her shoulder.

"Yea I run shit like that you know, it's all in a day's work."

"I hear you pimp." We all laughed as the bus made its way under the Vydoc. And like clockwork we all started singing. THE VYDOC FUCKING IT UP! The laughter caused the bus driver to snarl at us through his overhead mirror. I twisted my fingers and lips up at him as he rolled his eyes.

Cuz I know you not geeked about fucking with Terry? Tasha turned sideways in her seat rolling her eyes and head my direction.

"And if I am?" She questioned.

"But you not; though." I said stuffing my pager back into my Dickie pocket. I tooted my lips and nodded my head towards Tee; sitting on the opposite side of the bus from us, putting her lip-gloss on using her lochs as her mirror. Tasha leaned over her seat towards me. "I don't give a fuck, if she fucked him, who haven't she fucked though." I felt my eyes squinting up.

"Don't say that about my friend." She lifted her hands up and started chuckling.

"It is what it is, ain't no fun if the homie can't have none." Tasha Harlem shook her shoulders. I laughed and threw my balled up pal gum wrapper at her.

"Give me a piece of gum!" Tee said, fixing her lochs on top of her head. I unsnapped my backwards fanny pack buckle that substituted for my belt to hold up these baggy ass dickies. I pulled out two gum balls and through one at the each of them.

"What yawl talking about?" Tee asked looking out the window as we approached Hudson.

"Tash' not fucking with Cheesy or Terry and fucking with Big."

"Is that right?"

"As a matter of fact we didn't say nothing about Big, CJ." Tasha said in her matter of fact tone.

"Well that's who we should be talking about, the boss not the help. You know Big mad nice to you every time he see you." I mean Big always looked out. He was OG. He sat me down in front of the Triple Beam in Ms. Monroe's basement.

"Don't write this shit down. I will show you two times each measurement. This is an Ounce 28-grams. A half ounce is 16-grams and it's half the cost. If you charge \$125/\$100 per ounce; than you charge \$65/\$50 for a half. Your dimes are \$10, Twinks \$20 and your quarters are \$30. If you hustle right you can make \$300 off each ounce. I'm giving you 6 ounces. I want you to bring me back \$300."

I looked at Big puzzled for a second. I flicked my blunt in the mild filled ashtray.

"Big 6 Ounces \$600 if I make \$300 on each ounce that's \$1800 my nigga."

"Yea you're smart keep the math at the top of your head." He said picking up his white rag whipping his sweaty face off. "So I don't know if you're high or what not, but your giving me 6 Oz I owe you \$300 and I got \$1500 profit." I was geeked for a hot second until he smacked me on top of my head.

"No forehead! How you got \$1500 profit?" I opened my mouth and then thought your right.

"I got \$500 profit because I need to flip the Rack." I said like I've been hustling for years.

"There you go Forehead." He laughed lighting his Black.

I ran upstairs to grab my book bag. I wondered why he gave me this weed out of nowhere. When I got back down stairs Big looked as if he was lost in thought, like the walls were playing a movie that I couldn't see.

"Big! Why you give me this weed?" He shook his head and whipped his face again. "CJ, Heavy ain't shit; you always need to have your own money. You want to do your music with your Cousin? Then you got to have your money to do it. Don't ever have to ask a nigga for shit. Yea make him do for you off the rip, but always do and be able to do for yourself."

At thirteen this was some of the realest shit I've ever heard. That was nearly two years ago, since I've watched him move like a boss. This is the type of nigga my cousin should be dating. I thought as I watched him turn down all the neighborhood groupies when he came through to drop my work.

I snapped back to reality. Tasha pushed the bell as we approached Capital Park.

"Geah, geah, geah!" I loved going over to my Aunty Lisa's house. She was the youngest aunt; the youngest sister of nine children. We grew up like sisters, Aunty Lisa was our dog. We use to get over on her, with our little girl bs, but we'd fight the world for Aunty Lisa. We single-filed off the front of the bus and I flicked my gum wrapper at the driver as we got off.

"Yea your little skinny ass won't be laughing if I close your ass up in this door now would you?" We laughed rushing off the bus.

"Bye bus driver!" I yelled.

"Yawl be safe and young ladies." He smiled as he closed the doors to the bus. I wondered if they noticed I was secretly crushing on the thick fine, baldhead yellow-bone bus driver; then again probably not.

"So back to the convo:" Tee said popping her gum in her mouth.

I don't know why she bringing this nigga shit up...

"Ok it's time to stop dancing around this shit." Tee probably low key wondering if Tasha about to move in on her side dick.

"Girl Tasha is not about to fuck with your side dick." I pulled the pre-rolled swisher out of my fanny pack. I lit it real quick and stated: "As a matter of fact when we get back to the Doc, I'm going to try to hook her up with Big."

"Big? What Bitch? You must be tripping." Tee dismissed.

"Why am I tripping Tee?" I was really taken back by her comment. "You tripping nigga because Uncle Big John is a grown ass man and Tasha lil ass only 12 years old." Tash looked at Tee.

"Quit hating bitch you only 14 and you fucking all the grown niggas. Besides everybody think I'm 14 too just that CJ a few months older than me, feel me?" Tasha said taking the blunt, French Inhaling like she was Snoop Dog.

"Alright Bitches." Tee shook her head and her pointer finger sashaying ahead of us twisting her narrow ass.

"Ho!" Tasha screamed at her. I took the blunt from her laughing.

"You just mad because your Captain Save a Hoe Cousin CJ the only reason you still got your V card."

"Fuck You Bitch!" Tasha Yelled.

"You hear this shit dog?" She said hitting me on my upper arm forcing me to choke on the weed smoke.

"Mufuckas think you got my pussy hostage? What type of shit is that?" Tasha was getting pissed by the second while Tee laughed walking back towards us.

"Cuz it isn't even like that nigga." I said passing Tee the blunt whipping the ashes off my khakis.

"Man I didn't tell Tee about Ahmrod if that's what you saying?"

"No nigga I'm glad you didn't, but that's not what I'm saying!"

"Nigga Ahmrod told me about Ahmrod!" Tee interjected. He told me, CJ busted up in the crib while he trying to put it down." This bitch busted out laughing real hard.

"Woo shit, Nigga- said you was beating the door down. Like Nigga don't put ya dick in my cousin. I'm-a have them boys take yo fucking head off. I'm about to kick this fucking door down. Tash You should have seen the nigga face, he was like: I thought me and CJ was cool, she always hook me up with the fat sacks." They laughed hysterically as I was their favorite butt of their bullshit jokes.

"Fuck yawl"- I said turning up my face, rubbing my abs, fidgeting with my Looney-Toon character boxers.

"Fuck yawl Bitches! Fuck yawl! Don't talk to me when we get over Aunty Lisa's either I ain't fucking with yawl!"

"All look; she salty, she walking all fast." They were still laughing. I stopped mid stride. Turned, took a few paces and snatched my blunt from Tee.

"Thank you, Hoover. Now look at yawl face." I said turning around to my own little cynical laugh. Tasha now a few inches taller than me, leaned over & threw her arms around me.

"I love you too Cousin, quit tripping, ay we should start calling you To-Spaz instead of Topazz." They began laughing again.

Walking up to Aunty Lisa's door we could hear her and Uncle Ray arguing.

"Oh shit, its Friday he trying to argue so he can go run the streets, Nigga Shit."

"But on everything cuz, when we get back to the fort I'm going to introduce you to Big, don't be acting all young and shit, Boss Up, Big-Money. I never see him with nobody and he's always about his money. He's my nigga Big Brother." I continued my story while pounding on Aunt Lisa's door.

"He put me on, I told you bout that. That's the nigga I think my cousin should be fucking with. Not the foot soldiers. I'm just saying!" I decided to try and open the front door.

"Oh My God!" We all screamed in between deep gasp. Aunty Lisa and Uncle Ray were fighting again.

"Stop this Bull Shit!" I yelled Jumping a-little to the sound of Tasha slamming the front door behind us. "Uncle Ray What The Fuck? You don't got to hit her cause you want to run the street. Get the Fuck outta here!" I fan motioned toward the front door.

"I'm sorry niece, ya Aunty..."

"-Man fuck all that Uncle Ray." I cut him off.

I'm glad we got here when we did. Aunty Lisa's red ass stood in the middle of the floor looking like the devils daughter. With her medium length, coarse, black & blonde hair; blown back like Wolverine. Her eyes red as fire and her hands balled into tight fist, breathing so heavy it look like an exercise of her lifting and dropping her chest.

"Leave your wallet bitch or I'm calling the police." She said wiping the running snot from her nose.

"Man Lisa you fucked up." He said, looking like he fingered through five hundred petty dollars.

"No you fucked up you cheap ass nigga get the fuck out Raymond with your Hoe-Ass! Go on! Take ya dirty dick around! Its Friday fuck the hoe day! Bye Ray!" She screamed.

I grabbed Uncle Rays arm. "Do you need me to grab anything?" I questioned slowly walking him to the front door of their three bedroom town house dead smack in the middle of one of Columbus most ratchet apartment complex. We loved Capital Park. We grew up too fast watching all the shit that went on out there. Uncle Ray stuffed his wallet deep into his oversized Damaged Jean pocket, reached in the refrigerator grabbed him a cold beer, shifted his baseball cap a couple times and hopped his ass in his car and peeled out.

This was bullshit; I hate this nigga type shit. I'll never trust these niggas. I use to think Uncle Ray was a good man until I seen him hit Aunty Lisa the first time. Damn Domestic Violence.

"You good Aunty Lisa?" Tasha wrapped her arms around her shaken, battered aunt.

"Yea that bitch ass nigga wasn't really trying to turn up Annie. He knew yawl was coming; his bitch ass just trying to make a fight so he can stay out late. Stupid ass nigga just come in drop the money; turn yo O'l ugly funny looking, skinny, weave wearing ass back around and out into them streets, Simple like 123." We laughed as she dusted her hands together, fuck'um we concluded.

We ordered a couple pizzas then walked to the Neighborhood bodega. The menu; Gum, New Port Kings, Swishers, Black & Mild's,

Strawberry Hill Boone's Farm, Grape Mad Dog 20/20, Ice Cream Sandwiches, Doritos, American Squirt Cheese and Dill Pickles. Same shit every time. We were about to pig out, watch flicks, play cards, serve dope, talk shit to the local neighborhood rats, entertain these niggas while getting high as fuck.

Now that was the life for 13, 14 &15 year old hood chicks. Looney, Cheesy and the rest of our niggas was on their way to Aunty Lisa's said my pager.

"Tash I bet Cheesy gone be acting funny about you kissing Terry."

"WHAT?" Aunt Lisa yelled behind us.

"Yea Aunty Lisa" I turned to grab her black. "We waiting for the bus earlier, Tasha there with Cheesy ass and Terry just mob up to her and stick his tongue down her throat." Aunty Lisa started laughing pouring a mouthful of Doritos as we crossed Agler Rd.

"Girl you better go scrub your tongue. Better yet just chill tonight because I'm hooking you up with Big tomorrow."

The night was young and so were we. They brought so many bottles of Boones Farm and Mad Dog. My Aunt's house looked like 5 smoke-machines were blowing at the same time; all we could see was the red and blue light stand she had in the corner.

"Star I really need to talk to you ma." I leaned back putting my head on Joes shoulder.

"I've really been trying to figure out how to tell you this."

"Just tell me babe." I said as we stepped onto my aunts back patio.

"Baby I've been dreaming about a lot of Fish, and I've really been sick every morning. What I'm saying babe, Star, Queen (He took a forced deep breath) is I want you to take a pregnancy test, to see if you're pregnant."

"What! What would make you think that I was pregnant? We always use condoms!" He looked at me as my heart and soul dropped to my feet.

"I mean, I don't feel sick, I haven't got my period yet, but periods always change. But why are you so sure I should get tested?"

"Star let's just say I have a very strong feeling! I mean I don't know if you were lifted or not but a few times we didn't use any condoms."

§O§
§~Chapter 9~§
Time to Face the Music

I was too afraid to even go into the drugstore so I sent Joe in to get the pregnancy test. I couldn't believe this motherfucker was purposely trying to impregnate me. I glanced at him from the side of my eye, watching him wear this dumb somber look on his face. I guess me spazzing out about him thinking I was pregnant wasn't the loving happy reaction he was waiting for. I didn't give a fuck how he felt as we pulled up to G'Man's crib in Olmstead. I stood by the door as he asked him could we use his bathroom.

The entire apartment including the bathroom was dimly lit. Joe sat on the tub as I placed the test under my rushing stream.

"Hurry up Star!"

"Nigga what you mean hurry up, I'm still pissing. I need for you not to say anything to me right now, Joseph, Joe, Heavy whoever the hell you feeling like."

"Oh that's how you feeling?" He looked at me angry but shocked. I shook the excess from the test and sat it on the paper towel on the sink. Before I could even pull my pants all the way up the test was reading: PREGNANT.

"Dam fifteen and pregnant, my mom, Oh My God, what the fuck am I going to do?" The hyperventilation was something I never experienced before and passed out right in the bathroom. I woke up the next morning in his mother's basement wondering what the hell happened to me. I had to get an abortion before my mother found out, was all I could think of. How could this happen to me? I was always careful; I didn't want nobody's baby. How the fuck was I going to take care of a baby? What about my music, what about Tasha?

My life was over and I knew it. We stood in front of the trap caddy corner from my mom's house laughing shooting the breeze when the Police pulled down on us.

"Joseph Monroe! You have the right to remain silent!" The officer began pulling the cuffs from his belt holster.

"What! What are you doing? What are you talking about? Heavy what's going on?" They put him in the cruiser without anyone saying a word to me, not even him. The look of disappointment on his face as they drove him off cut me to the core.

"Damn C that's fucked up." Tee said consoling me, wrapping her arms around me as I feel into her chest.

"I got you homie, I'm-a hold you down until Joe get back."

"But we just found out that I was pregnant last night." I sobbed into her chest, upset that I let the truth slip out. My plan was not to tell anyone so no one would ever know I had an abortion. It would be mines and Joes secret to the grave.

"What did you just say CJ? Hell No! This is Really Fucked up." I think my friend's anger and frustration helped alleviate my own stress as I watched for her next reaction.

"Does your mom know?"

"No and no one is telling her either!" She grabbed her mouth and shook her head at me, as she walked with me into the unknown future. I walked into my house, I just wanted to lie down and cry until I fell asleep, as I walked through the living-room the phone rang:

"Hello!"

"You have a collect call from "Lisa!" An inmate at the Franklin County Jail; to accept this call press 0. To deny these charges and block this caller press;" I pressed 0 before the operator could finish her automated speech.

"Is this Aunty Lisa?" I yelled into the cordless receiver.

"I would have never gave that big fat-ass bitch my cigarette if I knew she was going to press charges on me." Yep this is Aunty Lisa.

"Who?" I screamed into the phone: "What happened Aunty Lisa?"

"Where is your mom CJ?" I recognized she was not hearing me.

"She's down at Aunty Darlene's. I can run and go get her. What happen?"

"You know that one new big bitch that just moved into the Neighborhood, with all that mouth?"

"Yes." I stammered, wondering which big bitch, all the project bitches looked big to me.

"Well it was a fight, she continued, she got dat ass beat up, that shit wasn't assault and she bigger than me, she needed that ass beat. That don't make sense she came to my house! I had to spank her ass! If I let her do it, everybody else would do it! She felt like she was Billy Bad, I had to make an example of her; your honor."

"That's what you said to the judge?" I couldn't believe my Aunt was in the county jail. "Hold on Aunty Lisa, I cut her off mid rant. I'm about to go get mommy, give me three minutes." I slammed down the phone darted out the front door down two houses to my Aunt Darlene's house; bursting into my Aunts front door:

"Hey!"

"Ah shit!" My Aunt flinched dropping ashes from her cigarette onto her lap, as both the twins sat smoking cigarettes playing Super Mario Brothers, pausing the game only to look up at me.

"Mommy; hurry up, go get the phone, it's a collect call from Aunty Lisa, and she's in the County Jail!"

"WHAT!!!" They both screamed at the same time.

"Oh hell no!" My Aunt Darlene murmured forcing herself off the couch. As they both rushed past me out the door, I lingered behind, dropping the pre rolled joint I was on my way to sell Aunty Darlene. She always gave me five dollars when I only charged her three. The fact that she was still keeping my secret from mom made me love, respect and look out for her that much more. I grabbed the five dollar bill placed under the pack of cigarettes and decided to take the pack to her down at my mom's.

"You left your cigarettes Aunty." I winked, handing her the pack, as they both stood huddled together sharing the receiver. "Hun Un, no she didn't, what" ...they continued.

Man this was fucked up, first my baby daddy, now my aunt, fuck the police! I'm going to sleep.

~§~§~§~§~§~§~

I hid my pregnancy from everyone for nearly four months, my parents, Tasha our managers. The only ones privy to my bun in the oven was Big & Their sister who was supposed to let me use her identity to get the fake id to get the abortion. His mom called for me to come visit him in the workhouse with her. She wanted to go first and speak to him alone, so I waited, scared of what the hell he wanted to talk so badly about.

"Ok baby girl he's all yours." Rita smiled to me signaling for the door. I walked into the visiting room with my head down, only lifting my head enough to see which glass stall he was locked behind.

"Hey Star." He smiled as I picked up the receiver.

"Hey"

"Damn that was dry as fuck." He quickly gained a frown. I stared at him as he went through his emotions.

"Ma I have this same dream over and over. You, me our little man that you carrying, we ducked off in our own crib out in Cali. You're still in law school still doing your music; I own two or three business including your record label, Big & Stinky both moved out there too but not with us." He chuckled a little scratching the side of his nose with his pinky. I felt my tears slowly stream down my face. At the sight of my tears he snapped: banging his hand and the phone against the wired glass; until three officers snatched his ass up.

"What the fuck is wrong with you? You don't want my fucking baby? You think you too good to have my baby Star? You better not kill my fucking baby Cernitha!" He continued yelling as the officers forced him out of the visiting room. I sat on the cold stool with my eyes closed, feeling the piercing glares of all the entertained jailbirds and their family & friends.

I couldn't believe this nigga screaming down on me behind the wall. I'm 15, just 15, No I didn't want his baby, my baby anybody's baby. I just wanted to go to school away from it all. Teen pregnancy wasn't popular and MTV sure wasn't following my ass around with no camera, as a matter of fact the cameras faded to black.

I whipped my eyes, gathered myself so that his mom wouldn't notice my fucked up disposition. During the ride home his mother continued to ask me what was wrong with me. As strong as I tried to be, I just couldn't stop weeping.

"No thank you." I sobbed as she offered me a cigarette.

"Well I got a joint in my cigarette pack if that will make you feel better honey." She laughed turning up the radio.

"Girl I know Joseph probably said something to piss you off with his silly ass, girl he just mad that he in the box. His silly hot head ass keep fighting, then getting caught with drugs; he just asking to go to jail. But you stay strong for your little boyfriend honey." She laughed ashing her cigarette out the window.

"I'm pregnant mom!" The word vomit flew out my mouth, I couldn't help myself, and I had to tell somebody who could help me. I realized I was going on four months pregnant and this nigga was stalling, his brother was stalling everybody involved was stalling about putting together this ID situation so I could get the abortion. I didn't understand where the fuck the red tape was coming from.

Big's friend worked at the DMV, his sister had her social security card and birth certificate and I was going to use Joe's stash money to pay for it. It wasn't until now as I cried silently to myself that I knew I wasn't going to get an abortion if Joe had anything to do with it.

"Oh My God, Joseph is about to be a father, God help us all!" She laughed holding her heart with one hand and the steering wheel with the other, before grabbing and squeezing my hand. "Have you told your mom yet CJ?"

"No ma'am!" She looked at me with a pity that I've never seen again. "It's going to be OK baby-girl Momma Rita got your back." She rubbed my back as my soul tried to soak up all the comfort in her touch. It was time to face the music. It was time to get that ass beating of a life time. It was time to talk to my parents and tell them at least some of the shit that was going on with me. Time to tell my managers that their teen dream was about to be the new teen welfare recipient, drug pushing baby momma.

I had to figure out how to move out of my parent's house. I had to talk to my counselor about getting emancipated. The bible said it's a time and a season for everything, a time to sow and a time to reap. I knew it was reaping season in my life, this shit was all way too much, way too real for me. I couldn't go home tonight, I couldn't hide it tonight.

~§~§~§~§~§~§~

I couldn't take much more of this lifestyle. It was time for me to go home, Tee, Tasha & I had been on the run from home for about two weeks. My Grandmother was posting missing pictures of us up and down Courtright Road, at all the corner stores; the shit was really getting to be too much. I was looking for an outlet for my pain and was really trying the hell out of the Universe. A few weeks back I was so mad at Joe cussing me out about our decided choice for abortion and the fact that he was in jail and I see bitches posting money on his books, so I fucked Andre around the corner out of revenge and spite.

Big put us up in a suite at the Radisson Hotel off 161 for about four days. He knew I needed to get my mind right. It was the worst time of my life, Joe was locked up, everybody was coupled up accept me the silent pregnant chick. G'Man let me hit some Dro that made me go temporarily blind.

Big was damn near drowning me, trying to rinse out my eyes as if that was going to bring my vision back. I decided rather or not I was going to keep this baby that I was going to stop smoking for a while.

I had Big drop me off in the alley and I walked around the corner to my house. To my surprise my dad was walking toward me from my Aunt's house. He began a brisk run towards me, I didn't know what to do but brace myself.

"Chachi is that you? Chach?"

"Yes Sir." I closed my eyes as he approached me with tears in his eyes. He grabbed and squeezed me so hard. His gasp in between tears melted my heart.

"I love you lil nigga, you had me and your momma fucked up here, your momma gone be so happy to see you and finally get some sleep. Chach don't ever do that shit again." He squeezed even harder. "Whatever you be going through we can all work it out together, quit shutting us out Chach."

My mom pulled up beside us in Grandpa Harvey's car. Opening the door before he pulled to the curb, I ran to my mom and grabbed her as hard as my father squeezed me. I needed her, I needed her help, I needed her love. My dad went into the house as my Grandfather drove off.

"C'mon mom walk with me." I grabbed her hand and headed to the gas station. I didn't know if she had any cigarettes but I figured she was going to need some. "Do you have any cigarettes?"

"I got a couple." She reached in her shirt pocket and pulled out her half pack. I looked at the ground then back at her.

"Can I have one?"

"Are you serious, how long you been smoking Cernitha?"

"For about seven months Mom. I lit the cigarette and just decided it was best that I told her. Mom first I want you to know that I love you and I'm sorry for hurting you, I'm scared to death to tell you anything but I feel like me not telling you got my life all fu-messed up." I corrected myself before she had to.

"Mom I've been selling weed for about two and a half years. I've been selling a little bit of crack here and there. I don't do drugs, I do smoke weed, been smoking about a year now and I'm stopping cause I'm pregnant I was supposed to get an abortion."

"-What'd you say Cernitha. Oh no God." She stopped and grabbed her heart and head. "Oh, Jesus not my baby not CJ. CJ you were supposed to escape this hell-hole, I wanted so hard for you to make it out." My mother grabbed me crying harder than I've ever seen her cry before.

She held me and I could feel both our hearts shaking and breaking together. We stood hugging and crying at the corner of 5th Ave. & Sidney for about 5 minutes before continuing to the gas station. When we got home we talked all night until the morning came. I fell back in love with my mother and really for the first time seen her for who she was and not who I thought she was or should be.

I moved in with Ms. Monroe, I figured it would be less of a financial strain on my family if I took care of myself. I was no longer able to sell drugs, for fear of being incarcerated while pregnant.

Since moving in and at least twice a week, I would have the same dream: It would be pitch-black and I was in a room. Big begins to appear to me as a hologram (the only light in the room), but his lightened appearance flickers in and out as I walk towards him I see two distant spotlights way up in this dark place that we're in.

"Go you got to save the Joe's save the Joe's CJ, you got to in this life time!" I ask him repeatedly what he meant, and then his hologram faded to black. A light to my far distant right appears shinning down on 3 small steps. As I walk on the path towards the three small steps, Joseph begins to appear as a hologram. We reach for each other but unlike Big I can't hear his words. As he fades to black I stand and cry wondering why Big told me to save him and I couldn't reach him.

In the dream the pain before those steps always repeated before the steps.

Once I walk up the steps I'm no longer pregnant, I'm never pregnant in the dream. As soon as I start the first step different places begin to lighten. The steps lead to a very large stage and on the stage waiting to take my white fur hand shawl is this beautiful woman. She's 5'5 thick built, light skinned with my dark features. She's absolutely beautiful and she's Arailya; she's the woman version of my soon to be daughter. I remember thinking in the dream, (I knew I was going to have a daughter regardless; everyone around except my mother believed I was carrying Joseph Jr.) My mother stands be-side her looking beautiful the both of them, dressed in beautiful white linens, hair, and makeup snatched.

My mother hands me a book and I turn around to look, at that moment a glass podium lights up. Instinctively I go and lay the book on the podium. I look down at my White & Gold two piece white pants suit, the trench jacket looked more like a gangsters Zoot Suit. While in amazement of what I could see of my clothes more lights begin to appear and I'm about to address a stadium full of people who begin to cheer.

I awake at the same point every time. Always with the feeling of; what was I saying, was I doing music? Why was I dressed like that, Why did so many of the woman in the audience have white things on their hands, everyone was dressed very nice, where was I at? Was Heavy there, was Big there? What did the book say?

The first time I had that dream I was six months pregnant, I was living with my incarcerated baby dad's mother around the corner from my mother, Aunty etc. Joseph was on his way home through the work release program. I began to buy all girl clothes even though Ms. Monroe kept telling me that she had a dream that I had a boy. I kept telling mom, I had a dream and I've seen my daughter; Arailya in the future.

It was a fun ongoing debate. After our Sonogram appointment the doctors was unable to tell the sex of the baby because the baby's legs was closed, and its fist was up pushing the scope. One thing for certain whatever the sex of this child it's going to be a stubborn fighter like its parents.

~§~§~§~§~§~§~

The evil ass judge let Joseph out of Jail two days after my expected March 9th delivery date. My body was under so much stress from carrying this 7lb 8oz baby in my gut, living with his mom without him and the fact that my sweet 16 was actually my baby shower was joyous but heart breaking. And again a milestone that he missed.

He walked into the Living room grabbing my hand.

"What's up babe?" I asked him puzzled at the tears in his eyes. Something was very wrong.

He led me into our bedroom and turned out the light. "Sit down Star." He patted next to him on the bed. I sat down nervously because even in the dark through the lights I could see tears streaming down his eyes.

"Baby what's wrong, what happened, why are you crying?" I caressed his face with both hands, kissing first his lips then both sides of his tears.

"Star, why did you fuck André, Pregnant with my son, man?" He broke down holding himself slightly at the stomach.

"Are you serious?" My mind began to race, damn how the fuck, who told him that? Moe told him, because she's the only one who knew besides my cousin who really didn't like him once she started spending more time with his brother.

"Star, I know shit fucked up, I know I did some stupid shit and left you alone as you say, but you know…" He struggled to pull himself together through the tears.

"You don't got shit to say Star?"
"What you want me to say, I wish I never did it, I'm sorry, I was mad, I fucked up. I was starting to hate you. I was tired of the Hoodrat bitches talking about which bitch you was fucking and who was saying they missed you type shit."

"Man fuck what a bitch say!" He yelled at me.

"Exactly fuck the bitch that told you that. I just went last week me and Tee over Janet's and she took us to meet your Fugly ass Side bitch Nish. I know you fucked probably just fucked when you disappeared, and I know Big fucking her aunt!" I felt the baby kicking and decided to be the peace maker.

"I'm-a beat Janet's ass, taking you nine months pregnant over that bitch house!"

"Damn, I can't believe I got you pregnant!" He screamed toward the wall.

"I never asked for your mother fucking nut; are you serious? Fuck you nigga! Big was right, yo ass ain't shit! Heavy… when the fuck did your fat ass become Heavy? You're Joe or J Looney, the whole time I've known you. Ok, so now since I'm Pregnant, done fucked up my contract and a fucking chance at life, then I get to meet the real you, the real dog ass nigga hun? Hun!" I struggled to my feet.

He rushed all his 6ft 2 inches, three hundred sixty pounds up in my 5ft 2 inch face, gripping my jaw like a clamp.

"Bitch don't forget you dogged me first, you cheated on me first since we're talking about Dog mutha-fuckas."

"Fuck you nigga, you'd like me to believe that lie!" The tears and the spit flew between us. I fell back sitting on the bed, Baby Monroe was not happy, kicking and stretching so hard it caused me to instantly throw-up.

"Oh shit Star, Damn!" He grabbed the trash can and put it in front of me, pushing aside the bang on my asymmetrical bob.

"I'm sorry Ma' damn it hurt thou Star." He whispered behind my ear as he tried to hold me and rub my back.
"I'm sorry Daddy, (I whaled) I didn't mean it, the shit you were doing just hurt me real bad though, cut my heart to the core..." I sobbed before throwing up one last time.

This was not the welcome home I expected. I went to the bathroom brushed my teeth and drunk some orange juice. Heavy grabbed his mom's bottle of Remy and we sat in the middle of the floor in the dark crying and talking until we found peace, understanding and acceptance.

"I Love you, you my baby daaadddyy!" I said in my most ghetto voice. We laughed, we kissed and this kiss was easing the pain. We tried to do as many positions as I could with my oversized over stretched belly in the way. Two hours later while getting fucked Doggy-style 5 O'clock in the morning; I had the worst contraction I've ever felt. Immediately I fell over on my side and off his dick. I knew once I got strength I needed to go shower.

Heavy decided to walk me to the gas station to time my contractions. Everyone told him that I was accustomed to false labor and after every pain I was ready to go. We got halfway to the gas station when the next pain dropped me to my knees.

"C'mon baby, get up Star. Damn… He continued patting his self in search. C'mon Ma get up I forgot my strap at the crib."

"Uh you forgot the Strap? I forced my pained weakened legs to stand straight. Are you talking about the Gun? Oh My God!" I screamed leaning as far back as I could without snapping my back. This is what back labor must be.

"No, fuck this walk; I want to go to the hospital, NOW!" The walk back to the house was painstaking. His mother & my luggage awaited me at the door. The joy in her teary eyes gave me strength to make it down the walkway into her awaiting Green Ford Escort.

~§~§~§~§~§~§~

The whole hood was in the waiting room, along with two security guards who must've been assigned to watch my entire rowdy, weed smelling, Styrofoam cup carrying hood family. My mother ran back & forth from the waiting room to the delivery suite to tell me what was going on and who showed up next, and who was all turned up in Grant Hospital.

Boxes of Kentucky Fried Chicken, Chips, Pop's and junk food filled the waiting room; it was a kickback without the weed. Everyone took turns walking me up and down the hall, teasing me with the food I wasn't allowed to eat. Finally! After 12 hours of labor, two bags of morphine drip, the heavyset white Russian Nurse in the delivery bed on top of my near conscious body forcing me to:

"Push this baby out!" Before 80 stitches; 40in 40out, my 7 pound 8 ounce, red-bone, big brown-eyed, thick dark curly haired: Arailya Mona was born. She came out swinging literally, fighting with the nurses trying to suction her nose and mouth. She didn't cry until the Doctor smacked her on the ass.

The relief of having my sore broken body back was overwhelming, I cried and thanked all 12 of the student doctors the 2 RN's and the Doctor as if they really did it. Heavy was pissed that I agreed to let all these student Doctors in the delivery room.

"Man hell no Star, I don't want all these crackers looking into my pussy, what type of shit is that?" He cursed to no avail. I didn't care; I was drugged out of my mind. The entire State of Ohio could've been in the delivery room as long as one of the motherfuckers got that heavy baby out.

I lay in the dimly lit maternal suite looking at a sleeping Joseph and Baby Arailya thanking God for what will forever be my family. I'm barely 16 and for their sake I have to become a woman. I thought about the phone call I got from my home-girl telling me Heavy's side bitch and her angry mob was parading around the hood looking for me. Knowing everybody & they momma was at Grant Hospital. I'll give it sometime & then he's going to have to fry that fish bitch.

§O§
§~Chapter 10~§
The Fire Inside

We just got back from Atlantic City and Heavy called himself being on the run staying down at Shy's sisters house. Whatever nigga; he was down there fucking them chicks, and one of the hoes gave him Syphilis. Momma Rita had Arailya and told me to go enjoy my beautiful self. I love mom, she knew how I felt about losing my youth to mother hood. I loved my baby unconditionally without a shadow of a doubt, but I would forever wonder what if?

I walked down to Shy's sister deciding to go over Ray-Rays to check for Tee after I seen Hev.

"You just in-time CJ, we bout to fire up the Dro we just got." G'Man stood smiling rubbing his growing naked belly, with his head cocked to the side, and gold teeth shining.

"Lock the door we in the basement." He said turning to walk to the basement. I had a love hate relationship with all these niggas. I hated how they fucked so many women and still laid down with my friends their children's mother telling them they loved them. I hated that some of my other friends wanted to be on the gravy train so bad that they would fuck with them and still smile up in their main chicks face. The grime is real, bitches.

"What's up Ma?" Hev said before kissing me.

"Shit, just got back from my trip." I said looking around at the three other niggas weighing weed counting money.

"I'm thinking about going to the east side to see Tasha for a while, Mom said she was going to keep Raily." I sat down beside Ray-Ray on the futon.

"Where is Tee?" I questioned G'ing up with him.

"Her high ass around here somewhere with Tracy and Sparkles, I think they still at the store."

"Ooh." I said grasping the blunt that Heavy was pushing in my face.

"Hit it slow Ma, that's the water weed, the Dro, that Hydroponic shit." They all laughed as I hit the blunt like I would any other blunt. Instantly I started chocking, my eyes began watering. Ray patted my back and lifted my arm like I was about to pass out. I snatched my arm from Ray-Ray embarrassed at their mockery.

"You silly niggas act like yawl don't choke. I still have lungs thank you." I hissed inhaling another big drag. I quickly passed the blunt to Ray-Ray as I felt another chocking spell coming on. Whoa that shit was strong. The strongest shit I ever tasted. I felt my entire body getting hot.

I pulled a wrinkled $100 dollar bill from my pocket. "Give me an ounce." Handing the money to Hev.

"These Ounces cost $150-$175." He mocked.

"For who? Boy quit playing." I snatched one of the ounces from the 6 they had rolled into baggies on the table. It read 28.3 I stuffed it inside my fanny pack and leaned over to kiss Hev goodbye.

"Babe you sell each gram for $10-$20, it's not the same as the regular weight. Here give me that bag back and take the bag that's been already broken down into sacs." I gave him back the bag and dropped the new bag onto the digital scale.

"Damn!" Ray-Ray laughed.

"Ya wife don't trust you at all my nigga." They all laughed as he sat blushing picking up the joy stick.

"Yawl crazy I'm outta here." I turned to proceed through the basement and was stopped dead in my tracks.

"Weee!" Out of nowhere a little garden gnome appeared in the middle of the basement floor. I started shaking my head.

"What's wrong Star?" Heavy yelled from the backroom in the basement. As I opened my mouth to respond the gnome made a window in the middle of the concrete basement.

"Come On." The gnome said as other gnomes began to appear, jumping as if there were a trampoline on the other-side of the window.

"Come on, Weeee!" The gnomes chanted.

"Nooo, they're trying to make me commit suicide!" I yelled holding my head.

"What! Who? Babe!" Heavy questioned, grabbing me.

I started screaming. "The Gnomes, do you see them jumping, he made a window."

Everybody burst into laughter: "Man she tweaked out, the gnomes; they made a window in the basement bruh?" They taunted all taking different shots at me.

"CJ don't commit suicide sis, we love you, fuck Heavy's shitty ass." Shy chimed in.

"Fuck all of yawl, what did you put in that blunt Joseph?" I was literally about to cry.

"You know I don't do drugs!" The homies fell out, which was my key to go, I had to get the fuck out of that basement.

~§~§~§~§~§~§~

After six months of being parents, six months of him cheating on me, wanting me to believe I caused it by cheating first: Heavy and I decided to break up. We've been through so much shit in the past three years. I was done with the gang fights, the in and out of jail stunts. Shit the night that I was delivering our daughter, his bopper-side bitch really had about 13 bitches with her walking around the hood talking about she was looking for me and Tee.

That bitch knew everybody who was somebody was at the hospital. The little homies called to tell us about the mob looking for me while I was on the slab with my hip splitting apart having his child. The oddest thing to me about that whole situation is two days before I went into Labor Janet took me to her house, I confronted her just me, Janet & Tee. The bitch swore she never fucked with him and if anything he was like a big brother to her.

Whatever bitch, she didn't want war with me, was her very own words. She acted as if she wanted to try Tee, but the frog never leaped. Ironic how hoes get powered up off their home-girl courage; I laughed crassly thinking to myself. That hoe never surfaced after my six week checkup.

After the last shoot out with some Bloods from our neighborhood I was done. This was not the life I planned for myself. But one thing for sure I had a beautiful daughter that I had to take care of. With our without him, and I planned to do it to the fullest, regardless. I stayed with my Gan-Gan for about a month until I had to move. She ran a daycare from home, and since I lived with her Welfare wouldn't pay her. So as much as she said it hurt her, I had to move out, but she would continue to babysit Raily.

I stayed with my Uncle's Junior & Timmy for about two months, before I took over Ms.V's old house. I never thought I'd be living in Tommy's old house but 1111 Sidney St. in North-side Columbus was home. While helping Tee pack her mother's belongings who abandoned the place, I ran across her rent receipts showing that she paid Mr. Thorton between $225 & $275 per month for rent.

I called Mr. Thornton and told him I'd pay him $250 per month and I was taking over the rental starting today and that he could come meet me with a lease because I had the rent and deposit right now.

Tonight was crazy. Weezy came across the street to sneak and smoke her stolen cigarette and a blunt with me. I really didn't want the company. I've been feeling really melancholy, & was enjoying spending time alone. Not hustling, not performing, not dealing with Joe or Heavy as he's now calling himself. We're really starting to settle into the co-parenting thing, especially after the fight.

"How you feeling cuzzo?" Weezy asked, interrupting my thoughts, as she rushed in my front door.

"I'm still a little fucked up in the head behind fighting with Heavy the other night. I still can't believe he slammed me on the car, chocked my ass out; and then dug in my eye in-front of Tina & Nem's mom's house. I'm just so sick of his fucking ass Weez, that's it."

"Well if you good my nigga fire up before my mom come over here and fuck shit up for me. You feel me?" She looked at me in her comedic undertone. I laughed with my cousin as I opened the Swisher Sweet Box, containing my stash and my 10 pre-rolled blunts. Pre-rolling blunts; was like a ritual.

Every Wednesday and Saturday night I'd roll ten blunts. I considered myself weaning off the marijuana, so I cut back to only smoking three blunts per day. I'd grind & separate the weed into ten fat perfect lines; and bust the Swishers down one by one. Every Wednesday night Solomon would bring my delivery: 3 bottles of White Zinfandel, 2 bottles of Chardonnay and 1 bottle of Absolute Vodka and a Cigar Box of Swisher Sweets from his families Brothers Drive Thru.

"(Sea-Shay)." He would say in his strong African Accent.

"I got the goods, you got my Merch?" I'd always trade him a quarter for the drinks, shells and cigarettes. Then I'd smoke one of my own with him before he left. I secretly wished I would have picked him instead of his cousin. I tried to hook him up with my younger cousin and a couple of my home-girls.

Our relationship disappeared after he confessed his love for me. If I only would have re-choose I could have had the good cousin. I made a mental note that I'd always consider my own feelings and wants first instead of giving a fuck about what something looked like or felt like to someone else.

I had way too much power for a 16 year old pint size little hood chick. All the Hood Niggas choppers were in my basement. They couldn't hide the real heat over their momma's house. I had connects to buy/sell whatever I wanted, I could still stand outside my door and call the hood. Aunty Darlene still lived across the street, and I was grown as fuck. Fucking when I wanted; in my own bed, paying my own bills. Meanwhile I craved other bodies; I wanted to explore grown men on my own terms.

My Goal was to quietly stack 50 to 100 thousand dollars and move to California during Spring Semester as soon as I turned 18. At the rate I was living, I prayed I'd be living for my 18th birthday. Looney was always on the run from the police or different situations, I was living diagonal from the family we had gun play with and shit was just never too sweet for real comfort.

Joe made it appoint to want to come and get an AK or Saw'd-Off whenever he seen I had company. I knew deep in my heart that he was always going to try hard to control my life in some form or another. After our fight, I quit getting money with Joe all together. Whenever he'd try to come run my pockets I'd hit the nigga with:

"I'm my own bitch, Mr. Baby Daddy, now go find something." He hated my mouth and loved it at the same time. I loved the fact that I had my own crib and he didn't. Yea his grown bitches had cribs; as they should've, but me ha ha ha born stunting on him.

~§~§~§~§~§~§~

I caught the Holy Ghost around April 7th, 1997; while sitting on the Lazy-Boy in my living room. My cousin Weezy freaked out, I freaked out. I just walked back home from smoking three baseball bats with Chicago. This shit had my head spinning. I had just copped six pounds from him, he couldn't believe it. After I stashed it in my safe and tucked the safe in my downstairs closet I locked the door and went to celebrate with the bottle of Moet he gave me.

We were on our third blunt & my second drink when I realized I was past woozy and needed to go home. Before I hit the corner of Sidney

& Shoemaker I threw up everywhere. After six rounds of vomit and dry heaving I wiped my mouth and waived off crazy Ms. Eve as she came up to me patting my back.

"Tee-Tay, Tomebody tole my vatuum tweeper." I made a mental note to go talk to Ms. Eve later. She didn't have her teeth in and she looked fresh off a hit.

"I can't right now Ms. Eve. I'll come by later." I locked the door and fell in my chair. This overwhelming feeling of gratitude for my life came over me as I sat in my favorite chair trying to grab a hold of my head as this feeling and my cousin Weezy walked in the door.

"Thank you Jesus; thank you Heavenly Father God, you are the Most High God, I thank you for my very life, thank you for my daughter's life! Yes God thank you for keeping me all those times, all those times I risked my life, thank you God!" My body felt hot like fire and my cousin threw down the blunt.

"I ain't smoking that shit, it got your ass catching the Holy Ghost!" Is the last thing I heard her say as she slammed the door.

~§~§~§~§~§~§~
THE FIRE
~§~§~§~§~§~§~

I awoke to, 1-year-old Arailya pulling the covers off my head.

"CJ, CJ, Eat, Eat!" She yelled.

"Lay down baby girl I'll fix you something to eat in a little while." I moaned groggy, not ready to wake from my sleep.

"Eat, Eat, CJ!" She pushed at me before digging her nails hard into my neck.

"Damn it Arailya!" I yelled grabbing at the pain in my neck. As I opened my eyes to a thick cloud of grey and black smoke filling my bedroom.

"What the fuck! I yelled jumping out of the bed. Larry, Amos what is burning?"

"NOOO!" I heard one of my cousins yell from down stairs. I ran towards my bedroom door attempting to run down stairs to see what was causing all the smoke. I instantly felt like I was trapped in a bad dream. The boys raced up the stairs in lightning speed as I watched the walls engulf in flames.

"NOOO!" I yelled as the fire came rushing up each side of the wall towards me. Watching as the steps slowly caught fire. The fire was like a beast coming for me. I wanted with everything inside of me to get downstairs to my closet where I just stashed the pounds of weed I got last night. To no avail; the fire continued to race towards me, a fight I couldn't win. I rushed back to my bedroom and grabbed a noticeably frightened Arailya off the bed.

I quickly wrapped her in the yellow blanky to protect her from smoke inhalation. *(OK girl; grab the Diaper Genie and bust out the window.)* My self-talk was rushing through my head at a frantic pace. I grabbed the Diaper Genie with my left hand as I clutched Arailya with my right. I reared my arm back to swing at the window, as the glass burst in my face. The fire from down stairs crashed its way into my window; setting my walls on fire as if by magic, instantly I lost my mind and began to scream. I heard another window break and my Cousins screaming for me to come to where they were at.

I panicked. *"Oh God, Oh God please don't let us die today. Please help me out of here. Please!"* I screamed to the burning walls. My entire room was engulfed within seconds.

"Now!" The still small voice in my head demanded. I looked around at the fire surrounding us; a small walkway leading from my room to my daughter's room was the only path untouched by the fire. The path to my daughter's room was God's grace and mercy on my life. I had to move slowly through the hellacious fire because the flames were out of control. I felt my eyebrows and hair being singed from the heat. Her room was only five steps from mines but the journey through the flames seemed like a lifetime.

"Hurry Up CJ Please!" Larry yelled as they made their way through the broken window on to the roof top.

"Ahh!" I screamed as the flames caught the end of my daughter's blanket. I unwrapped the blanket threw her on the bed next to the window and the blanket behind me to the fire. The blanket didn't land on the ground. The fire consumed it in the air like a peace offering, disintegrating it right before my eyes. Amos reached in the window to grab Arailya from the bed, pushing her through, making my way out behind her.

Uncle Charlie and Uncle Marcus stood screaming to us from the back yard as we took turns jumping to safety. I threw Arailya down after Amos landed on the ground. The fear in my baby's eyes shook my soul. They passed her to Amos as they yelled for me to jump down.

A sound of hell, yelled through the fire behind me as I gauged the distance to land. My house was right at the freeway, if I jumped too far, I'd surely jump to my death, landing or rolling rather, down the slope to the freeway. A thin flimsy fence was the only divider between my porch and the freeway. The singeing of the back of my hair was my catalyst to jump. They caught me in the most awkward position. One grabbed my neck the other my leg, as the right side of my body hit the edge of the concrete porch.

The pain raced through my body like lightning, instantly I started my period. Everyone rushed around the burning half double and across the street to Aunt Darlene's house. My attention shifted to Uncle JR, illegally parking his semi-truck on the curb, screaming, running towards us; as if I was in a movie and the scene was being played out in slow motion.

"No, not baby girl!" Uncle JR cried, hands on his head running towards us. The thought of his children dying years ago in a house fire shook me back into reality. He embraced me screaming, crying and shaking. Giving me the hardest hug I've ever felt in my life.

"It's ok Uncle JR 'I cried hysterically' she, she's over Aunty Darlene's we all made it out!" I yelled into his embrace. The news broadcasters were relentless, shining their lights in my face, asking me questions I couldn't hear. I don't remember the next few days, just the heavy feeling of losing everything I ever owned.

~§~§~§~§~§~§~
Summer 1997
~§~§~§~§~§~§~

17 years young and well accustomed to this new strenuous routine called my life. It's been four months since my house burned down and I lost everything I owned. I sat in my basement bedroom enclosed by the white sheer fabrics from JoAnne Fabrics. My mom's basement surely wasn't home but it's where I live. I sat on the edge of the bed smoking a joint. I couldn't believe I was smoking a joint! All the corner stores were closed so I got a few Zig Zag's from the white neighbor-girl Stephanie. Of course I combined all four sheets to make me a blunt.

I thought about the six pounds I lost in the closet during the house fire. The tears began to race... That re-up was supposed to change my life. That was going to be the money for my apartment in California. I was going to use my scholarship to go to UCLA. It was a full ride scholarship but I couldn't have my baby girl in the dorm. I wasn't going to leave her in Ohio, so I had to get my own place. I cried harder as my counselor's words echoed the shadows of my mind.

"Cernitha You missed too many days and by law your teachers had to fail you for the semester. I'm sorry about the terms of your scholarship and your house fire."

"Bitch you wasn't sorry!" I screamed out loud, looking to make sure no one was coming down the stairs. The washer & dryer sat directly in front of my bedroom space on the opposite side of the room. I wiped my eyes to no avail, the tears wouldn't stop. If the bitch was sorry she would've help plea my case to the scholarship board or the Gifted & Talented Program Directors. I know I messed up and under my current circumstances I wasn't able to make it to school on the opposite side of town every morning after working an afternoon and evening job, then selling dope all night.

Thankfully this is Heavy's two weeks to have Arailya or I'd probably lose my mind. I felt like tonight my mind was my enemy. Why am I conjuring up all these negative thoughts? I can't see past the trees, I can't see the silver lining; there is no fucking silver lining. I couldn't help myself I screamed inside and let out a full blown cry, tremors and all.

I lost record of all my childhood show, studio and recording memorabilia, I lost all of Arailya's pre-birth up to her first birthday all burned away as if my life never existed. I looked at my mom's new washer & dryer and thought about Heavy's evil ass not picking me up to do my laundry. All of Raily's things the uniforms from both my jobs and the three outfits I owned.

I caught a-ride to the Doc with Uncle Charles over his & Aunty Darlene's house. This fat ass nigga was still ignoring me while I'm around the corner. I sat, smoked, shared a few hugs with Aunty Darlene thanking her for washing my clothes while my mom's washer was down. I decided to throw caution to the wind and go over Momma-Rita's house to see if Heavy was really not there.

I walked down Sidney St. just as I had a million times; I looked back across the street where my house once stood. Tormented and traumatized at the empty lot with the three concrete walk-up steps still intact. Leading to a yard of charred burnt ground, where grass once grew.

As I made my way to the corner of Sidney & Leona my heart dropped. Even though Mom's house was three blocks ahead I could see clear as day her green four door ford escort parked at the curb.

"Motherfucker; lying, fat-ass motherfucker!" I picked up the pace throwing the Newport I got from my aunt to the ground.

Stay calm girl, my self-talk kicked in. *So what you going to do, if he is there?* I questioned myself. *He didn't come and pick you up like he promised wasting your time, while he's doing God only knows what! Since you recognize this, what is the point of going over there?*

Before I knew it I was knocking on Mom's door. After the third round of knocking my cousin Tasha answered the door.

"How long you been here Cuz?" I asked surprised.

"I got here this morning; I decided to go to first period only." We both laughed as she handed me her blunt. I couldn't read the look on her face as she motioned me into the kitchen.

"What's up Tash?" I asked bluntly.

"Your boy's downstairs; with his manly looking girlfriend." She twisted her lips awaiting reaction. I inhaled the blunt deeply, feeling my anger began to boil from the crown of my head slowly perusing down to my feet.

"Is that right?" I responded upon exhale.

"Yea I remember you telling me you were going to be here this morning, so I had Big come get me from school, I walk-in pull the curtains and see this nigga face first in o' girl. I ain't say shit; I knew what it was after that."

"So why didn't you call me?" She knew I was pissed.

"Because; I didn't want to add to your problems Cuzzo; so what are you going to do?"

"I'm going to sock this nigga in his lying ass mouth, that's what I'm-a do." I lowered my voice on instinct grabbed the blunt from her for one last pull. I took the Tahitian Treat from her left hand and took a big gulp.

"DAMN MC' Thirsty!" She laughed. "Sure have some." I looked up at her whipping the excess from my mouth.

"Gotta be refreshed Cuz." I smirked opening the basement door. I heard some shuffling as I crept down the steps, hoping to catch this nigga head first in some pussy, while I got to be at work tonight and this sorry fucker couldn't come get me to wash my dirty ass uniforms, like he promised.

The shuffling continued as I opened the curtain, both these stupid motherfuckers lay on the bed with the covers pulled up to their necks. On instinct I leaped on the bed fist clinched aiming to hit this bitch in the mouth. Like clockwork Heavy jumped up grabbing me around the stomach mid leap. Him snatching me mid launch caused me to barely hit her chin.

"Let me go bitch!" I was furious bucking my body and hitting him with my one free arm, causing us to land hard on his mother's cold basement floor. He pulled us both to our feet trying to block my attempts to fight.

"Bitch, that's how you wanna do me? After everything we been through, you can't even help me do fucking laundry? After you lying saying you were on your stinking ass way." I tried to swing again.

"Quit tripping Star." He repeated in his low aggressive tone.

"Tripping, Tripping! Fuck you Joseph, Let Me Go! LET ME GO!!!" I screamed as loud as I could. We both paused as we heard his mother screaming his name from the top of the basement steps. I looked over at the bed where his stupid girlfriend still lay clutching the sheets up to her nose for dear life.

"What the fuck is going on down there Joseph?" Mom screamed again from the top of the steps.

"Yea what the fuck is going on Joseph?" I screamed just as loud as her as he released his bear hug from around my arms and waist.

"Is that CJ?" She yelled. As soon as I gathered my bearings on the ground I swung and hit him square in the mouth.

"Fuck you Joseph!" I yelled barely budging him off his stance, as he grabbed his mouth. I turned and ran towards the stairs past Tasha who stood looking in utter shock. As I made it to the top of the steps mom grabbed me by the arm.

"CJ why the fuck are you down there fighting, you trying to have a heart attack? You're under a lot of stress."

"Stress, Heart Attack?" I snatched my arm from moms grip, shaking my head and headed to the door.

"Nah-Un you not going to walk away from me like that, I am not Joseph! She argued. Go, go on back to my room, I promise it will only be five minutes. Come on baby five minutes."

I walked in the door and sat on the edge of the bed, my favorite spot in the house for the past 4 years. She handed me her personal pint of Remy as she pulled her neatly rolled blunt out her cigarette pouch. She made her way past me and sat down on the bed. I motioned Mom the bottle as I fought back the tears.

"No go head baby drink some more. You've been through enough. I know Joseph is my son but that nigga don't know his head from a whole in a wall." I laughed a little on the inside but the hurt was too thick, too deep to let the laughter escape.

"So when did you start your new job?" I took another gulp of the Remy since she didn't want to take the bottle.

"You know I started the cleaning job a month ago, it pays nothing every two weeks. I started the position at KFC this past Monday. Since I started on the second pay period; I'll be able to get a one week check next Friday. This idiot cook bumped into me spilling flour all over my uniform. I have to work tonight and I only have that one uniform. My mom's washer and dryer got repoe'd. I talked to Joseph last night and he said he would come and get me. He's been ignoring me all morning."

I started to cry. Wondering why he didn't give a fuck that I just lost everything! Why didn't he give a fuck I just lost my scholarship, my house, my money everything but my life.

"It is ok Baby..." She said now handing me the blunt. "Fuck what a nigga say; how many times have I told you that? Remember before you got pregnant with my little angel and he took you out shooting and shit?" I glanced at mom surprised that she even knew that.

"I remember him leaving you in the basement crying because he didn't know how to console you. So he came to me told me what happened then hit the block. I held you in my arms all night, that night you became my daughter. I let you cry for about two hours in-between joints." She laughed. I just looked and listened to her quietly.

"Honey you don't need Joseph, you never have and you need to learn when a nigga is no good for you. He doesn't know what love is or he wouldn't do half the shit he does. He can't handle you and you're younger than him. Girl he was so jealous I mean so jealous when you took over Tee's moms double."

-How the fuck she got a two bedroom and she only 16?-

"I was tickled just laughing at his jealousy. He secretly wished you'd let him move in but you were already past tired of his shit so he kept playing house using and aborting these stupid little girls he's dating."

"Mom I love you thank you for trying to make me feel better."

"You need to smile; I brought you in here to give you this." Digging into her bra she pulled out a wad of money. She peeled four hundred dollars off the top and handed it to me.

"Here baby hopefully this can help you out. You're smart I know you will make it do what it needs to do." I clutched the money in my hand and hugged her tightly.

"Thanks mom I love & appreciate you."

"You're welcome babe." She said stroking my back up and down. It looks like you and I will be raising this child in the long run."

"Imagine that…" I said standing to my feet to exit.

"How did you get over here?" She asked passing me the remainder of her Remy. I turned to grab the bottle.

"My Uncle Charlie stopped by my mom's this afternoon and I asked if I could wash a load of clothes around the corner at his and Aunty Darlene's house."

"Oh, Un-Hun, I see. She said shaking her head. Well baby girl I'm rooting for you, you are one of the strong ones, un-hun I believe that shit right there. Girlie even though things look bad right now, you keep your head up, you hear me?"

"Yes ma'am." I sighed giving her a final hug and kiss on the forehead before hitting my cut.

"You Geechie cuzzy!" I heard Tasha say from the kitchen as I opened the front door.

"Yea Cuz, born that way." We shared a laugh as I mimicked quietly but over dramatically how I socked the shit out of Looney as I excited the front door.

"Ahh I hate that motherfucker." I sobbed coming back to present day as I watched my mom shove a load of clothes into her new dryer.

"You OK over there babe?" I knew she was concerned with my outburst.

"Yea mom I'm good just stressing, struggling, trying to fight this depression."

"Yea you're going to win, come upstairs have a cigarette with me, I want you to hear this song, I was listening to it earlier and it's just for you." I hesitantly rose to my feet and followed my mother up the stairs. She grabbed two singles from her pack, passing me one then grabbing the DVD remote to press play.

-I've gone through the fire, and I've been through the flood, I've been broken into pieces, seen lightning flashing from above, but through it all, I remember that he loves me, and he cares, and he'll never, put more on me, than I can bare.-

I listened intently to the lyrics from Kirk Franklin & The Families newest album. Yes I have gone through the fire and the flood literally, at this current moment I'm shattered into pieces, but I'm going to believe in what the song says: that God is not going to put more on me than I can bare. But does that same term still apply to a sinner like me?

I took that $400 that Rita gave me, brought me an eight-ball of work for $125, brought an ounce of weed for $100 flat I brought Raily two more outfits and me a new crisp pair of black jeans. I gave my mom $25 just because and set up shop on her back porch. I was still working these two dead-end ass jobs; does God credit effort or must I be holy before the blessings flow?

"What you thinking about CJ? You looked stuck out of space." Mom quizzed.

"Just wondering if God helps sinners like me mom."

"God loves you CJ, remember that' nobody is perfect and sometimes you have to go against the grain, but never lose your faith in God, rather you're a sinner or a nonexistent saint." I hugged my mom tight around her neck, wishing I could fall back into her stomach and start this entire life over again.

~§~§~§~§~§~§~

Bird & Autumn convinced me to hang out today. It was summer 97 and it's been awhile since I hung out with my Day 1's. We went back to Birds apartment that she shared with her Baby Dad, which was In the same general vicinity of my mother's neighborhood, and I was proud that my friend was doing good alone. I wished the abusive nigga would stop his BS, but it seemed like being abused by these half-ass niggas was the new common denominator.

These bitches clowned me over a bottle, a few blunts and a home girl make over. I never dressed like a girl, Heavy would never allow it. I didn't want to argue and fight about being a slut, putting my ass on display for niggas, Thotting around.

"He is not your nigga C, or you'd be over his momma's house instead of your mommas house."

"Shit he grown already yawl should have had your own house." Bird went on. I felt her on some levels, but she was fronting for Autumn like she was running shit, with her baby dad, when we all knew.

"Wait why you turning here, this nigga be on this street!" I asked Birda ducking down into the backseat of her car when I swore I seen Heavy.

"Girl you scared as fuck, of that nigga for real?" Autumn said as I looked up peeking out of the backseat window hoping we didn't run into him. I just wanted to be cute & girlie for a change hanging out with my girls, while we were making our way to Big who I decided to connect back with on the weed.

I thought for sure that Heavy was over his other baby mothers house, after I spoke to him on the phone this morning. They laughed so hard at me.
"Girl we'll jump that nigga, he ain't nobody, bitch your CJ your grown as fuck, he wish he could still control you."
"Your sch-medium as fuck and he got you wearing 6x!" We all burst into laughter. I couldn't help but respect their truths, my truth. This nigga had me shook eternally and I needed to break free. Who the fuck do he think he is, controlling the way I present myself? Fuck his opinion!

~§~§~§~§~§~§~

My eighteenth birthday came quick and it took until last month on Christmas for me and Heavy to start speaking again. I was determined to never say a-word to his scandalous ass ever again. Yet he had to bring Arailya home on Christmas Eve so she could open my presents. The bastard had the nerve to give me a diamond tennis bracelet. I can hear his lying ass like it was yesterday.

"Star I know I fucked up, and you probably never want to fuck with me again, but on the strength of our Daughter and on BOS I really apologize for not holding you down when you needed me the most. You've always been there for me, and I put the game in front of the queen. A Thousand Pardons Star." He begged me but I just looked at him silently in my resting bitch face as he placed the bracelet around my wrist. I accepted his offer to take me to the Nasty Neon for my birthday.

In the meantime at work, my sister Michelle was getting real chummy with the two white manager ladies, I was noticing that she was getting raise after raise, while I haven't even been sat down to get my first raise. Shit came to a head on my birthday thou. I worked first shift and Michelle was supposed to come in second shift until 10:30 closing. However as the hours passed I realized she wasn't coming nor was she answering her phone.

"Ok you wanna play me on my birthday you fat, jealous, hateful, ass bitch. See if you go with me tonight." I was pissed, not only did I log into the cash register under her log in, but I was taking KFC up-top, I walked out that night with her drawer only short two dollars and $250 cash. I don't know how much Robbie made off with, the little 18 year old black boy fucking the old white ex-whore.

Fuck yawl tryna play me, was my thought as I hopped on the COTA bus to go home.

I hopped off the bus in-front of my mom's house, and raced to the shower. Heavy hit me up on my pager and told me he was on his way in my messenger.

Word, I rolled me two blunts for the road. I pulled my Black & White Jordan's from the box under the bed, my fresh pair of black Guess jeans out the drawer, a black T and my white hoodie. I looked in the mirror while putting on my shower cap. My finger-waves were still intact and my blond highlights were killing the game. I tucked the wavy blond and brown tracks that hung to my shoulders in the back, I knew I was looking good. I raced in and out the shower as fast as I could. Raced back down to the basement before getting stopped by Michelle.

"Hey girl." She sashayed up to me.

"Hey my ass! Why didn't you come to work today? Why did you leave me stuck working a double on my birthday?"

"I just didn't feel like it sis."

"Oh you didn't feel like it on my birthday? That's cool." I laughed going back down to the basement.

"What time are we leaving?"

"We, bitch ain't no we, I don't know what time your leaving, but I'm leaving soon as Heavy get here."

"So you saying I can't go with you?"

"Oh dear I'm saying when you left me hanging you choose your night, BYE BITCH!" I said slamming the basement door behind me. Who the fuck do she think she is; besides stranded in the house tonight? I laughed hard, amused at how this hating ass bitch just tried to play me.

She watched me with devilish eyes as I hugged and kissed mom goodbye. I gave Mom a twenty dollar bill, and Michelle that I wish you would side-eye.

"Here Mom this is courtesy of KFC and Michelle's short drawer at work."

"What you mean my short drawer?" She questioned.

"That's exactly what I mean. Bye now enjoy your weekend." How the fuck they think they gone clock her in like she showed up to work, and registered her drawer like I was going to be the simp working for this bitch on my birthday, Ha!

"Happy Birthday Queen Star." He smiled pulling a pin with $300 attached to it, pinning it to my white hoodie. I kissed him customarily as I shut the door.

"Ay I told Mannix not to pick your sisters hateful, mean ass up no more." I hit his dap and kissed him again as we pulled off.

"Off to the nasty Neon."

That was some foul shit; almost as foul as me loosing Hev on the dance floor and finding him dancing with some other chick. Did I trip? Not at all. I made my way back to the pool table where this group of niggas stood.

"Oh you back Shorty? I see you rocking that whole bottle of Moet."

"Shorty a Baller!" Another dude from their group said.

"Let me holler at you for a minute." I stepped in between the pillars leaning my back against it, while turning up the bottle. Dude was leaning over me but I still could see Hev's evil ass rushing towards us from my peripheral.

"Nigga you better back the fuck up that's my baby's momma; whose face you all up in!"

"Man get the fuck out of here. I said before dude could open his mouth. It's my fucking birthday and your whorish ass over there grinding on some chick. True I'm ya baby momma but I'm not your chick, you can holler at bitches on my time, I'm gonna start hollering at niggas on your time and I'm going to start with this sexy one, right here." I said pulling at the dude's shirt.

"Oh Star you got me fucked up."

"Man, go back over there and dance with your bitches, you're here up in this bitch all the time, this is my first time, I know you didn't expect me to let you shit on me on my birthday?" He snatched me by my arm, "We out this bitch the party is over."

"Hold up nigga! I yelled, yanking my arm free. Let me at least get Mr. Sexy's phone number." I said simply to add insult to his angry ego.

"I'm taking your ass home." He yelled & snatched. I decided to guzzle as much of this half-filled bottle as I could.

"Here Happy Birthday!" I said to some random nigga pushing him the remainder of my bottle.

"You really trying to get your ass whipped for real on your birthday hun Star?" Heavy grabbed laughing in my face. Knowing he was every bit of pissed. I prayed that his bitches; was watching him make an ass out of both of us.

"Sure, right before you go to jail on my birthday nigga." I walked out the club into the freezing cold 15° January winter. As I slammed the car door to his Blue Bonneville I laughed. "Can you drop me off over Birds house around the corner from my mom's?"

"No I'm taking your ass home!"

"Really? I questioned. Well you can just leave me here, I'll ask that sexy nigga to take me there I'm sure he won't mind."

"Bitch you about to go home." He said pushing the car in reverse screeching the tires unnecessarily.

"Bitch… Right, I'm about to link up with my bitches come back up here and scoop up that nigga. Who the fuck you think you are playing? Me, on my birthday! I can't stand your fat little dick ass."

"Fuck you bitch!" He grunted hitting his black with a vengeance.

"Yea, fuck you, and fucking me is what you're not going to do." I pulled my last blunt out the ashtray and fired up. I ignored every question every statement and smart ass remark he made.

"You wanna go over my mom's for a minute?"

"Hell No I know you heard me ask you to take me over Bird's house. Listen I'm not even tripping, thanks for acting like you gave a fuck on my birthday. Drop me off at Birds the faster you do the faster you can go back to the club and grind on your Hoodrats."

"Aw, she jealous." He snide, trying to grip my chin.

"Get your hoe ass hands off my face." I said punching him in his arm as hard as I could. We pulled up to my moms and I was pissed. I allowed him to watch me walk over Stephanie's because I wasn't going home. I offered her ten dollars to take me around the corner. He sat and watched as we walked to her car before calling my name.

"Star, man get your ass in this car!"

"Fuck you, Pay me!" I fell into her car and slammed the door. About 15 seconds later he was snatching open the door and snatching me out. We drove down Whittier to High Street before he booked us a room at the Westin. Oh the bitch want to splurge tonight I thought as I always wanted to stay at this hotel.

We fucked that night like we loved and hated each other. The rougher the sex the more I wanted; I slapped him he chocked me and it continued until the hot sweat dried, and the tears formed slime pockets in the corners of our eyes.

"I fucking hate you, I hate that I love you." I said pushing his exhausted head off my shoulder.

"I love you more than anything Star, Happy 18th Birthday Queen." He kissed me on my forehead before rolling over on his side, leaving me with his back.

What am I going to do with this nigga? This shit is never going to change. *Happy Birthday Star.*

§O§
§~Chapter 11~§
Cinnamon

I pulled my stash box from under my dresser, called my Uncle Marcus and asked him to take me back to his connect.

"Am I gone get a little sample for hooking you up?"

"Uh don't I always give you some free work for taking me, don't I let your try it before I buy it? What's the point of that stupid ass question can you take me or not?"

"Damn calm down little Chucky he laughed, give me ten minutes and meet me at the car."

I went upstairs to the living-room watching as my mom stood shivering in the front door blowing her cigarette smoke to the wind.

"Mom I made a decision?" She turned slowly to look at me.

"And what decision is that?"

"I'm going to start dancing; I'm tired of working these two jobs. I'm 18 now, which means I should be able to get me an apartment now with no problem. So I'm going to go dance up the rent and deposit."

"I thought you were saving money from your checks?"

"Yes ma'am I am but that's slow money, I need some right now money so I can buy furniture Raily a bedroom set and so on."

"Well it sounds like you got your mind made up, do you have shoes and clothes."

"Uh- No ma'am I wouldn't even begin to know where to find them."

"Well I'm going shopping with your Aunt Karen tonight she should be pulling up from work soon, and I'll see if I can find you something."

"Thanks mom you're the best!" I said hugging her before walking past her out the front door.

"Where are you going?" I wasn't ready to answer her question truthfully so I lied.

"Down to Stephanie's to watch a couple movies, Raily don't come back until Monday so I'm going to enjoy my first weekend not working two jobs."

"So are you going to keep one of the jobs?"

"Yes ma'am I'm going to keep the KFC job for in the mornings and the needed paycheck stubs but I'm going to dance at night instead of cleaning that building."

"You know I wish you wouldn't put yourself out-there like that, but I know once your mind is made up there is no stopping you."

"We'll talk about it tomorrow mom!" I yelled down the row of townhouses to where she stood shivering on her porch. I dipped into the split of the two buildings appearing as if I was going into Stephanie's back door but made my way to Uncle Marcus car. Surprisingly he was already in the car ready.

"Ok gangsta you trying to get another eight-ball a quart or a teenager he asked. Nah Unc I just want an ounce 28.35 grams.

"Of the hard?" He asked stunned with his one good eye stretched in amazement and his lazy eye twitched and closed as usual.

"Do you have enough money for an ounce?" I pulled out my wad of money and stuffed it back into my jean pocket.

"One thing is for dam sure niece; you are a hustler, you are about your money. Now he charges a thousand dollars for an ounce."

"I know Unc, I'm good." I laughed to myself as my Uncle was trying to come up on an extra two hundred dollars on me; Dude told me he'd give me an ounce for $850 because he respected my hustle. I planned to sell each gram for $55 to these strippers.

We pulled up on Atcheson into the apartment complex. Coming here always scared the shit out of me. So I always came with my Uncle, I'd never take the chance of coming alone getting took up-top by one of these thirsty 8ball niggas. Uncle Marcus knocked on the door as usual and I followed him into the kitchen.

"Oh you back again Shorty?"

"I guess so." I replied.

"So what you trying to get today?"

"Well I thought I'd take you up on that $850 an ounce deal on that soft, and get an ounce of Dro from you."

"Man nigga you could learn how to enterprise from your little niece." Train said to my Uncle Marcus.

"Yea she about her money, I was just telling her that."

"Yea and I'm grown now 18 so please stop calling me little niece my name is CJ."

"Bwahaha!" They laughed in unison.

"I know ya name 'lil niece' and you know I'm Train but when we conduct business your little niece and I'm dude."

"Yea I feel it." I responded separating the money into two piles, one pile consisting of $850 and the other $150. I can't believe I was spending $1000 on drugs myself and Heavy had nothing to do with it.

I liked getting my work from Train, because he never tried to short change, nor hit on me, and I respected that, I respected that he was always on. Most of my plugs fell off every now and again but Train aka Dude was always connected. We sat and smoked blunts while he helped me weigh and bag each gram. He showed me how to cut the coke to make it stretch, after giving my Uncle Marcus a gram he disappeared.

"Where are you going? I hollered after him.

"Oh, oh niece I'm going to my peoples next door, yawl haven't even sacked up the green yet, so I'll be back before you're ready."

Out of all the times he brought me here this was his first time leaving me alone. I was a little nervous but I rest assured knowing some of my school buddies lived in this hood. If the beef was to jump off I wouldn't have to go far to reach some hitters.

"Ay, you gone have to start giving your Uncle smaller portions, you don't need to give that nigga a gram each time you come thru, in the long run that fucks up your profit. You cool Shorty you can come through on your own, save yaself 50-60 bucks. So how much you letting your grams go for?"

"$55." I told him.

"That's cool; but if you get repeat customers, raise the price after a while to $65. They gone buy it because the shit sells itself."

"True." I replied forcing the gram of Dro into the small bag

"And how much you letting you Dro go for?"

"$10 a gram."

"That's cool too, same shit apply when niggas start coming back towards the end of your sack charge them niggas $15-$20, remember the dealers need the weed to stay high to sell to the Feins, your selling to everybody and ain't nobody buying from you your friend, their all dollar signs. You feel me little niece?"

I watched him scoop the remainder of the gram into the packet before throwing it onto the table.

"Yea I hear you Big Dude." We both laughed at my crass since of humor. "So are you going to try to rock some of it up or you selling straight pow."

"Straight powder" I replied.

"Do you have the clientele?"

"Not yet, I'm about to try my hand as a stripper and sell to the bitches that work around me."

"You know what if my bitch's stomach didn't look like it went thru the meat grinder I'd have her ass doing the same thing. Well be careful youngen the jail time is different for the pow than it is for the weed, you know that right?"

"Yea I know."

"So how long have you been fucking with the power?"

"Oh I never took it; if that's what you're asking, I smoke weed and weed only, I'll never take this shit, I don't want to end up geeked up somewhere so I choose not to tempt the bear."

"Yea you smart Shorty, don't ever fuck with that shit, not even on a bad day. I've seen it ruin many lives. I'm going to keep a look out for you." With that he took a wet dish rag across the table cleaning up the residue.

"Why you do that, you know my Uncle wanna lick the table?" We both started laughing.

"You want a beer Shorty?"

"No thanks but do you got some Remy?"

"No I got some Hennessey though; you want some?"

"I never had Hennessey before."

"Try it." He grinned pouring me a shot into a small white Styrofoam cup. He slid the can of Pepsi over to me as I downed the shot of Hennessey.

"It kind-of reminds me of Remy a little bit."

"Yea a little bit, only the real gangsters fuck with the Hennessey." He poured me another shot and I took it to the head, drunk damn near the whole can of Pepsi.

"Ay, ay, ay, yawl still working in there?"

"Nah we good O.G. just wrapping up." Train said to my Uncle. I put both bags into my fanny pack under my hoodie.

"You stay up Shorty!" After giving Train dap; I headed to the door.

~§~§~§~§~§~§~

I called Heather the white lady who worked at KFC with me, who always bragged about her Biracial daughter and how she use to be a stripper when she was younger.

"Hey girl. This is CJ were you still going to take me to check out the strip clubs tonight?"

"Girl I forgot that was tonight, well your kind of in luck, were up here at Dreamers off Cleveland Avenue now, I'm trying to find me a couple grams."

-"Hey, Hey wait- I interrupted her- I just got home. Don't cop from no one, I'm about to come up there, I just re-upped so I got you." Oh no CJ I like the soft I don't mess with the Rocks."

"Yea I know I got the soft already sacked up, fifty five."

"Wow that must be some good shit if you selling it for $55."

"Yea my tester told me it was pure as he's had in a long time. My plug told me not to sell it any less than 55. I'm on my way Heather; don't leave and don't buy from no one else." I was scared to death. I didn't have a driver's license but I brought a car last week a four door Chevrolet my little G ride was two toned Sky blue at the top and navy blue at the bottom. Hood I know but it was $500 bucks and I couldn't resist. I decided to pre-plan my route; I'll take Champion all the way up until it turned into Joyce. Then I'd take my chances on Hudson to Cleveland Ave. The police lived on Hudson and I just prayed that they didn't get behind me.

"Hey, CJ come here!" (awe shit) I heard my mom yelling from my Aunty Karen's car.

"Where are you going?" She questioned, before I made it to the car. I waited to help her out of the vehicle before I gave her my answer. I didn't want my Aunt Karen to know that I was going stripping, even though my mom probably told her already.

"I got something for you." She said as she opened the back door.

"Hey Aunty Karen." I waved.

"Hey Baby Girl how you holding up?"

"I'm good Aunty." I winked. "I'm-a go put this stuff in the house Marlene and then I'm going to come down to your house."

"Alright K!" Mom said shutting the car door, handing me two shopping bags. "Bring these into the house for me."

"Yes ma'am." Already in-tow walking two steps behind her.

"So you are driving your own self tonight, in your car?"
"Yes ma'am, Uncle Ollie checked it out, did the oil change, tune up, brand new spark plugs, fluids the whole nine."
"The whole nine hun?" She laughed to herself.

"Hold on mom. I stopped her taking the cigarette and its one inch ash from her mouth. You're about to drop all these ashes on ya coat." I vaguely laughed & took a drag.

"So where were you going to right now?" She questioned seriously.

"Oh I'm going to Dreamers on Cleveland Avenue mom." I opened the screen and unlocked the backdoor.

"So where is your bag what did you decide to wear?"

"I just got the sky blue one-piece sheer and lace, that Heavy brought me for my birthday."

"Oh that's cute, what color thongs and bra?"

–"Uhh Black?" She laughed as she took her coat off.

"So what were you going to audition in?"

—"Audition I didn't know they would want me to audition tonight?" She burst into laughter. "Were you going to give them a resume?" I laughed with her. What was I thinking?

"Too much going on girl. Open this box." She pushed the box reading Steve Madden, Silver six inch Stalks' with platinum colored Butterfly's embossed on the heel and top of the toe. I loved these shoes!

"So try them on." She smiled, self-pleased.

"Oh My God Mom!"

"What?" She jumped.

"I never wore heels I don't know how to dance in no fucking heels." We both started laughing as I took off my Jordan's and my black ankle socks. I buckled the shoes and nearly broke my neck with my first step.

"Oh Shit!" I hollered crashing into the wall.
"I wish I had my camera." Mom laughed hysterically.

I mean the shit couldn't be that hard. I know how to dance. I've been dancing forever on the stage, in boots or tennis shoes though, dayum, dayum I mocked myself, still laughing when mom turned on the CD player: STOMP! ALL MY PEOPLE SAY STOMP!

"Oh no mom, not Kirk Franklin!" We both laughed before she paused: "Um hum maybe Kirk got a message for you."

"Mom not tonight. I practiced walking back & forth from the Living-room to the dining room. Alright I got to go mom. Thank you so very much."

"Wait girl! She said as I rushed to un-strap the heels. I got you this too." She handed me a white thong bikini set. Yesssss I was ready. I paused in all the nerves and adrenaline.

"Mom you really just prepped me for the stripping shit."

"We'll you know me, I don't like you out there fucked up."

"You my nigga mom."

"No you my nigga witcha black ass, looking like ya daddy." We laughed hysterically, I didn't care that I was one of the darkest women in my family, Honey I was, is, am and will be the (**S**)ugar (**H**)oney (**I**)ce (**T**)ea, even on my bad day.

(God baby; Embrace your beautiful brown skin. Queen Melanin).

Moving on, I placed the two piece and shoes into the small black duffle-bag she handed me as well as my purse. I was still getting use to carrying a purse. Which I had stuffed with baby wipes body spray, & deodorant, I grabbed my boobs double checking the work in my bra.

"OK mom I'm out of here, thank you sooo much." I exaggerated.

"Consider it a birthday present."

"Absolutely!" I smiled.

Dear God,

Please watch over me in my comings and my goings. I know my path is filled with sin until I find a way out this is the life that I live. I ask your grace, mercy and forgiveness in advance and I ask if I get too close to the fire, send your angels to grab my hand. Give your angels charge of protection as they watch over my daughter. Please keep peace and prosperity with my mother, for my sister and brothers. I pray that you deliver my father and me, these things I ask in your son Christ Jesus Name. Amen.

I started the car and in motion Cinnamon, my stripper identity was born. I was so paranoid on my ride across town that I didn't turn on the radio. I felt a panic attack every time I seen a police car anywhere in sight. I hoped out that dam car so fast after pulling into the parking lot. Whew I'm glad that trauma was over. I can't believe I drove from the Southside to the North-side at night alone. I was really on some gully shit.

I grabbed my bag, locked the doors and took a deep breath. I walked into the smokey club, literally feeling my knees begin to shake.

"Hey Sunshine!" Heather called out to me from the bar stool on my far right. Oh my goodness I was so happy to see her.

"Girl I thought you left."

"Hey Barbie! Heather yelled to the bartender -This is the young lady I was telling you about; my co-worker."

"Oh yea CJ!" She said pointing her finger at me nodding her head up and down.

"Yea so now I'm-a little nervous I don't know what to say."

"Oh don't worry about it. Come on, come to the bathroom with me, use the bathroom relax, it's all good." I gave DeDe her roommate my other co-worker a hug and headed to the back behind Heather. I looked at the naked white chick on stage, and even though she was dancing to Princes: Pussy Control she was dancing super-slow.

"She's not even dancing for real." I whispered to Heather.

"Oh but she is honey." She laughed pushing open the door to the dressing room.

"I thought we were going to the bathroom!"

"This one is much better darling, besides we got more space." She gave me her drink.

"What is this?" I sniffed.
"Hennessey & Coke."

"Oh yea this is pretty good I had two shots earlier."

"Let me see the Christmas present." She smiled.
"I don't know about Christmas presents, but it looks like snow for the holidays." She laughed opening the small packet.

"Ah ah you try it you buy it, where the money at, you know it's good." She handed me a fifty and a five dollar bill rolled up. Dipped her fingernail into the bag and rubbed it across her gums. I watched her slowly lick her top teeth and smile.

"You like that shit right?" I asked her taking off my shoes.
"Yea let me get two more." She moaned. I was excited that she was excited.

"$110 please." I held her Franklin in the air more so for jokes. I gave her two more packets from my bra. I was going to wait until she left the room to put my work into the little purse my mom got me.

"Nice doing business with you boo."

"Ay I need a favor; I don't have one of those things to put around my leg like the girls got their money on."

"It's called a Garter Belt babe." She laughed rubbing and squeezing her nose.

"I'm going to go talk to my friend and see if she got one for you." As she turned for the door, I raced out of my clothes. I kept my socks on because I didn't want my bare feet on this dirty floor. I took off my tan full booty panties, I had no need to wear pretty panties I wasn't seeing any dick on the regular. I grabbed the baby wipes and began my ritual. Grabbing the dry rag from the plastic bag and wiped behind the baby wipes.

I put the bikini bottom and top on while still wearing my t-shirt. I propped my titties up as best I could. I was still skinny from the stress & hustle. I stepped into the one piece short teddy that snapped at the crotch. It was lace around the breast and waist; I felt a sigh of relief as I spread my t-shirt across the chair to sit down.

Three girls came in the door behind Heather.

"So you're the new girl?" One of the blonds asked.

"That's exactly why I'm here, I'm about to audition."

"So what is your name?" The bleach blond asked.

"Cinnamon, call me Cinnamon."

"Awe that's cute, well Cinnamon my name is Charity. She shook my hand and stepped closer. I'm friends with Heather, we've been friends a real long time, so I'm cool you can trust me. You can trust us; I can't speak for everybody else though you know what I mean?"

Yea sure I said to myself I don't trust none of you bitches, I just gave her the resting bitch-face.

"So you got any more snowflakes?"

"$55 each."

"Ok give me two Honey. You don't mind a few ones do you?" She laughed as I sat back down to finish strapping these heels that already had my legs shaking.

"You look like your shaking baby girl are you that nervous?"

"Yea actually I am, I replied, I've never danced before and I really don't know what to do, say or expect." I pulled the two packets from my purse, collected the $110 from Blondie and zipped back up the purse.

"Wait honey I'm Sarah." The Burnett said that stood silently behind the blonds and Heather.

"Hi Sarah."

"Hey I just want one but when business picks up for me later I'll get another one."

"Aiight." This shit couldn't be this easy, just to think I just made $330 that fast. These bitches looked like they were competing in the Vacuum Division of the Dope Olympics. Line after line, then they'd grab their nose. Then fast to bend back down and snort like they had the Holy Ghost. Some coughing and choking others head back draining. I was done entertaining this spirit. Guess I'm ready to take my chances out there.

I placed my little purse in the cuff of my arm, grabbed my duffle bag and started for the door. I inhaled quickly and deeply as the bartender burst into the dressing-room. Oh My God, I hope she don't ask where it came from.

"Let me try some Heathen Heather." She laughed. I silently let out a deep breath as my initial fear subsided. Damn I was super paranoid tonight, like never before; something damn sure was in the air.

"You want the job Cinnamon?" The bar tendered asked softly grabbing my arm. I looked down at her hand slow but aggressively up into her eyes.

"Oh no offence dear I just didn't want you to rush past me. Any how I'll give you the job if you give me a sample."

"Oh, consider me hired." We all laughed in unison as I dropped my duffle bag to the floor and scrambled in my little purse for the sample sac. I used my little sisters Yellow Highlighter to draw a neon happy face. I figured the mother fuckas should be happy for a freebie. I took out the sample sac, turned the smiling face toward her.

"And it even comes with a happy face." We all laughed.

"Ok first things first honey, I'm Debbie, I'm the bartender slash manager. Have you ever danced before? Sexy dancing?"

"No! Just Hip Hop mostly choreographed dancing."

"Ok do you know any dancers?" She asked rubbing the coke coated finger across her gums.

"Uh just Heather from work."

"Well here honey the girls make their money three ways, in most go-go / topless bars. First you make money off the drinks. If you sit with a guy and he wants to buy you a drink, your small drinks begin at $10 you get $6 the Bar gets $4 until you make your $100 daily drink quota then we only get 20%. Second you make your money from tips. If the customers like you or your dance they will come to the stage and tip you. Finally you have your table dances; you can charge whatever you like but not to defeat the purpose of your VIP dances where you dance in one of the private rooms for the customers. Most girls charge $30 per dance because we charge $15 per song for the room minimum, you can buy the rooms by the half hour and hour as well."

I guess I was looking extra nervous to her so she decided to wrap her arms around me.

"It's no reason to be nervous really, every girl in here started on day one just like you, relax you're a very pretty girl, a little on the skinny side for a black girl but you're going to do just fine. Come sit at the bar for a spell, I'll make you the house drink."

I was going to need a drink or something. I couldn't believe I was in a public building in my lingerie. I don't know what had me shook the most, the fact that I was in here naked or the fact that I had all this dope on me. For a chick that was just riding high on a full scholarship just a few months ago, I really do have a "stupid as fuck" side to my brain. How did I talk myself into this?

"Here take these shots, very quick, if any of your customers ask you just turned 21, and as a matter of fact tomorrow we are going to have you a birthday party, that should make you a shit load of money. Just make sure to tip your bartender." She winked at me and the bond was set. I was going to continue to feed her this dope and have her feed me the club. All the way around I won. She knew I was just turning 18 so the fact that she just gave me this shot and whatever the hell is in this mixed drink gave me leverage over her too.

"Go put your name up on the board under the last girl, that's who you will follow during your shift. Look China is up now, over there in the pink. Then Ecstasy is after her and you will be after Ecstasy and then the list starts over again." That reminded me I had to buy a jar of pills.

I took the first shot to the head. "Whoo!" Straight hard absolute vodka, this shit just put a hair on my chest. I grabbed the second drink and walked to the juke box. I signed my name on the board in neon blue, I bent over to scan the jukebox and out of nowhere I was lifted off my feet from behind.

"Put me down!" I started kicking and screaming.

"Are you out your fucking mind, Star?!"

"Oh My God! I couldn't believe this nigga. Heavy what are you doing here?"

"Man the little homie called and swore on G that he seen you walk in and go to the dressing room. Man what the fuck are you doing Star, you got bread you don't need to be stripping, what the fuck you still moving your weight?"

"Fuck you Heavy what you mean"...The bartender came over and grabbed my arm leading me to the dressing room.

"Cinnamon that is not what you want to do, you don't want to argue with any of your boyfriends or customers here at work, it will turn your other customers off."

"Girl that's my daughters dad, one of his friends seen me and now he's here. I'm about to take my name off the list, Go talk to him so he never comes up here again, or at-least on the days that I'm here and I'll be back tomorrow."

"That's cool Cinnamon but tomorrow you have to be ready to work, Kenny the manager will be here, don't ever let him know that you are selling anything. If he ask you tell him no, and ask me about the girls before you sell to them, I don't want you fucking with none of the narks or rats up in here."

"Cool Thanks Debbie." I gave her one of my perforated paper business cards. "Call me if you need me before the end of the night.

"Oh also for tomorrow Cinnamon don't ask for any liquor at the bar when Kenny's here just give me the money and I'll have one of the girls take the drink to the back for you." I was fucking with Debbie real hard, I like her operation, my operation, our operation. I pulled on my pants and in my pocket was the twenty-sack I made for CB my other runner who didn't pick it up. Crazy CB use to be a Golden Glove Champion Boxer before he lost the fight with crack.

I went to have a drink with Heavy at Jeff's Place. He had to understand that he or no one else would stand in front of my hustle. I had to come up then get the fuck out of Ohio, 270 was no longer big enough for me and him. After he complained at the bar for about forty minutes, we left, booked a room and I showed him a new trick I leaned fucking with my hidden nigga C.

"Look at you, I see you been practicing some new shit." His jealousy was cute but not really.

"I'm surprised with all your 50/11 bitches you would recognize a difference." I swear the doctors gave me a new pussy after they stitched me up. I had a serious obsession with keeping my Kegel strong and walls tight. I did Kegel's so much that I trained myself to do it unknowingly.

"Damn Star, Oh you be tripping." He moaned as I turned back around on his dick. "You need to bring this pussy back home to daddy." I kissed him gently out of habit.

"Sorry daddy lil' momma gotta keep an Uncle in the closet for when you get your urge to put on and go grab you a bitch or three." I chuckled to him.

"Baby we're going to stay best friends, and maybe in the future when we both up we can visit the idea."

(He paused) "Man Star you can't have your cake and eat it too."

"And neither can you, so I just want you to stay out of whatever club I'm working at."

"Star you get on my nerves man…You know I'm gone get clowned if niggas find out you stripping." The seriousness in his eyes showed a fight between his pride and ego. He gripped my ass painfully and I knew he was more hurt than angry. Reaching over him, I lit his blunt. "I'm getting this money baby, Flat the fuck out! Fuck your niggas and you getting clowned, you nor your niggas checked to see if I was eating or if I needed anything after you put me out a week after my house burnt down. Tell them niggas come buy a sack with their opinion." With that, I was done with this conversation and trying to chase that illusive nut, so I slowly slid off his dick.

I knew my stint dancing on the north side would be short lived for many reasons. I never thought I'd be getting arrested my sixth day working at Dreamers. I had that bitch lit like a Christmas-Tree. Instead of staying on my feet, I allowed a customer to get me drunk and in my drunkenness sold some blow to a new stripper. Who brought me her customer who was seriously trying to force me to sell him some work. I told him I didn't have any and the only thing I had was a pre-rolled half a blunt, my personal stash. After he tipped me $20 I figured if he was that hard up for some weed he deserved it.

It was Friday, the last song of the night. I was down to my baby blue bra and T-Bar's dancing to H-Town's: Knocking the Boots. I've grown mesmerized with watching myself seduce these men and women with my body, slowly slithering down their lust. I was working on perfecting my booty pop when the Mifflin Township Police Department raided us. I was instructed not to move off the stage and that I was under arrest for sailing (the equivalent of a pin joint) Marijuana to an undercover agent.

"Are yawl going to let me put my clothes on?" I asked frantically, feeling the fear of embarrassment of being cuffed in my bikini overwhelm me.

"Officer!" I yelled to the white cop who was using excessive pressure on my wrist. I felt the cold metal cuffs digging into my right wrist as I watched the undercover agent that was begging me to sale him anything, cuffing my bartender. A scary looking tall, bald head black officer cuffed the coked out manager.

He snatched my arms abruptly and began dragging me towards the dressing room.

"Listen I'm giving you 3 minutes to get your clothes on, try anything suspicious and I am taking you down." His sharp tone; sent anger down my spine.

I was secretly thanking God; that I sold the entire stash of product I brought with me tonight, incase these Rollies decided to check my belongings. The walk of shame through the club and out to the squad car was humiliating. The customers whispering to one another and the dancers pointing at me making hand gestures that they were going to call me. The Irony, I knew my days of dancing at Dreamers were over.

The ride to the Franklin County Jail seemed like the longest coldest ride ever. Booking was something totally different. They made me take off my clothes, dug in my mouth, made me squat and cough three times. What the fuck, this was humiliating and they weren't tipping for damn sure. The cold chill up the crack of my ass caused my nipples to firm.

"Someone seems to be getting a little excited." The Manish white female officer laughed to her partner in mockery.

"I bet you'd like to find out. This jail shit is for the birds." I sassed rolling my eyes standing back up in full stance.

I placed my blue little mat on the floor in the corner cell. The Franklin County Jail was over populated. I watched the news for the first time behind four different sets of bars. This shit was seriously fucking with my vision. I was the fourth name they called to prep for Saturday Court. Dam I didn't know I was going to court the very next day. My

Hazel contacts where damn near cracking in my eyes they were so dry. I strained to see through the haze as I combed my hair with the flimsy three inch super plastic comb they gave me in my welcome to jail kit.

I shuffled in the single file line into the courtroom against the wall as we were instructed. Hands and feet chained together as if I just killed 10 innocent niggas. Oh that's the police job except they stand on the opposite side of convicted. I thought to myself as I looked at all the unfamiliar faces filling the courtroom. There she was! Tasha Mac the only one in the courtroom who knew or gave a damn about me.

I said whatever it was I needed to say to the judge to get me out on my own recon-. I caught the #1 Cleveland Avenue bus to dreamers first. I had the key to my locker where the rest of my money remained. The bartender allowed me to go get my things but repeatedly told me that I was never allowed in their establishment again. The bitch stayed true and told me she would still call me for the bugger sugar but I would have to meet her prior to work. I gave her a pack in return for a good reference in-case any other strip-club where to call.

I got my very first income tax check that year and used the money to move into Colonial Village. It was on the bus line incase my car broke and it was in the vicinity of two strip clubs and close enough to my family. I furnished Raily's and my bedrooms and the kitchen. I gave the Rental Office three months advanced rent with my deposit, to give me enough time to make a new plan. I overspent and didn't have enough for the living room suite I wanted. After a few dick sucks Heavy agreed to help me buy the furniture, he was so selfish anymore, worse than a nigga off the street.

§O§

§~Chapter 12~§
The Mirage

Suki reluctantly hired me at the Mirage, the Go-Go Bar on Main St. near the corner of Barnett. The Club was a 15 minute walk from my apartment, and it was everything I needed it to be. Suki the owner A 40+ year old Asian woman who was a stripper turned wife, who divorced him and got three clubs out of the union. Very smart woman, she didn't want to hire me because she said that I was too skinny for a black girl. Blue, Suki's sister and Bar Manager and Anna another 42 year old Asian stripper who surprisingly was 4 foot 8 had 6 children, and very few stretch marks; convinced Suki that I was beautiful and they would teach me the ropes, since I didn't have any experience.

About two months later, I considered myself a professional; my operation was as sweet as my pussy popping in a hand stand. I danced that night to Celine Deon's "Seduce me" after Phil Collins "Feel It in The Air." That was the perfect song for my pole work. I scanned the room while slowly humping my way down the pole to find all the watchers that were too afraid to tip at the stage. I always catered to my stage crowd; especially the ones that made it rain. My kegel muscles were so strong that I could retract and press out my vagina and my rectum, protruding to the point that it could be seen through my panties. The customers loved that shit, begging me to please flash them my pussy.

After collecting all my tips I made my way down the isle of the bar; where sitting was this Michael Bolton/Steven Segal pony tail wearing, cowboy boot rocking' shirt sleeves rolled up like grease lightning white dude looking fixated at me.

"Hey honey, how are you? Did you enjoy my dance?" I flashed him a big smile, lifting my leg between his knees on his barstool pressing his leg open, while opening my garter belt.

"Yes, yes I did. I'm Dan." He smiled exposing his crooked nose and teeth.

"Hi Dan; I dropped a seductive smile and lip lick in return. I'm Cinnamon; would you like to give me a tip?" I nodded toward my leg and lifted garter belt.

"Yes, he said putting his white business card into my garter belt. The tip is you are going to be my wife." He grabbed my thigh and looked like he was going to cum on his self. I snatched my leg down and tried my hardest to hit him in the face with my auburn and blonde weave.

"You wish asshole." I snipped before walking towards the dressing room. I hated the guys that came in the club but only wanted to participate outside of the club, trying to force prostitution. I was jerked by my wrist to the red love seat where Anna (my Philippine, how to be a stripper Trainer) sat with this rude black dude who was gripping my wrist tighter.

"Get your fucking hands boy!" I frowned at the dude then at Anna. "I'm sorry Cinnamon I just wanted to catch you and tell you that if you're smart, you'll hook up with the white boy you were talking to, that's my boss and he brought me in here to see you, he really likes you and want to fuck with you. I'm James." He said while giving me the same business card that was sitting in my garter.

"He ain't gone do the club, it's not his thing, but if you hook up with him outside of here he trick easy."

"Hum thanks." I said snatching the card putting it into my silver tip bag, before sashaying my way into the locker room to drink my awaiting vodka & cranberry shots.

I took Sunday – Tuesday off work to focus on Raily and school, I didn't do Monday night Bachelor or Private Parties. This was the last week of Heavy's monthly two weeks rotation of keeping her. This nigga was a piece of shit. He hated my hustle, threw salt in my game every chance he could, but wouldn't put any money in my pockets. He figured if he kept Raily for half the month and I kept her for the other half that he was doing his job supporting her. So fuck it, stay out of my lane was the attitude I kept with him.

He wasn't daddy anymore; he hadn't held me down in a long time. He didn't give a fuck about my crib getting broken into, until he stayed the night and they broke into his Bonnie and stole all his shit. Then the nigga running in the Mexican's house with the pump out, hum, shaking my head, I decided to call Dan.

"Accurate Collision Repair." The man said upon answering my call.

"Hi sir may I speak to Danny please?"

"This is he, how can I help you?" I chuckled before replying.

"Oh dear I thought I was calling because you desire for me to help you."

"Excuse me?" He paused in the conversation but didn't hang up. I knew he liked the teasing mind-fuck.

"I would expect you to know my voice by now, if you guaranteed I was going to be your wife just days ago."

"Cinnamon, is this Cinnamon from the Mirage?"

"In the flesh, my baby." I could hear his mood lighten.

"Where are you can you come and see me, do you want to go on a date?" I laughed flattered at his rapid-fire line of questioning.

"I would like to come see you and go on a date; I am at home however my car is still supposedly being fixed at this garage in the hood."

"What's the address to the car? I'll send a tow truck to get the car; I'll fix it for you for free if you come see me." Hum is that right-I thought to myself.

"I'll get the address for you once we hang up and then I'll call you back. At the moment I'm immobile and I'm not taking a bus to the north side." I laughed.

"You don't have to; I'll take a few hours off and take you out. My boss is out of town so he won't know I shut down the shop. What is your address, I am going to send a car for you, and call me with the address to your car."

I gave him my address then called Moe to get Eddie Kane's address. The friendly neighborhood crack head who fixed everybody's whips had my car for a while. I called back with the information and the one way street instructions. We'll let the tricking commence. I said rubbing my hands together, darting to the shower, I didn't know how soon the car was going to come so I rushed myself.

I grabbed the red dress with the two slits up the front stopping at the bottom of my thigh. This dress was sexy, classy and red, I never wore red. I put on my flat red leather wrap up sandals and pulled my blond tracks into a back ponytail. I sprayed down in the bottle of Channel No5 that Heavy got me for Christmas, lined & glossed my lips and eyes and I was ready to go.

I turned on the kitchen light incase Janice was going to come back tonight. I rolled two blunts and wondered if he smoked. The guy at my screen door looked like a white 1970's time warped dope Fein. His dried, fried mullet looked like something off of Wayne's World.

"Uh, Dan with Accurate Collision sent me for Cinnamon." He said through my screen door.

"Yes that's me." Yea this dude was fried I concluded. I locked the door then followed him to the back of this black on black Mercedes with the platinum package. 'Look-a here' I thought as I seen the dozen roses lying on the back seat. This guy was good; I was becoming impressed after freighted by seeing this driver.

"Excuse me what is your name?" I questioned the driver.

"Oh, Yes, Hi, my name is Jake I been at the body shop for about a year and a half now." He responded.

"Oh, OK, so tell me Does Dan Smoke?"

"Uh No not that I know of, but I smoke, I think you should ask him that." I laughed at this weird dude before instructing him to roll the windows down as we made our way to Cassidy Avenue.

"Turn on the Air and the Radio, I'm about to light this blunt before we get there."

"Cool." He responded.

"I like you already." We smoked and rode to Biggie Smalls, I definitely wasn't expecting that. I sprayed down the car and myself with my Victoria Secret body spray as I watched the tow truck unhinge my car into the lot. Damn that was quick, this man don't waste any time. He opened the door and grabbed me by my hand kissing me like we were old lovers.

He gave Jake some money, instructed me to get in the driver's seat of the Benz and to pull it out of the gate because he was about to close up shop. About five minutes after I pulled his Benz through the gate he joined me after locking the gate behind us. We drove to Tuttle Crossing Mall in Dublin and the first thing he brought me was a $400 Silver Digital Camera.

I was impressed, I really wasn't attracted to him, but I was trained at being attracted to the money. He was very touchy feely, At Mitchell's Steak House, I promised him if he gave me $1000 and let me borrow his car until my car was fixed That I'd have sex with him tonight. We settled on me having his Benz for Three days only. He vowed to have my car fixed by then.

He told me that he was the manager of the body shop and he had an apartment here in Dublin. He went on about a black girl friend that he broke up with because he knew she was cheating on him. I felt sorry for the guy as he was apparently a hopeless romantic. We ended the evening at some Hotel off 256. This man was a driving ass, he literally took me all around 270 in the course of one day.

I fucked him hard, hot like I wanted to marry him, like I wanted the Mercedes as long as I kept my eyes closed. I just never preferred white men, to me it felt as if his penis was a decent size but through the condom it wasn't hard enough. Whatever the excuse I couldn't convince myself to be 75% into it.

I told him about my upcoming: Family Trip Friday and that I would bring his car to the shop Thursday Night before I went to work. He let me keep the car Tuesday and Wednesday but Came for it Early Thursday morning.

The annual family trip abroad was going to be the wildest ever this year. Even though we were going to Atlantic City again; Weezy, Tasha, Aunty Lisa, Uncle Tony, Lil Larry, Aunty Darlene, Mom, Cousin Niecy, Martika, Rika and I were all on the trip together. The 13 hour bus ride was long as usual. The bonus this year was the bus stop was at the Library at the corner of Livingston & Barnett which was a few blocks from my apartment.

This year we were staying in the Trump Taj Mahal I was 18 and had a lot of money to spend. My client that had ownership stock in the Columbus Dispatch took me to Macy's to buy all new luggage and a few new outfits. These white guys where easier to butter than toast. Dan the body shop guy still had my car, so I was forced to tell my client where I lived. I allowed Dan to pick me up to take me to the bus stop even though I could have walked with my super cute luggage.

He insisted he wanted to give me something before my trip. I really didn't want to see him, he annoyed me wanting to do everything his way as if I never been giving shit by a white-man before in my life. I'm glad I let him come to get me. He gave me his calling card, a thousand in cash and fifteen hundred on a prepaid card. This one was seriously trying to win the trick of the month award.

Everyone oohed and aahh as the bus pulled off and Dan was riding beside us with his sword stuck out of the sun roof of his 1996 Tan Toyota Land Cruiser.

"This nigga, what are you doing? Are you some knight in white shining armor?" I mouthed to him through the bus window.

"Girl you better snatch up that white man, if you know what's good." Rika said to me, pregnant herself, rubbing her belly full of my Uncle JRs baby.

"Girl that nigga is the bottom nigga on my white boy totem-pole."

"Not that you call the white boy nigga." She laughed.

"Sis all ignorant motherfuckers are niggas, not just the black race." I shook my head at him as I slid down into my seat. I was upset that he still had my car; he was causing me to go against the grain too much. I felt he was keeping my car to force spending more time with me.

I never had so much fun in my entire life. On the first day we all went to the ship for shopping, smoking the entire way down the boardwalk, in and out of bicycle carts. Aunt Lisa brought some gin & juice and we were all lit by the time we made it to the Boat Mall. We all brought the biggest head set controlled super soakers and was going to split up into teams and go dumb in the fancy hotel.

I went to the store Fredrick's of Hollywood and fell in love. This store was sexy. I brought a few colorful wigs, some lingerie, one all Black & one all White with Star Diamonds on the Nipple and Bikini front T-Bar Sets to go with these robes honey, yes I brought two of them a white and black floor length sheer, feather trimmed robe. The robes put me in the mind of Dynasty, something those old Divas would wear. I'm definitely going to wear this to work.

"Bitch come look at these shoes!" Weezy yelled, fixing her yellow wig that she just purchased to match the yellow, blue and green sundress she was rocking.

"Oh Yes I'll take those in size six and a half." I pointed to my cashier. These opened toed, calf high stripper boots was the bomb. All rhinestone, silver mesh-net and silver leather with strings of rhinestones hanging from everywhere, they were bright shining, stunting disco balls and I had to have them. I laughed to myself as I tucked my blond weave into the Stocking cap putting on the white wig. I was going to wear the wig and the white robe down the board walk. I was already wearing an all-white skin tight jumpsuit with lace and satin squares up the sides. And my clear four inch square heels, I got from the stripper store.

That Cinnamon bitch was in full effect. Diamonds and Gold on every finger $55 dollar 2.5 inch nails. All the attention was encouraging me to wear this hair and robe to work next Wednesday for my Loan Clients as I like to call them. Hop & Reece who came in on Wednesdays, they'd buy me the $100 fish bowl to kill my quota. I'd sit in between them for the majority of the night and they would just rain the tips on me.

Of course I'd give them hand jobs and rub my bare pussy on their hands while giving them lap dances. Hop would always sneak in a bottle of Vodka and pour it in my Fish bowl of cranberry and orange juice filled with cherries. Mrs. Suki's alcohol free rendition of my under 21 sex on the beach.

We always talked about having a threesome and what it would be like. I never had a threesome and they always begged me to let them break my threesome virginity.

"I thought threesomes where two girls and a guy." I would always say to them. Taking turns whispering, licking in each of their ears.

"Baby threesomes are sex with any group of three people. I myself would absolutely love to have your green little ass for myself, and I'd damn sure would love to have a threesome with you. Let's make a fantasy come true." Hop was the smooth Good looking Cousin.

He was in his late twenties early thirties, but I knew this was the kind of man I wanted. My "Loan Cousins" kept this splurge up every other Wednesday for three months before I decided to give in to their offer of a thousand dollars each and they had to both buy an ounce of Kush for $175 each. I did it for all the reasons. And because I kept dreaming about it, thinking about what it would be like while I was dancing. I knew they were closing on a property so taking a band from them each was child's play. They spent about that much on me per month any way.

~§~§~§~§~§~§~

We decided to sit our tired feet and bags down at this Fancy German Restaurant. Before deciding to take our food to the top deck of the Mall-Ship and enjoy our bagged Gin & Juice. We watched a few people play shuffle board and miniature golf, as I surveyed Tasha, Weezy & Aunty Lisa deciding if we should play either attraction. The Atlantic City Ocean One is a nice distraction from the crowded board walk.

"I loved the parquet floors here." I admired aloud as I sat my bag beside my chair, in the mezzanine this Boat Mall was nice.

"I have a confession yawl." I said looking sneakily back and forth between them. Feeling relieved to finally get off these heels.

"What's your confession, I hope you're not pregnant and you're just getting your money right." Tasha scouring her: you better not face at me.

"No Honey, never mind." I sighed shying away from the confession.

"Oh yea, girl tell us, what it is, if you're not pregnant." Weezy chimed in realizing we hooked her drink up.

"I had a threesome a couple of weeks ago." I smiled sipping my Gin laced orange juice. We spiked Weezy's orange juice while she went to the restroom with Aunty Lisa. Weezy was only 15 and Aunty Lisa didn't want her to turn out like Tasha and I so she said.

"So are you going to give us the juice or what?" Aunt Lisa looked at me still shocked.

"Ok so I have these two customers that come and see me every Wednesday or every other. They say that they're Cousins. I call them Hop and Reece they're loan officers, they're doing pretty good for themselves."

"Girl get to the juicy shit." Tasha interrupted fanning her long colorful finger nails at me. I laughed at her annoyed face, she knew I was trying to set the bullshit up real nice and pretty for Aunty Lisa.

"Alright so both these cousins are my nigga per say. I really like Hop, like on some real shit but I'm not about that life right now. They've been spending some nice money with me and I told them I would. Hop came alone to pick me up, we got Gengi Take-out; went to the Liquor store for Condoms, Vodka, Orange Juice and a carton of Swishers. All the while, I'm facing this loud ass Dro, I just got a pound of FYI! (I pointed to my Aunt and Cousins in laughter). Hop kept rubbing on my thighs and my neck saying that he wanted to penetrate me first and he was having second thoughts about letting Reece join. I told him I already put up Reece's money and I wasn't giving it back. I assured the nigga that I had extra feelings for him as well but you know the whole life in a different direction type shit.

He kissed me hard as we parked at their condo. I felt proud of them for having their shit together legally; regardless of how much shit they do illegally, these brothers were smart enough to pursue the cover. Hop was feeling in a way, It was all over his face when we walked in the door.

I sat down the bag of ice and Styrofoam cups, pulled open the bag of ice, grabbed three cups and made two strong drinks, and a huge shot with a dash of chaser. Bent quick was the recipe. I put the ice in my mouth as he was taking off his dress shoes. I took a swig of the vodka from the bottle chased it with the drink, stuck a few chunks of the ice in my mouth and started at his dick.

He didn't get the second shoe off by the time I had his dick out. Girl he fell back into the wall & scarring the shit out of me. I crawled over to him crouched down against the wall and started sucking him again, thirsty to make it hard against the cold ice. The ice turned to warm saliva as his dick grew harder in my mouth.

"Ooh Cinnamon, ooh baby girl." He moaned repeatedly until jealous Reece came in.

"Oh, so yawl gone start the party without me?" Reece whined with his hands in the air, I stood to my feet, whipping my mouth, closing Hops still open mouth.

"No baby, the party became the party when you walked in." I blew him a kiss, took off my pink FUBU tank top and threw it at him as I went over to grab their drinks.

"Here you go baby." I said to hop while he quickly took off all his clothes. Reece began gulping as soon as I gave him his cup. I pulled down his gym shorts.

"Ooh Reece has a big dick too." I said rubbing the spit I just spewed on his quickly excited dick."

"Damn, two big dicks Niece?"

"Two big dicks Aunty, so I sucked Reece's dick a little bit as Hop began to walk towards me. "No nigga!" I yelled pointing back at him.

"Yea, no nigga!" Reese laughed pointing at Hop causing us all to burst out laughing.

"Baby you roll us up a big fat one." I placed my fist in an O to show him how big to roll the blunt. I was trying to get faded fast, just in-case I began to think I couldn't handle the shit. I went back to the island in the kitchen and made my own straight double shot of vodka. I cracked open the 2 Liter of sprite and made me a lighter mixed drink as I watched them pour Medicine into two new Styrofoam cups.

"Girl they was sipping that cough syrup shit, your Uncle Ray was trying to tell me about."

"Anyway what happened girl?"

"Right, but I see the waiter about to come over here, can you order a Glass of Gin and a shot, I'll order the rest. Yea my munchies are kicking in them little crabs and shrimp wasn't shit girl." We laughed because we couldn't pronounce anything on the menu so we went with Crabs & Shrimp. I flagged the waitress over to expedite the process.

"Hi we'll have 4 refills of Orange Juice, 4 orders of the Filet Mignon well- done, with the Asparagus, the loaded Baked Potatoes, house salad with separate Ranch & Sweet Dressing and the Chicken Quesadillas for the Appetizer and whatever my Aunty wants."

"Aunty Lisa!" I said snapping her back into the conversation.

"Oh I'll have a glass & a shot of Gin, or two Glasses of gin Hell were on vacation from Ohio, most of my family is here and were having a good time!" We all agreed in unison; looking at the waitress for her reaction.

"That's great ladies, enjoy your stay, my name is Shelly and I'll be your server for tonight, I'll be right out with your two tall Gins." She nodded and smiled as I tipped her a twenty dollar bill.

"C.J I'm not paying for the Filet Mignon shit, you ordered, I'll be fine on that crab and shit we got from down stairs." We all looked at Aunty like what are you talking about?

"I got it Aunty, and we're going to move this party over there and smoke, so we're going to need to eat some more to sop up more of this liquor; that shrimp didn't do it for me, besides Dan is paying for it." I said smiling at the Credit Card I waived in front of her.

"You are something else girl." She said shaking her head at me sparking her cigarette. "I never expected you to turn out like this?"

"Like what?" Tasha said taking the words right out of my mouth as I was saying them.

"Like all turned out and shit, having threesomes getting a whole bunch of money from different guys."

Me and my cousins looked at each other and busted out laughing. "The fuck you mean, you taught me a lot of the shit I know, why get hung up on one nigga when you can have plenty."

"A plethora."

"A gaggle of niggas."

"Not a Gaggle of niggas Weezy?" We laughed so loud and hard at Aunty Lisa trying to have a conscious through Amnesia.

"Man Aunty Lisa quit tripping; CJ, Cinnamon quit bull shitting and finish telling the story." Tasha interrupted after the waitress sat down the Quesadillas and Three Glasses of Gin.

"Yes I like her!" Tash purred, scratching at the waitress slipping a $10 tip on her tray for the third glass of Gin. She knew we were under age, she knew I was paying and she recognized we were balling. She barely looked 21 her damn self.

~§~§~§~§~§~§~

"So Hop's rolling the Stoggie at their dining table. Reece is turning on music, diming lights, lighting candles and I'm sitting nervously on-top of their island. In my Pink Bra & T-bar Set with Pink G-string suspenders, some white ankle socks with the pink cotton ball on the back and my white and pink Adidas shell toes. I've downed about the equivalent of 3.5 shots of vodka and I was slowly sipping on the vodka and orange juice, when Hops 6 foot 1, 180lbs of pure gorgeous dark brown, chocolate heaven spread my legs and blew me the biggest shot gun ever.

After chocking on the smoke for a while I grabbed the blunt as he slid my legs around the counter top onto the side of the island. He pulled the dining room chair up sat down, moved my panties over and started sucking my pussy. Sucking not licking, I began to moan instantly as I moved the bags and clutter aside so I could lie down.

I flicked the blunt ashes into the empty Styrofoam cup and studied my body as this man took my clitoris to places it's never been before. It felt like he knew I was beginning to come so he started squeezing my pussy lips together sucking my clitoris even firmer. Oh I wanted him to stick his finger inside of me so bad.

"My pussy was yearning for me yet?" Hop questioned. I watched Reece approaching, massaging his noticeable bigger dick in his hand, guiding it towards my mouth.

"You ready to let go and get turned out Cinnamon?" Reece asked taking the blunt, rubbing his dick across my chin.

"Yes." I moaned as Hop worked on building my second orgasm. I purred sucking Reece's big fat chocolate dick; while rubbing on Hops soft waves, licking and sucking circles between my legs.

"Damn that feels good girl." Reece complimented as I tried my best to swallow his unswallowable dick.

"She taste good too cuz." Hop whispered licking his lips coming up for air.

"Damn, stand up on the counter, I want to taste you too baby." Reece demanded pulling his dick from my mouth. I stood up on the counter barely catching my balance, noticing the liquor had kicked in. I stepped out of the T-bars and g string suspenders whipping the excess moisture onto the suspenders.

"-Nah don't wipe it off, let me taste you." Reese continued pulling my ass into his face sticking his tongue directly in my asshole.

"Ahh." I definitely wasn't expecting that and I damn sure wasn't going to stop him. The moans ripped out forceful as he intentionally ate my ass with delight. Hop lifted the bottle of absolute to my mouth and what I didn't drink spilled down my chest and stomach. He didn't seem to mind as he licked the drippings, climbing on the island so he could suck my pussy sitting sideways while his cousin ate my ass.

"Ooh, Ooh…" I moaned repeatedly my body and legs shaking from the forced orgasms; I've never felt this double oral sensation before. I mean I've been licked clit to booty before but never at the same damn time. I was seriously in my head reviewing some of the conversations we had about them financing me a huge ass house, where the three of us and my daughter would live as roommates & lovers. We'd have a couple extra bedrooms for the lady friends who were willing to take dates and work the webcam rooms. I opened my eyes as I orgasmed and the image of my baby dad crashed my fantasy. I know that shit wouldn't go down if he had anything to do with it.

"Come on baby." Hop said jumping off the island motioning for me to lie in his arms, while his big dick stuck straight out at me, begging me to jump on it. I lay in his arms as I watched Reece make another round of drinks and began to roll another blunt. This could be the life, I contemplated as Hop grabbed the bag containing the condoms and carried me into his bedroom. His black & gold triangle patterned bed set, curtains & decoration was manly and sophisticated. I really liked his style. He laid me atop the King Size Pillow-top on my back; licked and sucked my pussy as he fumbled with the plastic bag and the condom box.

I drifted into fantasy as he fiddled his dick into the condom, Heavy could continue to keep Arailya for his two weeks and when he would come to pick her up it would have to be during business hours while they were at work. I wanted to do it, I wanted to live it.

"Umm." I cried gripping his arms as he stuffed his hard curved dick slowly into my pussy.

"Ah baby, this, um, this juicy pussy is tight." He trembled, still very slowly stroking trying to fill me with all of his dick. I pulled him into me, slow thrusting my hips firmly into his pelvis as if my pussy could drink his dick. His size was just right not to big not too small. But just right, he was about a 8/3 where Reece was like a 6/4.5 his dick was wide and thick.

He kissed me passionately as we moaned together when he reached the bottom. My pussy danced like a parade on his dick, throbbing up and down as I thrust and twirled my pelvis and hips. I wanted him to touch all of me, feel everything.

"Baby let me take off this condom." He whispered in my ear before sucking & licking the top of my ear.

"No baby, you know I got love for you, but I love my life, & you are not mine." I flipped him over positioning myself to ride him, as I checked for the condom. I rode Hop like I loved him, like the dick was mine forever. I smelt the weed before I knew Reece was in the room. Blowing me a shot gun rubbing on his dick. He handed me the blunt after he ash'd it in his cup.

I blew Hop a shot gun and continued riding him in slow motion. I hit the blunt a few more times before giving it to Hop. I heard Reece Fumbling with the box of condoms right before he pushed my head down on Hops chest, lifted my butt up so Hops dick was standing straight up in my pussy and Reece once again was eating my ass, licking the back of my stretched pussy. I wondered if he was touching Hop's dick. I didn't care.

It felt so good him tongue fucking, licking my ass, I wanted his big dick, I wanted him deep and slow. My toes craved it, my hairs craved it. He climbed on the bed straddled squatting over me as I rubbed his dick from behind, checking the condom. He rubbed his dick against the back of my stuffed dripping pussy and now contracting asshole. He spit in his hand before rubbing it against my ass, after a few repositions he slowly, painfully, penetrated my ass. The burning sensation was temporary as he massaged my ass and rectum with his strong hands.

"Ooh, ooh ahh, oh my goodness ahh: I moaned, I cried-out in pain, pleasure and ecstasy. Hop fought to kiss me, Reece pulled my ponytail, gripping my neck with the other hand. I gasped, I moaned, I spilled my juices like never before. The juices kept churning inside of me, these orgasms that would stain my body's memory forever, a feeling like never again and never before, amazing!

Them grabbing, biting, kissing all over me, ravishing my flesh like animals, the thin line between love and hate must've been as thin as the lining between my pussy and my ass. Their dicks moved in unison, gliding inside me against one another. I came so hard; I thought my toe bones were going to break from being squeezed so hard together.

Hop came and not even 5 pumps later Reece was Cuming hard. I felt the explosion in the condom inside my ass; my wet Cumming ass.

Reece fell off me onto his back. I rolled off Hop to give my entire body a break I couldn't believe I came like that.

"I can't believe you were throwing your ass back like that, Cin." Reece huffed slapping me on my thigh.

"Man Cuz, her pussy good as fuck, I was trying so hard not to cum, when you came in, saved me from busting right then." We all laughed at my goodness, as I found myself thankful for having a child. I bet if I didn't have a daughter so early, with my sexual appetite and lack of giving a fuck, I would've made my own line of porn. I lay rubbing my stomach as Reece drew me a hot bath.

I had to shrink up whatever was left of my ass and pussy and call off work, tomorrow. I had enough money and I could enjoy my new furniture and move some of this and work to these niggas. Reece carried me to the tub; honestly I don't even know if my legs would've made it, had he not. He kissed me on the forehead as I planted my feet in the hot bubble bath.

"Can you roll me another fat one?"

"Yes your highness." He winked smiling then blowing me kisses. That tickled my fancy and he knew it. I am that bitch that queen bitch, gangster, hustler, diva, porn star, consummate mother, ahh I am definitely the queen bitch.

"Girl I can't believe you." Aunt Lisa sat in utter disbelief.

"Sometimes I can't believe myself."

~§~§~§~§~§~§~

I started my period the day we were leaving Atlantic City and my flow was super heavy. I put on my blue jogging suite with my grey t-shirt and my blue and grey Nike air max. I brought a neck pillow and an "I love Atlantic City" Pillow, to help on the ride home. I was too threw; The running through the entire hotel playing Super Soaker War, Trips walking up down the board walk, swimming, gambling, the mid tissue massages, shopping, shows, I was done I was ready to sleep for two days.

We smoked the last blunt at our first rest stop in Pennsylvania. I let my Aunt's friend hit the blunt, I didn't know she smoked. I knew she was the Aunt to Nish, Raily's daddy & the hoods side bitch and she was the sister to Big's side chick. I didn't give a fuck, that chapter was over anyways. The sick part is Tasha new all the stories and used that as fuel as to say that she was no-longer messing with big, that girl was always smart.

Dan kept paging me so I called him from the payphone.

"Hey baby it's me how are you." I said as soon as he answered the phone.

"I'm better now that I hear your voice, I was thinking about you and how you made love to me on that shopping trip." I moved the receiver so he couldn't hear the long sigh of frustration that willingly escaped my mouth.

"Yea I was thinking about you too, I'm not feeling so well baby, I got my period this morning and I just want to go home from the bus stop."

"I'm still coming to pick you up from the bus stop, right honey?" He questioned with a demanding undertone.

"Yea sure."

The driver was hauling ass through those mountains. We arrived to the bus stop at 11:45pm as planned. Dan was standing in front of his truck looking thirsty as ever.

"Ugh." I sighed to myself, I just want to get home, pop some Motrin and go to bed. He was at the luggage pit before the bus even came to a complete stop.

"Hi Honey!" He smiled and for the life of me I didn't know why I didn't like this trick, I mean he was nice per say and he made it clear to everyone that he would do anything for me. He told my mother that he was going to marry me one day.

"I know that's right honey, you better make her a member of the bar association." My mother replied causing me and my cousins to crack up.

"What's the Bar Association?" He questioned smiling waiting for the bus to arrive.

"You know the Bar B.A.R the Big Ass Ring association." They laughed at the joke, while I laughed at the expression on his face, priceless. The ride to the waffle house was quiet as we listened to Jazz.

I didn't want to entertain him because I asked and demanded to go home, instead and like for the most part he was in control in the driver's seat.

"So what do you think about being with me?" He turned facing me in the red leather Waffle House booth seat.

"I don't." I replied matter of fact.

"What do you mean you don't, you don't what?"

"I don't think about being with you Dan. I don't think about being with anyone. I think about saving enough money, and relocating to California and going to school there, that's all I think about."

"Baby you know peoples paths in life change; I know you said you lost your scholarship, maybe that's because you were supposed to go to school here. Maybe you'll meet your husband and start a family here."

"Maybe, I'm going to the restroom." I dropped the conversation and proceeded to the restroom. These cramps were so strong I could literally throw-up. My period was the worst. I passed so many blood-clots I wondered if I would have any blood left. After a good five minutes in the bathroom, I made up my mind, I was going to demand him to take me home, or call a cab to retrieve me and my things from the waffle house. I didn't feel good at all, and I didn't want to be bothered with him.

I sat to my order, Orange Juice, Grits, Toast, Two Waffles and Bacon. I didn't have the appetite for any of this shit; I was just forced to spend his money.

"Can I get a To-Go Box please? Thank You." I signaled to the waitress.

"Baby you need to eat something, here drink your OJ." He smiled pushing the glass up to my lips. I grabbed the orange juice and gulped it down. I always loved citrus fruit. I picked at the grits, while I loaded the rest of the food into the containers. Slowly I couldn't lift my spoon to my mouth; I turned to look at Dan who was smiling looking directly at me, it looked like his face dropped to his lap. I tried to open my mouth but I couldn't talk. I wanted to tell him it felt like it took me ten seconds to turn my head.

"Come on Honey, you are getting very sleepy."

§O§

§~Chapter 13~§
D.A.N
Dumb Ass Nigga

"Where am I? Am I still in Atlantic City? What Happened to me last night? What the fuck?"

"Hello!" I screamed standing to my feet on this bright pink carpet. I spent myself into a frenzy looking around in this huge white living room with only an oversized white loveseat. The panic set in as I felt the tears well up in my eyes. A silver sword, mounted on the wall was my salvation. I grabbed the sword and opened it, and to my surprise it was real and sharp. I looked around at this kitchen I've never seen before, the kitchen had two entrances one from the living room and the second from the Hallway.

A flash of Dan carrying me into this house penetrated my memory, along with a sharp pain out of nowhere. Am I dreaming? I remember seeing the stars clear as when I was a child in the fields laying watching them. The chill bumps on my arms were real. The sound of my hello's to no- response, resonating in my ears were real. I was not asleep. I couldn't explain, another flash like headache brought a memory of me lying on the pink carpet, fire to my left, slowly turning my head to see Dan rising smiling at me, a face full of smeared blood.

"That was real!" I screamed to myself as I ran back in the living room seeing what I imagined was a gas or electric fire place. How did I get here, I did not want to come to his; wait he told me he had an apartment in Dublin, whose house is this? I took the other exit from the living room leading to a sitting room to my left, a set of stairs and a dining room leading to more rooms to my right.

I had to get out of here, it was too many doors and I didn't want to find out what they led to. I ran out the front door, sword in hand and paused in my tracks.

Where the fuck am I? I surveyed the beautifully manicured lawns, with differing huge houses, looking like they started from Two Hundred Fifty Thousand and up. Mercedes & Lexus Coupes lined their driveways. I definitely was not in Columbus. I ran to the end of the block, the street signs read Dark Star & Venetian Way. So I'm on Venetian Way, wherever the fuck I am.

I took off back down the hill to the house, 1065 was the address carved into the concrete. 1065 Venetian Way. I felt a-little better just knowing that much, where were my clothes, my pads.

"Ahh!" The scream ripped out of my mouth as I walked back into this huge empty house. I decided to leave the door open as I searched for a phone. After about 5 minutes, mounted on the wall, what looked like a black square box was actually a cordless phone. I fumbled with the receiver before removing it from the base. I dialed my phone number at home. My caller Id should be able to pick up the number and I could grow from there.

"Hello?"

"Janice this is CJ, did the number show up on the caller id?"

"No it's an unknown number, where are you I thought you were coming back last night, Rita has been calling wanting to talk to you about Arailya."

"Girl all I remember is Dan picking me up from the bus stop, taking me to the Waffle House and me waking up on the floor here."

"Where the fuck are you?"

"I don't know J!" I screamed into the phone, that was it, I couldn't hold back the tears nor the fit that came with it.

"If anything happens to me and I don't make it home tell the police, Dan the body shop guy picked me up, took me to the Waffle House and I'm at 1065 Venetian Way. I'm about to call the police.

"Yea girl hurry, up that sneaky, creepy, smiling motherfucker done kid napped your ass girl. I told you to quit fucking with that white devil." I really didn't need that; I abruptly hung up the phone on her; before I could dial 9-1-1 the phone ring.

"I thought you said the number didn't show up?" I questioned pushing the talk button.

"Hey baby, it's me, I see you found the phone."

"Are you crazy motherfucker, I called Janice and now I'm calling the police, am I in Dublin, where did you take me?!" I began screaming at this bastard who I could feel smiling through the phone.

"No, no, no baby calm down, don't call the police, what are you going to say to them?"

"I'm going to say this white man picked me up last night, I asked him repeatedly to take me home from the bus station, instead he took me to the Waffle House, and then I woke up at 1065 Venetian Way!"

"-Honey don't call the police, I'm 15 minutes away, I will take you home, please don't call the police." I hung up on him and called Janice.

"Girl this motherfucker says he's 15minutes away and not to call the police, I have this sword I got off the wall this motherfucker is going to take me home or its going to be a blood bath."

"Girl just call the fucking police!" She reiterated "Fuck what he talking about, Fuck his life."

I hung up the phone with her and thought for a minute. This bastard still has my car, I really need my car. I actually need to get my license while I'm bullshitting. I got to get the fuck out of here and I've got to get my car back.

I sat biting my nails on the front step of the house. How was I going to handle this? He pulled into the drive way on two wheels. Jumping out of the truck with his hands extended.

"Honey I didn't mean to upset you." He rushed towards me. I jumped to my feet still clutching the sword pushed past him and jumped in the truck. Inside I found my luggage along with my purse.

"Bitch you, you sick bitch you took my purse and I'm on my period!" I screamed not caring if any of the wealthy neighbors where privy to my kidnapping.

"Take me home." I yelled as he came back from locking his front door. I placed the sword in-between my seat and the door as I fumbled through my purse for my Newport's. Hands shaking while I'm trying to flick the lighter, I inhaled the first puff as hard as I could, watching him watching me, slowly making his way to the driver seat.

"Baby"- He began.

"Baby my ass Dan, your ass is going to take me home, I will come and get my car tomorrow, me and the whole fucking hood if need be and you are going to leave me the fuck alone period." I inhaled again pushing the button to roll down my window.

"Honey you know I don't like cigarette smoke."

I whipped my neck at him like the exorcist; I couldn't believe this bastard had the nerve to open his mouth with a request.

"I don't give a fuck what you like Danny, I don't like to be taken against my will, I don't like for a motherfucker to leave me on a floor in some house I've never been too. And how the fuck did I get there? I don't like that you've had my car over a damn month if you couldn't fix it you should have said so!" My anger was provoking me to smash my burning cigarette in his face, but my need to get to safety was much stronger.

"Yea honey I wanted to talk to you about the car, it was really a piece of shit, I got a surprise for you at the shop, maybe when you calm down, you can come talk to me rationally at the shop." His snide remark with his matching smile made me want to slap him. Hard!

I sat quietly smoking my cigarette playing out different scenarios in my head. As we pulled into the parking lot of my townhouse Janice came out the door. I pressed the unlock button clutching my purse and his sword as his gaze was fixated on Janice. I went to the back of the truck opened it and began dragging my luggage out. J grabbed the biggest dragger as I placed the smaller one on top of it, and the new one I purchased to hall all the new shit I brought while I was there.

"Honey let me help you with that, you shouldn't be lifting heavy things for a while, you might want to take the next couple days off work and then come see the surprise I got you at the shop." I took a deep breath and slapped the shit out of him. The force spent him halfway around and the shock on his face was still not enough payment, for how I felt this morning.

"Get the Fuck outta my face and stay there!" I screamed dropping his sword on his feet before rushing into my apartment slamming the door.

"I rolled you a blunt, it's on the end table, C." Janice said looking at Dan through the curtains.

I swore I was never going to see that fucking creep after I got my car back. I wasn't going to answer or respond to his bullshit. I just wanted to know when my car would be fixed and how much it was going to cost me.

~§~§~§~§~§~§~

He persistently called my phone, all morning since 9 o'clock. I felt like calling the police. It wasn't that much weed hangover in the world. My Aunt Lisa, Weezy and I blew through an ounce of Dro like it wasn't nothing; blowing them Louisville-Slugger Swisher Sweets. I wrapped the ounce real tight and placed it in my luggage, which I was praying didn't stink up what was supposed to be a make-up case. I had a quarter in my purse that I was going to wrap up in something at the next rest-stop. I stayed away from my Gan-Gan who kept asking "Do Yawl smell that, it smells like pine cones on fire." I knew she knew it was us smelling like Pine Cones on fire. We blew through that entire ounce and quarter before the bus ride home.

Still it wasn't enough to have me completely knocked out. I went over the scenario over and over in my head. How did I end up on his floor? Did he change my pad? Was I dreaming of seeing blood all over his face and chest, that had to be a nightmare. No man would eat a woman's vagina on her period. It couldn't be, I didn't remember seeing blood on the floor beneath me when I awoke. I know there was a fire beside me in the dream and when I woke up I seen a gas fire place, it didn't look as if any wood had been burnt in it. What the fuck was wrong with me? He had to put something in my drink. I remember him giving me the orange juice after I came back from the bathroom.

About a month later and after a lot of convincing, I caught a cab and met Dan at his shop. He was adamant about him paying the cost for my vehicle. Sending Couriers and Telegram Services to my house and job; singing bearing notes saying please let me see you again. I started looking into a lawyer after he told me he sold my car to Jake. How the fuck was he able to sell my car? I started to feel sick this week, so I didn't go to work at all.

I don't know if this creep and my car situation we stressing me out or if my body was just tired of working, I don't know how my body was tired, it hadn't been a full month and a-half ago since I came back from vacation? All I know was I didn't have the energy to keep up with Raily and Janice's daughter while she was in school in the mornings.

~§~§~§~§~§~§~

As I pulled up in the cab, I noticed he had another Land Cruiser the same year, color and model as his parked in-front of the doors.

"Come and pay the cab man!" I yelled into the customer service lobby of the building. He paid the cab turned to hug me as if shit was sweet.

"Hey baby I missed you." He tried hugging me again.

"Dan get your fucking hands off me. I pushed at his attempts. I don't feel good and I just want the money for my car." I shifted from side to side in my Nike Airmax.

"Money?" He laughed "Here baby, I got this for you." He said opening the door to the 2nd Land-Cruiser.

"What?" I questioned dumb founded.

"Yes baby I know you're mad at me, you have your reasons, but I still love you. (Love? This motherfucker is crazy!)

"I still intend on making you my wife. I'm going to let you drive the truck this weekend, but Monday Jake is going to take you to go get your license. I've put you on my insurance so if you get pulled over you won't be fined as much."

How did he know I didn't have a license? I didn't care, I was about to go floss this truck to my home girls.

"Is this my truck? Is my name on the title?"

"It will be after you get your license. Come back up here at eleven tomorrow, I want to take you somewhere. It's an appointment already scheduled so don't be late."

"Tomorrow at eleven." I kissed him and slammed the door; I smiled at the brand new collection of TuPac CD's sitting on the passenger seat. I grabbed the All Eyes on Me CD and played Run the Streets as I pulled through the fence. I took the right onto Agler Rd and the left on Sunbury; I was about to hit the hood. I opened up the ashtray to ten crisp one hundred dollar bills.

"You're welcome." I laughed.

I pulled up on Tee who was standing in-front of Ms. Wilson's house.

"Come on girl let's go!" I smiled waiving to her as the window rolled down.

"Hell no, this you C?"

"Yep, just got it; not even an hour ago." Rolling down all the windows and opening the sun roof.

"Here let's blaze." Throwing the pre-rolled & lighter to her; I dug in my purse and grabbed my Mac Lip Gloss applied it then passed it to her.

"We got to be shining when we ride down on these niggas." I smiled, geeked about my quick little come up. I went down Shoemaker and turned left on Sidney, I started blasting Tupac's: You Can't See Me as an added bonus to this stunt session, I was about to pull on Heavy who I seen sitting at the end of the block with all his niggas.

Tee looked at me and smiled as we recognized both our niggas at their favorite little stoop high-signing. Niggas can't see me!

"What up lil nigga," I said pulling up beside Heavy's turned back.

"Oh so the white boy let you drive his truck today hun?" He laughed hitting Bishop in the shoulder for back up.

"No nigga you see the thirty day tags, he brought me a matching truck." I smiled blowing the smoke in his face.

"Ay let me hit that Star and quit playing." I passed him the blunt as he made mockery about hitting my pussy from the back. I signaled to Tee to light the other blunt.

"Nigga please you better enjoy hitting that blunt, you know I don't fuck with you like that no more." I said dramatically ashing the freshly lit blunt out the window.

"Man that white boy got you tripping Star."

"Nah baby you got me tripping, & that's why I don't fuck with you. Keep the blunt, I'm good on where your lips been." Me and Tee both laughed as her baby daddy came beside the truck.

"Let me hit that nigga." Ray-Ray walked up reaching at Hev's Blunt. "Keep it!" I insisted

"Since you big balling little nigga let me hold something." Hev's sarcasm was thick and as forced as the fake grin he was wearing for his homies. That nigga was tight, I don't care how hard he was smiling.

"Ain't you still holding my furniture, oh I forgot you took my shit to your other baby's mother's. But I got you." I said throwing him about thirty singles.

"Have a stripper tip." I winked at his furious face, while Ray & Bishop bent down to pick up the ones. Heavy snatched the blunt from Ray screaming!

"Fuck You Star!" I mashed out on the nigga, throwing my Pitch up as I hit the corner of Sidney & Leona, today was a good day.

~§~§~§~§~§~§~

I met Dan at the shop at eleven sharp. I hoped in his truck as he was already inside waiting.

"I got you this salad." He insisted.

"Thanks, I could eat anyway, all the time I had the munchies. So where are we going, you know I still don't trust your ass."

"Honey you got to get over that shit if we're ever going to move forward. And before you start, I'm taking you to see my doctor."

"To see your doctor; for what?" I was instantly terrified.

"Just to make sure were both healthy, if you're going to be my wife, I'd like to make love to you without a condom."

-"Ok that shit was cute in the beginning but not now, I don't even like you. Let alone hold any concern about being your wife, I feel violated by you, kidnapped motherfucker. It's not like you stood me up for a date, you took me against my wishes. Then you sold my fucking car, the fuck you mean your wife."

"OK let's not talk about that, I see that upsets you." We pulled up to the doctor's office on Johnstown Rd. I decided to go along with the program until I got my license and title Monday. I could deal with this bastard for a few more days. We were there giving various blood and urine samples when the Doctor came in the door and congratulated us for having a clean bill of health, He told Dan that he had something equivalent to a yeast infection and he told me that I was pregnant.

"Pregnant? Did you say I was Pregnant?"

"Yes ma'am." He replied snatching his jacket sleeve from my grasp. I instantly started crying, before darting out the door, running to Dan's truck. I cried all the way to the steak house and then back to the body shop. He smiled quietly the whole time, like he knew all along.

~§~§~§~§~§~§~

It wasn't easy at all being with Dan, but it was easy to get infatuated, engulfed, and entangled with the lifestyle of plenty. Legally hustling and even when you wrong the customer the police was still on your side because you were the business owner and the dispute immediately becomes a civil matter. Staying with this pervert easily made since when there were Bills to break, lawyers to pay, and he really was a decent size trick.

I called off the wedding after all the money that was invested into it. I cut up the $1100 wedding dress that sat in the basement after he cursed my grandmother out. I was looking for any excuse to get away from him. I found out, he got his fortune from murdering his father. He did juvenile time then received the insurance benefits after being released from prison. If he could kill his father, he could damn sure kill me, was a constant thought traipsing my mind.

My heart couldn't stand this bitch, thou. I couldn't believe he got me pregnant, niggas are vicious. I was beyond tired of paying rent in Colonial Village and the neighbors repeatedly breaking into my house. I moved my home girl Janice and her baby girl in to watch over my house. But the watchers knew when she came and went too. She couldn't afford to keep up the rent payments so she moved to the Short North. I let the two bedroom townhouse go.

Colonial Village's Janky establishment charged the $3,000 plus left on the lease regardless of my three police reports. I was still pissed with my sister Michelle for laying on the floor while Hev & Big and whatever other nigga took my furniture. His spiteful ass moved it to his second baby's mother's house, like I wouldn't find out. I was upstairs knocked the fuck out recouping from working all night at the club and the bachelor party that didn't end until 4am.

All was well that ended well after the second break-in I got rental insurance. I received a check for five and a half bands. What didn't go to weed or legal cost went to the bank. Michelle as of recently has been super shady. Not only did she let the niggas rob me without telling me. She decided not to move with me at all. She decided living with the white girls was a better decision than living with her sister after all the wasted hours talking about it. The funny part is a couple years later she moved to Colonial Village with her dude. Your family be the biggest hating bitches, don't they; hilarious.

It was easy to leave that behind, and deal with Dan's bullshit. It was easy to fall into another abusive relationship at-least I could finally take a break from hustling & working so hard. Besides this bastard went through such extremes to entrap me, I felt it was my duty to make this motherfucker pay for stealing my freedom. Yea, it was easy in the beginning until the mood changed~.

The truck started having issues, which I really believe was Dan fucking with it trying to force me to stay in the house pumping out flyers and coupons. I really hated that I introduced the idea, but I was happy about the amount of business it was bringing. I refused to feel enslaved, especially by this Wing Tipped Cowboy I raised so much hell about being immobile that he got me this white 1998 GT Pontiac. I promised Tierra that I would take her to her interview off Fifth Avenue. We were geeked she got the job; we were on our way back to the hood.

-Bam! Out of nowhere this huge old-school car runs the stop sign and hits us so hard on the driver's side that we spent around in the street, hit the light pole, then spent until stopping diagonal in the middle of the street. The impact of the collision was so hard that it vacuum sealed all the doors shut, and the electrical system in the car collapsed. We were forced to climb out of the cracked windows to safety.

I awoke with the Paramedic placing my neck in a brace, pulling the gurney down to the ground beside me. The pain in my head caused my vision to dance back & fourth between blindness and distorted tunnel vision. The impact caused me to hit my head several times creating temporary memory lost. I heard Tierra's familiar voice as she told the Medics my name was Cernitha Jean I was 18 years old and three months pregnant.

"Pregnant! I'm pregnant?" Was the last thing I remember saying before awaking at OSU East Hospital.

"No she's coming home with us! The doctors said she suffered multiple concussions and contusions and she needs to be under extreme two hour watch for the next 72 hours. And you're going to be glued to that shop, and we ain't coming way to Gahanna to care for her, she's staying with us."

"Ms. Marlene that is my wife laying there pregnant with my unborn child." Dan retorted.

"She's not your wife yet motherfucker and when you came in here the first thing you asked about was the car, we know where your priorities lie and it's not with my daughter." My mom was angry; I wondered why they were arguing. The look on all their faces as they walked back through the curtains was one of sheer relief.

"She's woke!" My mom yelled rushing to my side.
"Baby you were injured pretty bad; you sustained a lot of trauma to the head. We're taking you home with us. You need to be awakened every two hours, for the next seventy two hours; to help prevent you from slipping into a coma. Do you want to go home with me?" She looked at me then back at Dan.

"Uh yes ma'am." Was my only answer. Coma? Where was T & what the fuck was really going on?

This transition to my parent's house turned out to be a blessing in disguise. Things were already unbearable with Dan, I already Edward Scissor- Hands the $1100 wedding dress that I got on sale for $900 and hung the shreds in the basement. Truthfully I was unhappy with him and my heart could only take so much. I was 18 years old and 3 months pregnant with our Son, my second child and his third child by his third baby mother. During my pregnancy I found out a lot of hidden information about Dan. First thing was his other Black baby mother, whose son was only a few months old when Dan impregnated me. I also found out that he wasn't the manager of the body shop and he didn't have an apartment in Dublin. He was the Owner of the body shop and was the owner of the house that I awoke in on the floor.

He was also not 27 but 32 and the vilest of them all was he was all of a sudden being threatened with molestation allegations from his exes who he swore were plotting against him. That was for sure the icing on the cake until the day I got the yellow envelope package in the mail. Telling me that he murdered his father when he was 15 and spent the rest of his youth incarcerated until the age of 21 when he was released and given the insurance money that he was listed as the sole beneficiary.

Dislike turned to fear, and fear to hate, so moving back in with my parents, my siblings and again my sister Michelle was a welcomed distraction. During my pregnancy I gave Dan a total of 7 threesomes. I didn't want to touch him nor could I stand the sight of him, but my so-called friends were more than willing and ready. Some of them I paid some of them I didn't. Some snuck behind my back to get peanuts on the dollar. I grew tired of going to bed beside him, awaking to him talking to me about having a three some.

I put off selling drugs until after I had the baby. So I sat patiently on the money I had. Arailya seemed to love her new Queen Size bedroom and the common shopping sprees when I was depressed. I was trying to enjoy being pregnant with the father around catering to my every need, but I couldn't stand him.

Around my 5/6th month of pregnancy Heavy and I started bonding again. I helped him as much as I could with Big's case. Tasha turned shady on me as she was suckered into believing that I told the FBI or Crime Stoppers that she was on the run with Big in Florida. I never even knew the chick left town, so how could I tell anything. She always took the bait. But I had my own fish to fry rather than being hung up on some lie that had her panties in a bunch.

Heavy & I plotted on robbing Dan and moving down to Florida together. To let him tell it, shit done got cold in the streets after the body count start piling up, and it would be best for him to go set up shop elsewhere. So he could continue to feed the family and finance Big's Lawyer Fees.

~§~§~§~§~§~§~

I pulled up to Rika's house big and pregnant. I wanted to share with her the scheme we were masterminding to come up off Dan and for Heavy to raise the son I was pregnant with as his own. I told her that I would raise his other two children and we'd just be one happy family.

"Bitch I don't know if you've lost your mind while being pregnant, but what would make you want to rob Dan and go hustling cross country with this nigga?" Her question ran through my mind repeatedly as I called Heavy's cell phone and blew his pager for the hundredth time.

I was getting impatient. I was just going to ride down on his ass. I know he's right down the street in the hood. I grew impatient thinking about it as I remembered the last time I rode down on him, my daughter and his trap chicks daughter was hanging out of the second story window that didn't have a screen. He was all kinds of motherfuckers that day, and his yamp was every hoe bitch in the book.

I couldn't put my hand on it but something was really wrong, why would he be ignoring me knowing that we are supposed to be meeting right now? As I turned left from Cleveland Avenue onto Leona my heart dropped into my stomach. A school bus was taped off by the caution tape and I knew someone was dead. The car stuck behind the bus that wasn't moving was honking at me to go in reverse. I wasn't going anywhere I had to see whose body that was on the ground. As I got out the car crossing to the other side of the street the police began to flash me back to my car. I nearly fell to my knees as I seen a large black man's body lying on the ground.

Channel Six news reporters pulled on the scene as always, and decided to hit Camden go around and come up Leona from the other direction. I stopped at Momma Rita's house looking for answers but no one answered the door. The police wasn't letting any traffic through nor were they answering any of my questions.

"Oh my God, where is Arailya, where is my daughter? She was with her father; oh my God I hope nothing has happened!" My racing mind was driving me expeditiously towards insanity; I drove up Cleveland

227

Ave into the Terrace at-least 60 miles per hour. I pulled up to Rika's house frantic I couldn't control my emotions. My mind was moving faster than my reflexes I opened the truck door before putting the car in park; I tried to pull the keys from the ignition before putting truck in park.

I was pissing myself off. So I screamed at the top of my lungs: "RIKA!" Hopefully she would hear me in front of her house and come help me. I kept screaming her name kept crying.

"Calm down girl, please calm down tell me what happed!" She shouted at me, pulling me out of the whip.

"Oh my God, oh my God, I think my baby daddy is dead, I think Heavy is dead I seen a big guy on the ground the police wouldn't let me through they said they were going to arrest me if I kept going past the barricades, both Trap Houses are roped off, someone got killed over there. Mom's not answering the phone to tell me what is happening. The news was asking me what happened. I don't know what happened, what happened to my ooh haaaaa…

"Where is Heavy? God please send me some answers!" My head was spinning, spinning as fast as my thoughts could take me.

"I knew this crazy nigga was going to get his self-killed, oh my God!" I screamed. Dan called my phone about an hour into Rika trying to calm me down and find out what was going on.

"Honey did you see the news? It says the police is looking for your baby Daddy and his friend. Said they killed this guy in your old neighborhood, I'm in the office watching it right now."

I jumped up ran to Rika's remote and turned her big screen to channel six. Sure enough, Heavy & Eddie Kane was wanted for the murder of Kalif Vaughn. Rika and I looked at each other in disbelief as my cell wrung again.

"Hey sorry about that Honey, the call dropped, I want you to go home, I don't know where you're at but I want you to go home, I don't want you around that nothing ass nigga, he might try to use you as a hostage now that you're attached to money."

"Are you stupid motherfucker?" I screamed into the phone before hanging up. The phone rang again, I was just going to cuss him out until my heart's desire.

"Listen Motherfucker!" I began until I heard Heavy's crying voice on the other end of the phone.

"Oh my God, Heavy where are you at, what happened baby, why?" I cried into the receiver.

"Listen Ma, I need you to go to the payphone. You know when ever shit gets hot, the police come at you. I just bodied the nigga, I didn't mean too I should have met with you ma." He began crying.

"I want you to call Knights Inn on 161 and ask for room 113, I'm shook I don't even want to talk on your phone. Star please bring me some weed something to drink and some food, I'm all fucked up in the game right now Ma, I fucked up. I need you to come through for me." The sound of his cries broke my heart.

After we hung up the phone I asked Rika to ride with me to the Liquor store, I still wasn't old enough to buy liquor, so she got him a box of Swishers a pint of Hennessey a pint of Remy and a bottle of Merlot for me. I hated red wine but I surely needed a buzz. I figured I was already six months pregnant and they say wine is good for you. I stopped at my cousins and grabbed an ounce of weed. Then headed to the Chinese Restaurant across from Northern Lights Shopping Center and damn near ordered the menu.

I called him from the payphone as he instructed, and told him I would be at the door in less than five minutes. I struggled to carry all the items as I fought back the tears. I knocked on the door with my foot, listening to the sounds of him scurrying to the peep hole.

"Its Star babe, I'm by myself." The tears streamlined as the idea of me being by myself took on a new more permanent meaning. I never cried so much in my life. We ate drank, smoked and cried. He cried as he kissed my oversized exposed belly. Sharing his wish to be the father of the son that I was carrying, he wished we had ended up like this. We watched the tear drops land on our variation of brown skin as the moon shined through the motel blinds. We asked God, countless times for forgiveness as he told me how the fatality unfolded.

He jumped up in rage screaming grasping at the air, as he knew he wouldn't be here to help Big fight his case.

"What about my children?" He yelled, pounding on his chest. I sat quietly rolling blunt after blunt slowly sipping my nasty wine.

"Why did the motherfucker keep pushing Star? They beat Mousey Lil Brother the fuck down, I told the nigga that they could catch the little nigga in his hood but they wasn't gone just keep beating the little nigga since he ran to me for help! Star the motherfucker wanted it with me, he pulled out his strap, the fuck I suppose to do besides let the heat ring at that nigga. You know I'm going on the run right Ma?" He asked me falling on his knees in front of me.

"I know babe, so what am I supposed to do now, I mean I'm going to need Dan's money to be able to funnel shit to you, I can't work right now, I'm high risk, I'm supposed to be on bed rest."

"Stop stressing." He demanded standing to his feet pulling me up beside him. "No matter what happens Star I love you, you are my first real love, you gave me my first child. I'm going to always hold you down Ma." We made love for what would be the last time before he left Columbus. I met up with him three weeks later in Cleveland, Ohio delivering him my love and our daughter for a visit and my last package. Upon my return as soon as I made it within the confines of 270's freeway my cell service restored and my phone went off none stop. My other baby daddy, along with my parents, the police and crime stoppers was looking for me. I didn't tell anyone but Rita his mother, where I was going and what I was doing because I didn't know who to trust.

Dan was so livid with my disappearance that he moved me into the condo that week. I'm sure he figured that he needed to keep me close. I allowed my daughter to go on the run with Heavy and his other baby mother Christine, during my last two months of pregnancy. I figured this would be the last time she spent time with her father as a free man.

§~ I Can't Believe Her ~§

I hated being at home with Dan, my oldest daughter was over her grandmothers and I was out with my baby visiting friends. My good friend Moe, Her sister and I were smoking blunts in her bedroom. We were having girl talk, you know: What good sex you had lately, whose dick you miss etc. So Moe's telling us of her dude shaving her pussy for her in the bathtub before he eats it.

So her sister says: "I don't like that nigga, it's cool he pampers your pussy and all that but he don't treat you right. Fuck these niggas they only good for sex. I told sis fuck these niggas I'll eat your pussy, you don't have to deal with these niggas." I instantly began chocking. I couldn't believe her blood sister offered to eat her pussy. My friend shrugged it off calling her sister stupid. Saying she wasn't into that Gay shit that their Aunt had her sister on. The conversation freaked me out and aroused my interest at the same time.

I began studying her sister as if I never seen her or cut school with her years before. I looked at her tightly pulled ponytail, her bright yellow skin, wide almond eyes studying me, and her pink tongue and lips she slowly licked while watching me stare at her. I wanted to ask her to eat my pussy, I didn't want to say it in-front of Moe. How do you ask your friend to eat your pussy? I didn't want to say it at all. I didn't know what to do so I decided to leave.

"It's been real, but I'm about to go yawl." I said standing to my feet; I threw the remainder of the twenty sac on Moe's bed.
"Thanks Sis." She smiled raising from her bed to come hug me. "Don't be a stranger I know you live way out there in no man's land in that big beautiful house with that devil looking white man." "Devil looking is right." I chimed in. "I won't I'll come through more often, girl I just been stacking planning my great escape."

"I feel it; she replied opening the door to her bedroom. I didn't know if I should hug her sister or give her dap, but she was standing there definitely anticipating some interaction.

"You nervous?" She asked as I grabbed my sons diaper bag.

"Nervous; about what?" I replied walking up to her face; flashing her my infamous go-to half-grin.

"Just wondering she smiled semi tilting her head. I was wondering if you could drop me and the girls off, if it's not out of your way?"

"Sure Boo, let's go." I replied walking out the bedroom door down the narrow hallway.

I wrapped DP up in the car seat. Helped her load her kids in the truck and we were off.

"You got some more trees CJ?" I looked at her almost amazed.

"Of course I do." I looked in the rear view mirror at her nodding, near sleeping children.

"Can I ask you a question Boo." I nervously uttered pulling into her apartment complex. "Would you consider eating my pussy?" She laughed at me as she opened the passenger door to my Champaign Gold 1999 Toyota Land Cruiser.

"Can you chill for a minute or you out?" I put the car in park and began to gather my son & luggage. I went back to the car to grab her youngest baby & laid her in the playpen in the Living-room. I put my son and his car seat in the room with her sleeping daughters, I never wanted weed around my babies.

I went down stairs and rolled up while she did whatever upstairs. I tried to think about what I would say when she came downstairs since she laughed off my question. I took deep long drags of the blunt, hoping for cloudy courage. Oh yea I remembered the vodka I had in my sons diaper bag. I was still too young to buy liquor so I had Dan keep our Bars at home stocked. I reached in the diaper bag and pulled out the Vodka, took it straight to the head no chaser.

"Ok You was holding out at Sis's house!" I laughed handing her the bottle of vodka.

"I actually forgot I put it in the diaper bag."
"Well I'm glad you remembered!" She took the bottle to the head chugging like a pro. Pria couldn't be any more than 2 years older than me but she damn sure lived way faster. I inhaled the blunt before exchanging it for the bottle. I sat back on the couch, rubbing my

sweating palms against my pants. She fell down on her knees, in-between my legs and began biting on my pussy.

I instantly bent over to grab the bottle sitting on the floor. She stood up laughing as I chugged for courage. I watched her nervous but excited as she turned on her stereo and off the living room lights. I began unbuckling my boots when she got back on her knees, moving my hand aside, unbuckled and removed my boots. I unsnapped my belt buckle and she grabbed my hands.

"No, Don't touch anything. Here but touch this and sit back, don't touch me until I ask you too…"

Oh this was stimulating; her submissive aggression was turning me on. I felt my clitoris throbbing as I inhaled the blunt, I rubbed my vagina back and forth against my jeans while she unfastened my belt. She partially straddled me as I blew her a shot gun. I felt myself relaxing, horny, wanting this to happen so badly. She fell back to her knees pulling my pants off. She moaned as if taking off my clothes was giving her an orgasm. She licked around the tip of my panties when I passed her the quickly burning blunt.

I took another swig of the Absolute shocked that we drunk over a half of bottle that fast.

"Do you have anything I can chase this with boo? This shit is starting to burn my chest."

"Hold on." She went to the kitchen and came back with two Capri Sun Pouches. We laughed, but didn't care.

"The kids are going to be mad tomorrow." She laughed punching the straw thru the pouch.

"Nah were going to get the babies some more juice." I took a big gulp of the vodka and sucked the pouch until it inflated.

"Sit back and be still." She whispered standing over me again. She pulled my panties off slowly as I glanced to see how wet the center of my panties were. "Boo got that pussy wet don't I?" She smiled pulling my legs closer to her, causing me to slump on the couch. "Um that's a pretty wet pussy CJ." She closed her eyes and began rubbing her chin in circles in the center of my pussy. Softly blowing underneath my clitoris, blowing and gasping, like she was inhaling my vagina. I wanted to touch her, grab her head and put her mouth on my clitoris. Instead I allowed myself to be taken by this sensation that was running through my entire body. Her chin felt good and her teasing me sporadically sticking her tongue out was driving me nuts.

She lifted up on her knees placing her entire mouth around the circumference of my pussy. Her mouth was hot, hungry and extra juicy. She licked and sucked my pussy like the best lollipop she ever tasted. Um, um, um she moaned sucking firm but softly on my clitoris causing my orgasm to explode. I had to touch her. I grabbed her head and she wrapped her arms around my thighs.

"Ooh Boo." I moaned holding both sides of her head, as I rode her face. Her mouth was ecstasy to my clitoris. I never felt a mouth so good. Ooh she sucked my pussy with precision. I couldn't stop coming. I felt my legs shaking as she moaned loudly into my squirting pussy.

"Oh, Oh My God." This girl was turning me out. I wanted to fuck her face real hard. She locked her right arm around my thigh, pulled the skin back over my clit and began sucking and spitting my clit in & out her mouth; genius book of world records fast.

"U, Uuh, Boo." I whined loud, spilling what felt like three orgasms in one onto her swirling chin.

"Ah Fuck!" I yelled as the stimulation was becoming so intense it was creating a pained pleasure in my stomach.

"Boo Stop." I begged trying to pull her head from my vagina.

"No baby, this pussy taste good, I got this pussy coming like a motherfucker! Umm." She wrapped her lips firmly around my clit. Pulled my legs further off the couch until my back was my only support. She folded my legs back exposing my shinning, dripping, wet, throbbing pussy. She held my legs back with her left hand, and began three finger' fucking me in my pussy while licking my ass.

"Ooh"! I screamed, I couldn't take the pleasure anymore but I didn't want her to stop, she didn't want to stop. She thrust her fingers deeply, slowly as all the nerve endings in my pussy exploded.

She pulled out her three fingers spreading them; admiring my slime web of cum. I grinded her hand hard, shaking, wanting her to touch me, dig in me again. She rubbed her drenched knuckles around my butthole before licking the residue.

"Yes baby, yes!" I wanted this feeling forever.

"Yesss… I hissed as she placed her thumb in my ass, her three fingers back into my vagina and her mouth around my clit.

"Mmmm." She hummed as she stroked her hand up and down in my ass and pussy.

"Uh I couldn't take it I forced myself to my feet holding my shirt up with my chin. I grabbed her tilted head and fucked her beautiful mouth & trained hand as hard, as fast as I could.

"Uh, Ah." I couldn't catch my breath I was coming so hard. "UH" I moaned snatching my pussy from her mouth. Shaking holding my shirt and stomach with my left hand; physically trying to grip my head to make the room stop spinning.

-Bam! Bam! Bam! The knock on her backdoor scared us both. I grabbed my pants panties and shoes and ran into her half bathroom.

"Hold On!" she yelled towards her kitchen, turning on the living room light.

"Oh Shit I think that's my baby dad." She said rushing into the bathroom with me to wash her hands and face.

I put my clothes on runway model fast. My heart was beating really fast, this adrenaline was about to make me pass out. I wiped my pussy repetitively with her paper towels; rushing to sit on the couch before she opened the door. I begin to roll another blunt appearing to be busy.

"Damn what took your ass so long?" Her baby dad yelled busting past her in the door. "It better not be no niggas in here."

"What it do Corkey?" I said to her wild-haired, fat, yellow, deadbeat ass baby daddy. "Shit my nigga, I ain't seen you in a grip." He leaned over giving me dap. I lit the blunt fast deciding to take a couple more puffs before walking the blunt into the kitchen to give it to Boo. I reached in my bra and gave her a one hundred dollar bill.

"Here I'm about to go; have Corkey take you to go get the Juice."

"You leaving?" She asked starring into her Refrigerator; I'm assuming gaining her composure.

"I'll help you with the baby's bag."

"Cool I replied taking the blunt from her, hitting it as I walked back into the living-room. I reluctantly gave the blunt to Corkey. I hated supplying a bum Nigga, with anything more than advice.

"You still live in that mansion with that white motherfucker?" Corkey's rude ass questioned as I brought my son & car seat down the steps.

"Is it 1999?" I asked like Duh.

"Of course it's 1999 what kind of dumb ass question is that?" I took my blunt really feeling my allergies to bitch niggas beginning to flare up, I grabbed my Coach Purse & diaper bag and concluded my conversation with that dunce with: Yea that Champaign Land Cruiser is 1999 too, fresh off the showroom. Maybe one-day Boo will bring you by we can have drinks at my bar."

I knew that wack ass nigga couldn't stand me. I couldn't stand that nigga or any nigga that was jealous of a woman that grind harder than them; Sucker-attack ass niggas. I changed my still sleeping son, on my lap in the kitchen as I listened to him lie to her. Niggas with nothing to offer a woman has plenty of criticism, gas-lighting, degrading, and facetious talk. They don't have anything of monetary value to give you so they devalue you. Their Mental, Emotional, and Verbal abuse is called Domestic Violence.

"Keep the L, on me.' I winked at him and headed to her back door. For the past year and a half I got use to niggas hating in a nicety way (that's nice + nasty). It became the new norm for me.

~§~§~§~§~§~§~

"Hey Babe!" I yelled for Dan as my son and I made our way into the laundry room from the garage. AC/DC's "Highway to Hell" was blaring through the house.

"This shit is nerve wrecking, I shrieked to myself as I carried the heavy car seat & matching coach diaper bag through the hallway and into the Den. I sat him on the oversized white couch that was the only remainder from any furnishings he shared with his ex or last baby momma should I say. He could keep it, I was taking everything else when I make my great escape. I watched him twirling, spinning into the office, from the bedroom with his imaginary electric guitar. His thinning long brown/blonde hair flying up and down against the bare, pale white bird chest he was so proud of; ugh and those black faded looking jeans that he literally had 50 pair of.

This fool has got to be on something, I thought as I watched him entranced in his imaginary rock & roll performance. Ooh, he restocked the wine rack in the hall, just what the Doctor ordered. Coping juice, I laughed to myself as he dropped to his knees, then on his back. "High Way to Hell!" Screaming from every direction; I felt like I was on a sure path to hell, dealing with this devil. We just installed surround sound speakers throughout the entire downstairs including the basement bar, my favorite room.

"Dan!" I screamed again, I wanted him to hopefully busy his self with the baby while I whisked off to wash baby-girls spit and my dried cum off my body. His horn dog ass finding me gummy was the last thing I needed.

He was already threatening to sell the condo I was staying in. For the life of me I couldn't understand why he went through such great lengths to catch me cheating when I told his ass I was going to get me some black dick as soon as I dropped his child. He must've thought I was playing. I was tired of the transmitters on my car and the clicks from the taps on my phone.

My body was mines again, and my escape Ohio plan was back in full effect. He tried his best to take me out of town every other weekend, so I made sure to run my Marijuana Business Monday-Thursday. We took trips everywhere I wanted to go. The more I resisted the more he spent which later became a habit fighting, him for checks. This new lifestyle was very lonely. The more material things I purchased the less my so-called friends liked me, called me etc. It got to the point where the bitches would only call when they wanted something.

It was cool with me, I survived birth alone and I'm going to die alone. Fuck um, they think they're going to use me, I'm going to put them bitches to work first and just like that Real Ass Entertainment was back in business. I found myself spending more time with Boo, I don't know if I was infatuated with her head game or if it was my want to help her out of her rut, but I made it my business to help her, we enrolled in school together, shopped together and hit stings on the niggas together.

She moved from the Projects to the Short North, where our friendship came to an end. I nearly got in a fist fight with her sorry ass baby daddy. This nigga in my face screaming that he was going to tell the whole hood I was fucking his bitch.

"You can't be satisfied you fucking the white motherfucker, but your hoe ass gotta come over here and fuck my baby mother!" He screamed in my face.

"First and foremost Nigga, I'm not fucking your children's mother you are, and if you want to tell the hood she my side chick then go the fuck on and make yourself look stupid, nigga be my guess. But don't be mad that I'm doing your job for my friend." I threw the blunt I was smoking on his feet and made my way out the door. Looking back I caught a glimpse of Boo's sad face and her thirsty, broke, slum ass, nigga picking up the blunt from the floor.

She called my name asking me not to leave. I chucked my deuces at her. Sorry I'm not fighting no nigga over his bitch. What the fuck I look like, Get the fuck outta here.

~§~§~§~§~§~§~

"I need you to put the baby in the house and come listen to this tape." He said to me as we pulled into his garage. I walked through the laundry room into the hall that lead to the den; I placed my son safely on the oversized white couch, looking at the skylights as the rain began to come down. I could not read the look on Dan's face as the light from inside the house shined into the dark garage where he was still sitting in the driver's seat. My lack of trust encouraged me to leave the laundry room door open, in case I had to make a run for it for whatever reason.

I leaped into the truck as he pressed play and the sound of static thing ringing filled the car.

"Hey Girl!" I heard the familiar voice say. "Hold on I got Marquis on the other line." Instantly I knew this was my four-way conversation with Rika, Twink & Marquis. Dan looked at me with his eyes full of tears as I got antsy.

"So we gone have a barbeque at your place, we all pitching in for the meat, we'll do the sides and they're going to do the liquor and trees." The conversation continued. I opened the door in the dark truck as he grabbed my left arm.
"Honey you would just cheat on me like that, after all that I've done for you?" He squeezed my arm tight as his tears began to freefall.

"Are you crazy Dan? I gave you countless threesomes, and you still hit on bitches behind my back, now you want to cry, are you fucking serious? Motherfucker you tapped my phones, you cheated first, you can't control yourself." I hopped out the car and ran as fast as I could thru the garage and into the house where I felt safe around the weaponry. He came flying in behind me.

"I had a private investigator following you around and I got a transmitter put on your car, I know you was fucking around with that nigga, I know you went out of town, while you were pregnant with my mother fucking son, and you slept with that sorry ass drug dealing, death sentence motherfucker." As he raced up to me in anger the only thing I knew to do was swing. I hit him as hard as I could in his face before he leaped to attack me causing me to fall on the couch beside our now crying son. We fought for a good ten minutes before my distraction with my crying child caused him to pin me down.

"I'm not letting you go, you belong to me, you're my fucking baby's mother, and you still want to run after that sorry nigga that treated you like shit! I buy your rotten spoiled ass everything you want! You wanted a pool, you want new this I'm paying for your mommas shit! We're not breaking up! I'm selling the condo you have to move back here with me and be a fucking family! That nigga is going to get caught soon and you're not going to be with him when he does, you're going to be with me!" He shouted tightening his grip.

"I'm not playing with you CJ either you leave that nigga alone and come home and marry me or I'm going to tell the police where they can find him."

I couldn't swallow that shit, this life was becoming more than I could handle. I turned off my emotions and reverted to Cinnamon's game: In a soft voice I whispered to him.

"Baby calm down, I'm sorry, you've done so much to get me I understand baby, I'm confused honey let's take a trip this weekend, let's go somewhere to get our minds off all this drama. Do you want to go baby?" I whimpered as he began to kiss me. Any time he felt threatened he took me out of town, this time we went to Manhattan New York.

~§~§~§~§~§~§~

My cell phone rang. Who the fuck is that? I thought. No one knows I'm back in Columbus. I hope it's not Aunty Darlene. I wasn't ready to go pick the kids up. Besides I paid her to keep them until Tuesday. It was Sunday and we came on the redeye this morning. Dan had enraged ass customers, threatening him as usual. If they didn't get their car today they were going to call the Better Business Bureau, Six on Your Side, the police, file a civil report. I mean the threats never stopped. So he was dressed and at the shop by eight. The ringing stopped as I decided not to answer the unfamiliar number.

I laid back down in my oversized coal black throne, poster board, Queen-sized bed. I love Columbus in May; the weather is perfect the birds are singing. I listened to the sounds of nature, coming through my opened bedroom window, as I closed my eyes to relax into my sleep. "That's my bitch, that's my bitch, that's my bitch, that's my bitch. The sound of my best-friends Birds or Fall's ringtone repeated through my cell phone. We were all drunk one night at my studio session and started a: that's my bitch cipher. I had my engineer make it into a Ringtone; so whenever either three of us call one another "That's My Bitch plays.

"Wake yo lazy shopping ass up bitch!" Bird's drunk ass screamed through my cell phone.

"If I was sleep I'm up now bitch! What's cracking? It's not even 12 o'clock and you sound lit already." I sat up and adjusted my pillows behind me.

"You have no fucking idea doe, it went down last night, and you missed some major bread." She sounded very rushed and excited.

"Word?" I questioned her, excited to hear about the get down.

"Word bitch! These two Jamaican Niggas came in with a sexy faded nigga and a white nigga, dropping major bands. Somebody had just copped them a few keys or the whole fucking piano because them niggas was happy and generous bitch."

"Yawl moonlight with them niggas?" I asked already knowing the answer.

"Bitch you know we left the club, hit the waffle house on South High?"

-"Why the fuck yawl go way to south high's waffle house?" I interjected as I decided to get up and grab me a square. I had a feeling she was going to be awhile. I opened the double bedroom doors, off the office. I admired the shining hardwood floor silently wishing it was my house alone. I opened the back door, walked off the patio and into the pool. The heated water was still a little cool as it raced up my crack while I positioned myself on the oversized pink & clear floater. I listened to Bird scream at Shawn about not drinking all her bottle.

"This nigga rude as fuck." She said returning her attention back to our conversation.

"Oh yea these niggas had suites at the Westin Bitch. I'm talking about balling out not these lil five six hundred dollar baller's either. Sis I missed your ass so much last night I wish you was there. I made thirty two hundred and the nigga gave me like two quarters of some pure bitch. We linking up with them tonight, bitch I wish you were coming back today." Bird began to whine, like she was really saddened by my absence. I laughed, pushing my foot against the rim of the pool to add motion to my floater.

"Awe you miss me T.T? I mocked. Well bitch your wish is my command."

"For real, you gone come back early? I saved you one, I know you will like him. His name is Saga. He let Sex suck his dick, sprayed off all on her face and went to sleep. She cab'd it home."

"Ughh he was fucking with that white bitch?"

"Whatever Cinnamon, she igged me. Back to the real shit; you gone fly in today for-real?"

"Bitch bye, I'm already here."

"What! She shouted. Damn you made me spill my drink." I laughed so hard causing myself to choke on the remaining cigarette smoke.

"I thought you were coming back Monday?"

"Yea that was the plan so we could finally hit a club in NY but he ran to work as usual."

"Man fuck him and the drama he bring check it, Shawn bout to take me out west so I can pick my car up bitch, Zim Zima Candi bout to get back her beamer." We both laughed in unison at her break out song.

"I'm happy for you bitch, glad your bread up." I told her as I flicked my cigarette butt into the grass.

"You in the pool bitch?" She asked.

"How'd you know?"

"I can hear the water swishing in the back ground. Swish, swish ah ha ha... that's how my pussy was sounding last night when that nigga dropped me fifteen hundred to make it clap on his pole. So a bitch bout to go pay this shop and get my car back. Get the Kids layaway out- girl these mutha fuckas raped me like two hundred dollars extra in storage." Damn I thought about the irony, we be killing our customers in storage fees at the body shop. Storage fees and lapsed insurance policies was the main reason I got all those cars to flip.

"Aiight so it's on. They want a show tonight. We're linking up at 7."

"Dinner: at Game Works in Easton which is by us both. They got Limo Service! You better fucking come C.J, I don't want to hear no shit about Dan and the shop blah blah."

"Candi!" I yelled! "Get the fuck on with the Itinerary already."

"Don't be rude bitch! She snapped back at my sarcasm. Listen we going to take um' to the strip clubs up here on Cleveland and Shrock Rd. or where ever the fuck it is. You know the one with all the chicks with the fake boobs."

"Saga" I thought, hum the name alone sounds interesting enough. I hope the nigga didn't run out of money or a few mother fuckas gone be upset tonight. I slid off the floater thigh deep into the luke warm pool water. The contractors finally finished the pool last weekend and I was able to debut it at my Mother's Day Weekend Fish Fry; mouths to the floor.

~§~§~§~§~§~§~

I couldn't deal with Dan anymore I was tired of trading my soul for cash fastly spent. My home girl Tish told me I could stay with her until I found a place. I couldn't understand why these rental properties were failing to rent to me, I had fulltime gainful employment with the body shop, I paid my fine to Colonial Village so my rental history was back to A1 and they still were turning me down. I called Tasha and told her to call the body shop and act like an apartment complex and confirm my employment and rental history with Dan, since he was technically my last landlord.

She called me back with bad news: "Cuz I told this nigga I was calling from the Kimberly Parkway Apartment complex and I needed to verify your employment. Girl this motherfucker said that you didn't work there anymore that you only worked there for a week and you stole over two thousand dollars' worth of merchandise." She said laughing at his treachery.

"Damn he shady then a motherfucker!"

"Yea he dirty like Tweet said." She replied still laughing. I reached my peak, I just couldn't anymore. I called him and told him that I would be coming over Saturday to get something's for me and the kids.

"Sure honey, but I don't know why you make things so hard for yourself, were a family you should be trying to learn how to work it out with me, your kids father." I couldn't believe the nerve of this motherfucker. Shit wouldn't be so hard for me, if he stopped pulling the rug out from under me every chance he got.

I pulled up to the house with Raily & DP in-tow. I told Raily to go to her room and put all the clothes she wanted to wear in her pink Barbie Suitcase. I wasn't in the house for ten minutes before he attacked me. As I was walking from the master bathroom which held my walk-in closet thru the bedroom and into his office, he slammed the door shut. I had a large duffel bag on my shoulder, our son in my arms and a suitcase in my spare hand.

"Oh you really plan on leaving me; with my child hun?" He yelled right before punching me in my right eye. I screamed from the instant excruciating pain that was dancing inside my eye. As he karate chopped me across the neck. DonP began crying as I let the duffel bag fall off my arm with the suitcase. In one action I sat the luggage and my son on the ground and started swinging. I grabbed his back length pony tail and forced his head as hard as I could onto his glass desk repeatedly.

He back handed me so hard that I collapsed into the wall. As he turned to attack me I kicked him in his dick, jumping to my feet grabbing his head and punching him in his face as hard as I could. Fighting, watching in fear as he took his thumb and gouged my eye causing temporary blindness. I was done I snatched open the door and ran down the long hallway corridor into the kitchen. Dehydrating & hyperventilating, I turned on the faucet and stuck my son's empty bottle under it and drank like I was going back to war.

"Mommy come on let's go, let's leave Dan's house!" My four year old daughter yelled as she pulled on the legs of my pants.

"Ok Baby we're leaving right now, I'm going to go get your brother from the back." She stood beside Dan's office door with her pink suitcase ready to go.

"Here honey, take this." He said proudly waiving in-front of me a $1750 payroll check and personal check he wrote for another $1750.

Go get you a hotel suite and do a little shopping with the kids and come back home Monday after you calm down." I snatched the checks habitually grabbed my belongings and my crying son and rushed to my truck.

"This motherfucker got me fucked up!"

"That's right mom, tell the police that he hit you!" My daughter yelled as she fastened her seat belt. She's right I thought as I rushed down Hamilton Rd to get to the Gahanna Police Station. Jumping out the truck with my two children, I ran feverishly through the building until finding an available officer.

"I'd like to report a domestic violence attack that just happened." I fidgeted, repositioning my son on my hip. I wasn't all the way in the building before Dan came pulling his matching truck beside mines. I tried to tell them my story before he came in.

"He's tapped my phones, had private investigators following me around. He has transmitters on my vehicle and he just pulled up." He burst in the door screaming!

"This bitch attacked me!"

"Oh my God this clown is the devil."

Because physical bruises and blood was apparent on the both of us we both had to go to jail. I called Tish and asked her if she could have someone bring her to the Gahanna Police Department to get my kids and my truck and if they could stay with her for a couple of days or she could drop them off to Momma Rita's house until I got out of jail.

She made it to the station in less than thirty minutes. I gave her a one hundred dollar bill, the only cash that I had on me. I gave my four year old daughter the two checks and told her not to give them to anybody and to keep them in her suitcase. I cried, my baby cried like she would never see me again. She had already suffered watching her father get sentenced to 48 years to life and was well acquainted with the prison visiting system.

"Mommy please don't stay in jail, please leave Dan alone." She cried hugging me around my waist.

"Don't worry baby, I'll be home in a couple of days, be good for Ms. Tish and when I get home were going to get a new house of our own ok?" She was pleased with my response, but not happy at all. They cuffed us and walked us across the parking lot to the holding cells Dan kept trying to talk to me:

"Honey don't be mad, just look at it like a short vacation from the kids, when we get out I'll take you to California, you always wanted to go to California right?" I grabbed the bars in front of me squeezing them wishing they were his neck.

"You're crazy motherfucker, this ain't no vacation, no you will never see me or my kids after I get out, fuck you, fuck you fuck your life!" I screamed at the hell in his laughter. The holding officer brought us a hamburger, fries and small diet cokes from Burger King.

"Yea it seems we have to feed you guy's lunch, until we get the clearance to haul yawl down to the county jail." He laughed shoving the sandwiches through the bars. Wow this was the best tasting Burger King I've ever had, I hated Burger King prior to today.

I spent two days getting hauled between the Franklin County Jail and the Workhouse. My body was sore, famished and I was tired of sitting on the concrete slabs. I stood shaking over the disgusting metal toilet seat. A few of the prostitute-addicts I shared the holding cell with watched me fight through my pain to crouch over the toilet. The pain won as I fell full assed on the seat. I cried on the inside feeling hopeless yet again.

I left the county jail on my own recon with my ass and legs infested with crabs. This shit wasn't right and it wasn't fair. I was going to fuck Dan doggy style tonight just to infest his bitch ass and then I was going to stay at Choices Shelter for Battered Women. The two representatives from Choices had me meet them at the Greyhound Bus Station and follow them to the secret house.

I stayed there every bit of three days. I couldn't take the group sessions; one of the white girls shared her story detailing how her boyfriend beat her with a baseball bat while she was four months pregnant forcing her to miscarry leaving her Barron mind, body and soul.

Was my shit really that bad? Day 3 my Uncle JR Called me telling me that he and Uncle Timmy was moving out of their half double and I should come and talk to the property manager to see if I could get the place. The rain wasn't stopping me I flew to the onsite property manager's apartment. The middle aged black woman opened the door in her night clothes as I greeted her with my still blackened eye.

"Are you ok Honey?" She asked stepping aside.

"Hi Mrs. Stanley, my name is Cernitha my two uncles rent that middle double right there, I pointed to the duplex. Junior called me and told me to come speak to you in regards to renting the place out. Here is $1350 for the Rent, deposit and next month's rent. I have great rental history and I'm employed. I work for my children's father until next month when I begin my position with Buckeye Equity Service. I'll fill out whatever you need. But if you call him for a reference he is going to lie to you, forcing me to stay with him. Please Mrs. Stanley!"

I began to cry, "I just got out of jail last week for fighting him back, my Uncles can vouch for me, and I use to live here with them a few years back." I continued crying.

"I thought you looked familiar." She comforted me with a box of tissue sitting beside me rubbing my back.

"Well honey your safe now; pack up your things and your moving in. Fill out this application just so I can turn it in to the powers that be and give me a moment to write out your lease. I should have it for you by Monday." She gave me a receipt for the money I gave her and instructed me to get the keys from my Uncle.

God Thank You, I had a breakthrough.

FINISH THE STORY IN VOLUME 2

~§O§~§O§~ §O§~

§~Q & A~§
For Book Club Discussions

Describe the Main Characters Personality, Traits or what you believe is her driving force:

Where you engaged immediately or did it take you a while to gain interest in the story?

Do any of the characters remind you of someone you know & who?

What happened to CerSire?

What chapter, passage did you find engaging, profound or where there any segments you found humorous?

How did you feel about the ending of the story? Did it satisfy you?

If you could ask the Author one question what would it be and why that particular question?

How did you feel reading the book? Did any moments in the book touch your emotions?

Which Story would you advise to make into a full book?

What character did you dislike the most?

What is your favorite chapter and why?

Did you find any moments in this book Inspirational?

What would you like to share with the author?

Cernitha St. Jean Presents...   In This Lifetime **Vol1**

IN THIS LIFE TIME ORDER FORMS

Name: _____
Company: _____
Address: _____
City: _____ State: _____ Zip: _____
Phone: _____
Email: _____
Social Media Site: _____ (Optional)

PAYMENT METHOD

☐ CREDIT ☐ DEBIT

☐ VISA   ☐ MASTER CARD   ☐ AMEX   ☐ DISCOVER

Card Number: _____
Exp Date: _____ Signature: _____
☐ CASH ☐ MONEY ORDER ☐ CHECK ☐ PAYPAL RECEIPT #
#

DESCRIPTION	PRICE	QTY	TOTAL
In This Life Time Vol 1 (a novel)	$21.99		
In This Life Time Vol 2 (a novel)	$21.99		
In This Life Time Audio Book (2 CDs)	coming	2018	
In This Life Time Vol 3 (a novel)	coming	2018	
BUSABAND (Single)	$4.00		
Power's Pain (Single) CD	$4.00		
Too Much Juice (Single)	$4.00		
Shipping Charges Ground 1 book $4.95 /$1.75 each additional book $2.50 per CD	Sub-Total		
	Shipping		
	8.5% Tax		

Make Checks / Money Orders Payable to: Cernitha St.Jean c/o
Dynasty1 Enterprises, LLC
P.O.BOX 11166 W. McKinley St.
Avondale, AZ 85323

Total	$

www.CERSIRE.com

Thank You for Your Support! ☺

www.ingramcontent.com/pod-product-compliance
Lightning Source LLC
Chambersburg PA
CBHW070524170426
43200CB00011B/2314